KURT COBAIN
FOREVER IN BLOOM

KURT COBAIN
FOREVER IN BLOOM

THE LEGACY BEYOND THE TRAGEDY

KELLY CATLIN

Skyhorse Publishing, Inc.
New York, New York

This book was previously published by Genius Publishing as *Kurt Cobain: Forever in Bloom.* The book has been edited and revised since the original publication.

Excerpts from the article "Don't Hurt Girls When You Dance (Or Any Other Time)" by Juno Stump printed by permission of *Unwinnable* magazine.

10 9 8 7 6 5 4 3 2 1

Library of Congress Cataloging-in-Publication Data is available on file.

Cover design by Kai Texel
Cover photo credit: Getty Images

All lyrics licensed through Hal Leonard Corporation

Print ISBN: 978-1-5107-8654-7
Ebook ISBN: 978-1-5107-8942-5

Printed in the United States of America

For my husband and son, my two favorite people:
You're my best friends and my inspiration.
Thank you for your love and support;
I could not have done this without you.
I hope you're as proud of me as I am of you both.
I love you to the moon and back, forever and always.

CONTENT NOTE

This book contains discussions of suicide, substance use, abuse, misogyny, homophobia, transphobia, racism, and mental health struggles. These topics are explored through personal accounts, interviews, and archival material. Some chapters include firsthand accounts of trauma, discrimination, and violence.

TABLE OF CONTENTS

KURT COBAIN
FOREVER IN BLOOM

FOREWORD

When Nirvana was tearing the music world asunder, Susan Collins was the VP of A&R (Artists and Repertoire) at Virgin Music America, Nirvana's publisher. Her recollections helped me paint a comprehensive picture of the Nirvana frontman, providing valuable insight from another side of the music industry. But more than that, Susan's words proved just how missed Kurt is. The following is a personal memory Susan shared with me about her incredible time with Kurt and his lasting impact:

★★★

I was sixteen when I moved to London to share a flat off the King's Road in Chelsea. I could not believe my luck, as at that time, this area was known as the center of the punk movement, where Vivienne Westwood and Malcolm McLaren's "Sex" shop was based, where Johnny Rotten and Sid Vicious hung out. The years were 1976–1977, and punk was everywhere.

Before I left to go live in the States when I was twenty-one, I worked for Jet Records, a subsidiary label distributed through CBS UK. The biggest act—by far—on that label was ELO [Electric Light Orchestra], soon to be followed by Ozzy Osbourne, who would sit at reception with me while I worked the switchboard while he waited to meet with various record label people about his upcoming record, which I helped him name *Blizzard of Ozz*. Even though ska was just breaking through, Jet was primarily a rock label, home to Gary Moore, Randy Rhoads, and Girl. "Mr. Blue Sky" (ELO) had been huge for the label.

From this background, I entered the world of A&R and found myself working for Chrysalis Records on Sunset, the LA branch of the UK record company where we nearly (at least to my mind) signed Guns N' Roses. The colorized press photo stood out and their demos were amazing; they had taken hard rock and put a punk edge to it. When I listened to their music, I thought, *Here is a band who moves things along, a band who speaks to a generation*. Whether or not they would ever have signed to a label successful with pop artists like Huey Lewis, Pat Benatar, and Billy Idol was doubtful, despite the fact that the label was outperforming Geffen, but for that reason I believed we had a chance, and I left the field of battle with a heavy heart when they went on to sign with Geffen.

I then took a job doing A&R for Polydor Records in the UK, where I had been tasked with the job of finding a UK version of an American rock band. I made a valiant effort, but in a market dominated by Pete Waterman [record producer] and all his signings, I was not hopeful, until I went to the CMJ awards in New York (it could have been NMS) and saw a band that blew me away.

One particular night in New York, having seen all the bands ticked off on our schedules, a group of A&R people arranged to meet up for a drink. We decided to meet outside the Pyramid Club, which was not on our list of official venues. While we were waiting for some of the others to arrive, I popped into the club to see who was playing. It turned out to be a band called Nirvana, and finally—after days and nights of seeing bands in mostly empty venues—here was a band who actually had their own audience that was going insane for them. The venue was heaving and everyone was dancing and the band sounded great. Everyone was crammed up front.

When I got back to the office in London, the boss, David Munns (who had made his name with Queen and Iron Maiden), asked me if I had seen anything I wanted to sign. I told him about an American band called Nirvana and said they were amazing. He said, "I'm not signing any bloody American bands."

So that was it, until almost a year later. Bear in mind there was no internet; the only way to find bands was by tracking them down and calling on a network of contacts in rehearsal studios, managers, promoters, club bookers, lawyers, songwriters, buying independently released records, visiting small record shops, and so forth. When I found myself working for Virgin Music in West Hollywood some ten or so months later, I set about trying to find Nirvana. There was a lot of excitement over Mother Love Bone and Soundgarden, but damn if I could not find Nirvana. I even went to a gig at The Roxy by another band calling themselves Nirvana. I went home that night disappointed.

I had Nirvana's independent vinyl release on Sub Pop, "Sliver," but it had no contact information on it, and I didn't think Sub Pop would appreciate a call from someone they might view as a corporate person trying to poach the publishing out from under them and ferry Nirvana off to a major label. Sub Pop probably would have had a typical indie deal of splitting all the income, including publishing, 50/50.

I continued to look for Nirvana until I got a call from a lawyer I knew well: Alan Mintz. "Do you know of a band called Nirvana?" he asked. Did I know?! When Nirvana's cassette arrived, I couldn't stop playing it. "In Bloom," Kurt's vocals, the lyrics, the tempo, the power of the words, wow. The poetry of the lyrics, the musicality, the vocals, the performances, and "the sounds." I was so excited. It all had the energy and flavor of punk but was a lot more sophisticated both lyrically and musically than anything else I'd heard up to that point.

"Smells Like Teen Spirit" was not on the demos; I don't think it had been written and although others close to the band may disagree or say I'm wrong, I have to wonder if one lyric wasn't written about the band's experiences interacting with the music industry, as if the execs sat back with folded arms as if to say, "You want the money? Entertain us." It was no surprise that the cover was a baby trying to reach for a dollar. The corruption of innocence, Nirvana had signed their rights away.

Alan gave me Krist Novoselic's number, as there was no manager at that time, and I called him and arranged to go to Nirvana's next gig in Tacoma. Krist offered to pick me up at the airport, which I gladly accepted. They were there on time at the gate, and we drove to Seattle in their van. With Kurt driving, they drove me to my hotel. Kurt and I talked about music the whole way there. I felt like I had met my soulmate. We talked about Sammy Davis Jr., and I remember being impressed as Kurt had a broad taste in music, which I found rare. So many bands stick to their own genre. After the swagger and carefully crafted imaging of Axl and Slash, my impression of Kurt was that he was easygoing, friendly, and relaxed, with nothing to prove. He was comfortable being him. So punk.

I went to Nirvana's rehearsal, and at that time I was trying to quit smoking, so I was needlepointing to keep my hands busy to stop myself from lighting up. Now, in my day, punk was all about speed, pogoing, high energy, fast music with the tempos speeded up; it was not about heroin. Heroin was, to my mind, for the Ozzy generation: druggy, slowed-down music that I associated with the older generation of bands and musicians like Hendrix. Call me naïve, but I did not associate heroin use with Nirvana. I saw them as punks like me!

After their rehearsal, I went back to my hotel and then later drove out to see the show in Tacoma with Nick, a guitar player we had signed. Having arrived in Tacoma, I was shocked to find myself inappropriately dressed in a light summer grunge dress—it was a complete wardrobe malfunction. No one mentioned that a two-hour flight out of LA to Seattle could result in a drop in temperature from 90 degrees F in LA to 30 degrees F in Tacoma.

Then we were told that Nirvana would not be going on for two hours. This meant I was very much in favor of heading back to the warmth of the hotel, ASAP. In those days, neighborhood coffee shops were still hard to find, as Starbucks had yet to spread to every high street. Luck had it that we found somewhere to hang out for two hours, and it was, in fact, a coffee shop. I remember fighting a strong urge to head back to Seattle and prayed I was going to see the same band I'd seen at the Pyramid in New York.

By the time Nirvana came on stage, the venue was packed. I was so ready to leave, but as I turned to Nick to say "Let's go," I heard something and thought, *Wait a minute, is that a Beatles melody? No way.* But Nick heard it, too. So I stayed for the whole show. The energy; the performance; the true spirit; their fun, devoted, good-natured following. I was knocked out. What a privilege to have been in that audience that night.

There was a break—if memory serves me correctly—at 2:00 a.m. for the under-twenty-ones to leave because of the alcohol licensing laws, so I didn't see the second half of the show. I didn't leave because there was a break; I had seen enough to know I wanted to sign Nirvana's publishing. The audience was smaller but still rabid, and the band no doubt played into the early hours. I told Krist that I loved them, and he absolutely said he understood why I was leaving, and told me to go rest and call his lawyer the next day. I recall Krist being funny, friendly, and kind.

Then my memory blurs. I remember flying out with Jeff Fenster—who was doing A&R for Charisma Records out of New York at the time—to meet with Nirvana. We effectively worked for the same label, as Charisma was owned by Virgin's owner. After our meeting and on the journey back to the airport, I asked Jeff why he had brought up needles to Kurt, and Jeff said he'd been discussing his dentist with Kurt and Kurt's fear of needles.

My boss, Kaz, put a publishing offer together, and I took Nirvana's newly appointed manager, John Silva from Gold Mountain Management, to lunch, and soon after, the deal got signed.

During that time, industry interest in Nirvana caught fire to where they were being offered record and publishing deals by most of the major players in town. In those days, there was a controlled composition clause between major labels and publishers, so we had to wait for the band to sign to a record company before we could sign our publishing agreement. They ended up signing to Gary Gersh at Geffen, who had signed Sonic Youth, one of Nirvana's favorite bands. It was a wise decision, as Gersh understood the band and had the authority at Geffen to see the band's vision through.

My first job as Nirvana's new publisher was to sort out a lack of income from being paid through their *Bleach* EP releases on Sub Pop, which had been licensed out to a label in the UK that had done very well with it, but no income found its way back to the band. We got to the bottom of that, and Geffen purchased the EP rights from Sub Pop and rereleased it.

After the record was made, Kaz and I went to the valley to visit Nirvana in the studio, to hear the album *Nevermind*. I was concerned that their choice of producer, Butch Vig, would make them sound too polished. I need not have worried, as the new drummer, Dave Grohl, was great, and the finished record did not sound too far from the original demos. It was a happy group that went out to eat that day. Kurt and Krist told a story about how Donny Ienner, then head of Columbia Records, had tried to sign them. It made Kurt laugh, telling us the story of how Donny had slapped his thigh when the band said they wanted to have hit singles and be on the "Hot 100" chart. "That's what I like to hear," Donny had told them.

Now, as anyone at that time will tell you, any record company boss promising a band like Nirvana daytime airplay on a parallel one-pop station was winding them up.

I remember getting a call from John Silva, inviting me to the video shoot for "Smells Like Teen Spirit," and I so wish I'd gone. What a groundbreaking video that was.

After a few weeks of *Nevermind*'s release, I went to pick my car up at the garage and could not believe that the mechanic was listening to a Nirvana CD.

"You're playing Nirvana," I told him.

He said it was the best band he'd heard in ages. Oh boy, oh boy, when music filtered into people's boomboxes and you started hearing it out and about, you knew something big was happening.

Then I started to worry that the band might become too establishment; they were being offered opening slot tours with the Chili Peppers and Guns N' Roses and selling fifty thousand CDs a week. They were a phenomenon, and I remember calling Gersh to ask if it was wise to put them on the cover of such a mainstream magazine as *Rolling Stone* at this juncture, and he said, "Don't worry, Kurt is wearing a prom dress."

And then things changed. I remember seeing John Silva looking tired, trying to get Kurt out of The Whisky one night, away from people wanting to talk to him. It was around this time that Guy Oseary (who later went on to manage Madonna) had been in my office talking up an artist he thought was amazing, called Courtney Love. Her music was pretty raw, but I could hear what he was excited about, that distinctive voice singing "Doll Parts." It was a natural pairing, Kurt with the upcoming Queen of Punk, Courtney Love.

I hadn't seen it coming—the drugs, that is.

In all of this, I should mention that the world had slowed down for Nirvana. It was as though the Red Sea had parted for them. At that time, the FBI had finally succeeded in bringing some of the well-known independent promo guys to court on charges of racketeering/payola for receiving gifts, money, and holidays in return for airplay. They decided what records got played, when, and how many spins. In those days, record companies could expect to pay £100,000 to the indie promos to see if a record had traction—whether the public was buying the CDs, turning up to gigs, requesting video rotation on MTV, and whether the band was generating press. All of these elements worked together to keep a record on radio playlists. During the time of Nirvana's CD release, major labels held back their big releases until Joe Isgro and the other kings of indie promo were back in the driving seat. But it was during that lull in radio that Geffen leapt in and Nirvana got the radio play the band had been promised.

Nirvana's headlining gig at the Hollywood Palladium, with Dinosaur Jr. opening, was a nerve-wracking one for me, as it wasn't long after we had completed our publishing deal which, for an unknown band, was a considerable sum of money. Now, looking back on it, it was of course ridiculous to worry, but at that stage, Nirvana was still very much a cult band with a small, devoted following of grunge fans.

In those early days, I used to collect band T-shirts every time I visited the small independent record shops in Seattle. There were some amazing designs and slogans, none more so than Nirvana's shirt, which was a circle on the front of all the worst profanity. It was outrageously hilarious. I don't recall how my boss, Kaz, got a hold of one of these T-shirts (it's possible I gave him mine or John Silva or the band members gave him one), but he actually wore his out in West Hollywood and, at that time, there was nothing untoward about that, ordering a takeaway sandwich in a T-shirt that began with "Mothereffing" etc. Until one day, he got stopped by the police. He walked back to the office with the T-shirt inside out. I wondered how late Kaz had been out the night before because it was so not like him to come to the office with his T-shirt inside out.

"The police tried to arrest me!" he said.

I still wonder what happened to that T-shirt design.

Then there was the Reading '92 with Nirvana headlining; oh, the joy of it, standing in the wings, Kurt coming out in a hospital gown, and Krist giving us a bottle of wine during their set. It was an amazing show.

When the third album came out, *In Utero*, I remember quoting "Heart-Shaped Box" lyrics to Kaz, saying, "Who writes like that? It's so powerful." And along with the album came Danny Goldberg from Gold Mountain, into the office, to renegotiate the publishing deal. Sadly, Virgin Records was bought out by EMI Records, and Kaz and I moved over to the record company. John was asking me to research unlawful radio ads on record stations no one knew the name of. It was, of course, coming from Kurt, and he was no longer the Kurt I had met in Seattle that day at the airport. I, like any fan, heard rumors and read about him and Courtney in the press and their shenanigans on the road.

Then came Kurt's death.

Kaz and I—like all the fans—mourned the loss of this great talent. We flew out to Seattle for the funeral and went to Kurt's house where his family mourned and his baby, Frances Bean, unknowingly rested in her crib, fatherless. It was the saddest of days. Across town, unbeknownst to us, Dave and Krist held their own funeral.

The age of twenty-seven will forever be a landmark age in my mind. From the timber environment of Tacoma and Seattle and its burgeoning music scene so reminiscent of the UK with its night clubs, coffee shops, and independent record labels came this young genius and his talented close friend, Krist. Kurt had worked so hard for everything, and now, here it all was for him, all the success he could ever have dreamt of. I don't read books on Kurt, as I can't find in them the Kurt that picked me up from the Seattle airport.

Having been around a lot of musicians with drug dependencies, I know that to come off of heroin is one hell of an undertaking. There is nothing like heroin to destroy the human being. The idea of heroin as a recreation or taken indiscriminately has made it hard for sufferers the world over to get the true pain relief they need; this is because the drug has had to become so highly restricted. Everything written about it is true, and for those few who did manage to overcome its allure, it will never leave the body, mind, and soul of the person the way it was before they took their first hit. No addict will ever be that person again—it is gone forever, even for those who quit; for the few survivors, you have to live the rest of your life one minute at a time. For the small amount of escape heroin provides, the price to pay is either your life or the rest of your life. The fact that Universal has made fortunes off of stars like Amy Winehouse or Kurt Cobain is enough to put any future talent off heroin forever.

Boy, did that star shine bright. May you rest in peace, dear Kurt.

Postscript:

I have to thank John Silva and Gold Mountain's generosity in sending over what seemed like, at the time, a van load of Nirvana platinum, gold, and silver discs. One, in particular, I hung over the doorway to my flat in London, where every year, on the anniversary of Kurt's birth, the disc would fall off the wall, and I would find it in the morning on the front doorstep. The last year it happened, I came home and tried to open the front door. I could see just enough inside to see that it had wedged itself under the door so I couldn't open the door without damaging it. Then I remembered it was, of course, the anniversary of his birth. I have often wondered if Kurt was not trying to send me a message from beyond the great beyond. I look at pictures of Frances Bean, and, even if he had never recorded again, I so wish, like we all do, that he'd stuck around to see his baby girl grow up.

—Susan Collins, former VP of
A&R at Virgin Music America

INTRODUCTION

On April 13, 1984, my beloved friend, family member, and Veteran Marine, Walter, was born. The world welcomed a courageous spirit who embodied the best of this world. He was a son, brother, uncle, and a brave human being. He was charismatic and wildly funny. And he was loved.

But on July 20, 2017, I was startled by the ringing of my cell phone. It was 12:30 p.m. on a beautiful summer day. My husband was calling to let me know that Walter had left this world. He had died by suicide. His struggles were personal, his hardships painfully on display to those who knew him best. But his spirit is eternal, and his life is a reminder of all the love he had to offer and all the lives he affected.

I thought of ways to honor Walter but didn't know how. There's a quote I think of often that's widely attributed to Ernest Hemingway: "Every man has two deaths, when he is buried in the ground and the last time someone says his name. In some ways men can be immortal."

I knew I had to keep saying his name.

★★★

Four years later, I arrived home one day to the sound of raucous music emanating from my twenty-something neighbor's speakers, rattling my car windows as I pulled into the driveway. Kurt Cobain's raspy vocals caught me off guard, his lyrics somehow aggressive yet delicate.

I asked my neighbor if he was a Nirvana fan.

"Absolutely."

Later that afternoon, I found myself asking Alexa to blast Nirvana, suddenly eager to immerse myself in the music of my childhood. As I listened, Kurt Cobain's world unfolded before me with fresh eyes, pulled not just by the music, but by the person behind it—and the weight he carried.

I owned a handful of Nirvana CDs, the kind that transported me back to high school dances where "Smells Like Teen Spirit" blared from every speaker, kids headbanging in unison regardless of what clique they claimed. That was the thing about Kurt Cobain—he had an undeniable relatability, and once you felt it, something in you shifted.

The broad strokes everyone remembered—the struggles, the scrutiny, the overdose of fame, the devastating end—were not lost on me. But those facts alone never told the whole story. They didn't explain the impact, nor the deeply personal connection people had formed with him.

My thoughts turned to Walter. Could we have done more? Could his death have been prevented?

My family handled Walter's passing through all the usual channels—talk therapy, survivors' groups, and fondly recalling our best memories. Everything helped to a degree, but it's true what they say: sometimes the only way out is through.

Walter took his life shortly after my wedding. When the photographer emailed our pictures, the first image from the ceremony showed him smiling as he walked up to the chapel with my husband. It took us weeks before we could watch our reception video. It's difficult to comprehend how someone with so much light could decide they didn't have anything to live for. He had people who loved him and wanted to see him succeed.

I thought about ways to honor Walter, and it wasn't until Nirvana was blasting through my neighborhood that I finally knew how I would try to pay tribute to him. Hearing those songs again made me think of Kurt Cobain's death—one of the most high-profile suicides of the twentieth century, affecting countless people—and somehow I knew he could be the vehicle for my journey to help others like Walter.

Like many, I saw Kurt Cobain as a kindred spirit, not because I shared his suicidal ideation, but because I shared his empathy. As I dug deeper and began writing, "Kurt Cobain" slowly became "Kurt," a shift that happened as I worked intimately with so many of the people who loved him and still miss him. Over time, I formed genuine friendships with those who had been part of his life. Once you share friends with someone and learn about their life so intimately, the formality falls away. He becomes a human being again—not an icon, not a headline. Just Kurt.

So, I started paying closer attention to how people talked about him—what they claimed, what they assumed, what they repeated without thinking. I paid attention to what people had to say about his exploits, the same constant theme striking a chord: Kurt Cobain was doomed from in utero—literally. Be it in print or digital media, countless readers felt they were led down a dark, spiraling trail that aimed to prove his suicide was unavoidable and inevitable. The protagonist was his own worst antagonist, his fate sealed from every story's inception.

But I don't subscribe to this notion.

So, I decided I'd write a book.

I'd remind people that no one is destined to take their own life.

I'd visit dark, uncomfortable places, remove the stigma surrounding suicide, and donate profits in Walter and Kurt's honor.

My three-year experience was chaotic but powerful. I didn't know where it would take me, but I was certain about one thing: I didn't want to recreate Kurt Cobain's life—I wanted to remind people he was more than the sound bite he became. I sought out people who knew him—friends, musicians, photographers, recording engineers, and music management—anyone and everyone. I also wanted to speak with indie artists who were deeply affected by Kurt—not just in their work, but in who they became as people.

But these would be my interviews, my journey, my experience. I needed it, not just for me, but for Walter.

Along the way, I took the road less traveled because I refused to sensationalize Kurt's tragic passing. Just because he left his mortal coil doesn't mean we get to rummage through his personal effects, taking liberties and assuming we understand his inner dialogue. Sensationalism is often one-sided, reducing a person to flashy headlines instead of acknowledging their full humanity. Kurt deserves better.

Instead, I decided to celebrate Kurt's life and lasting legacy and focus on a man who, although he left this world at a devastatingly young age, liberated countless lives. For every obstacle he faced, we are reminded that he was more than his struggles. He had a fierce, unwavering belief system, and that can't be erased. Sadly, his empathetic nature was often downplayed, even though it largely defined him. But I wanted to explore the best parts of what he represented. My goal was to celebrate him for the man he was instead of the man the media needed him to be: a tortured artist caricature.

The internet is wildly invasive and intrusive to the point of contention. Every detail of Kurt's life was laid out before me: his favorite drink (strawberry milk), his childhood home (1210 E 1st St), and his favorite guitar (Fender Mustang). You can even read his personal journals—his private thoughts—for a mere $24.17 on Amazon. His suicide note and autopsy report are also readily available, both unfathomable documents that no one but his family should be privy to, let alone slapped on a T-shirt.

Kurt Cobain was a private man, and I wanted to keep it that way. I was determined not to focus on his whereabouts the week before his suicide or his last act of desperation. Instead, I decided to honor his enduring impact.

I knew writing this would be challenging since Kurt is synonymous in the public imagination with suicide. I was faced with discussions that were as difficult for my interviewees as they were for me, but I remained steadfast in my quest to shine a bright light on suicide awareness while reminding people that the romanticism surrounding Kurt's passing deserves to be put in a heart-shaped box and locked—tightly.

Enter *Kurt Cobain: Forever in Bloom*.

The individuals featured in this book have lent their voices to discuss a man whose ideology was selfless, empathetic, and wittily astute. Some people I interviewed expressed a sincere hesitation before speaking to me, feeling their words were previously misconstrued. This book is the product of painstakingly honest interviews, enmeshed with a celebration of life as we remember the man who gave voice to a generation and counterculture. Kurt's values and spirit emerge through a collection of stories and reflections from those who knew him and loved him. What follows is a collection of deeply personal dialogues, marked by honesty and introspection. This book also discusses pivotal Nirvana shows and what Kurt represented as an artist and as a human. I tried not to take liberties when writing and often took Kurt's words at face value. Many have challenged his musings, but I didn't feel it was my place to do so.

Gilbert Blecken, a fanzine writer and photographer from Berlin, once shared with me a striking photograph of Kurt. Taken on Sunday, November 10, 1991, the picture offers a glimpse into Kurt's soul, his eyes boring a hole into the camera lens. To me, it captures the Kurt I learned about along the way: warm, inviting, and effortlessly intriguing.

"Kurt was sitting on the stairs that led directly to the stage of the Loft club where they sound-checked shortly after I had taken the photos. Funny enough, it was my interview where Kurt said the iconic words: 'We're prepared to destroy our career as it happens.'"

For context, Gilbert asked Kurt, "So you're not prepared to become superstars?" to which Kurt replied, "No we're not, because we're not going to be. We're prepared to destroy our career as it happens."[1]

Gilbert considered the experience:

> "What I always stress is that I was just a twenty-two-year-old fanzine writer asking for a spontaneous interview, so I think he [Kurt] already showed a lot of class by agreeing to that. And even though he did have a good sense of humor, he seemed very serious about the interview and also didn't mind at all to be photographed afterwards. I felt very comfortable

in his company because he gave me the impression of a young man who rested within himself, which also gave him a very pleasant form of charisma. And I think he also felt comfortable in that situation because I probably came across a bit insecure—partly due to my Asperger's syndrome—so he didn't feel he had to prove himself. To him, it might have been a nice contrast to some of the arrogant professional photographers and journalists he usually met around that time."[2]

Years later, on his website, Gilbert reflected on Nirvana with the same clarity:

> "There's nothing really 'sensational' to reveal about this encounter. What stands out, though, is that even as the life of Nirvana was beginning to become complicated, there was still a friendly atmosphere around the band and Kurt didn't feel he had to prove anything when meeting someone who was a writer but also part of his fanbase. I'm aware that, during that same time period, [Kurt's] first difficulties occurred when it came to dealing with the mainstream media. However, even two years later, Kurt remained a man of integrity who would still talk to fanzines and support unknown bands that he loved."[3]

This book centers on the life of Kurt Cobain and the ways he inspired others—and continues to do so. The people inside these pages pay tribute to the man who, in more ways than one, sold the world. The point isn't to unearth scandal or reinvent the wheel. It isn't about chasing "new facts." It's about reframing what we already know and allowing room for a different kind of understanding. Some of the stories shared with me simply haven't been told in this way before, but the heart of this book is Kurt's legacy—his artistry, his decency, and the imprint he left on the people whose lives he touched.

This project came together because people wanted to honor him. They wanted to speak about the real Kurt—for the sake of mental-health awareness, to challenge the stigma surrounding suicide, and to deflate the romanticism that has followed his death for decades.

This book also celebrates Kurt and all his accomplishments, because he was—and continues to be for all who knew and honor him—a driving force to challenge the systemic injustices that plague our world. Despite his struggles, there is so much to celebrate. Kurt Cobain is more than a person. He's an ethos, a feeling. He's the desire to persevere despite the odds. So was Walter. That truth should not be overlooked.

And we should continue to say their names:

Kurt.

Walter.

Chapter 1

"TERRITORIAL PISSINGS"

"I'm so happy 'cause today I found my friends
They're in my head"
—Kurt Cobain, "Lithium"

Modest bungalows line the residential street. A pale-yellow house faces a hill of Douglas firs and western hemlocks. The sun threatens to make an appearance, but a perpetual cloud cover chases it away. The house is small and unassuming. To some, it's nothing more than a humble cottage, its quaint yard well-maintained despite its interior being devoid of life. The only life that resides within 1210 E 1st St in Aberdeen, Washington, is the ghost of a young Kurt—not the famous musician who sold the world with a single guitar riff, but the Kurt who longed for the nuclear family that divorce deprived him of. The Kurt who experienced what it's like to be unhoused, depressed, and in solitude. The Kurt whose happy childhood was short-lived, affecting the man he'd grow to be.

But it didn't start out that way.

The date was Monday, February 20, 1967. The weather was mild—perfect for the world's most unassuming rock star to make his grand entrance, even if no one realized it yet. Nurses in starched white dresses scurried about Wendy Cobain's hospital room, preparing for the birth of her first child—the son who would inevitably change the landscape of music for generations to come. At 7:38 p.m., Kurt Donald Cobain was born at Grays Harbor Community Hospital—an arrival that would eventually eclipse the small town.

Although Kurt had no love for Aberdeen later in life, his childhood retained a mirthful innocence. He had the one thing most children crave: two parents living beneath the same roof. Even though Kurt's time in a nuclear family was brief, there was a period when his cereal packet family provided a young, energetic towhead with everything he needed to grow and thrive. That sense of family stability was fleeting for the inhabitants of 1210 E 1st St, and a divorce rocked a young Kurt to his core. The house he once called a home soon became a point of contention. He would reference that pain during interviews after striking international stardom, and songs like "Serve the Servants" spoke to the effect it still had on him nearly two decades later. Rather than perpetual promiscuity, Kurt married young, which also hinted at his desire to return to the nuclear family he had lost early in life.

While speaking to some in Aberdeen about Kurt's childhood, I encountered conflicting opinions. Some said he was happy, full stop. But Kurt himself insisted that his parents' divorce deeply affected him, so I figured it was best to let him speak for himself. In an interview with Robert Hilburn, Kurt spoke about his home life and the profundity of his parents' divorce:

> "I was a seriously depressed kid," Kurt explained. "Every night at one point I'd go to bed bawling my head off. I used to try to make my head explode by holding my breath, thinking if I blew up my head, they'd be sorry. There was a time when I never thought I'd live to see twenty-one."[4]

The reminder is that Kurt's own words showcase a deep-rooted pain. It's no secret that Kurt was passed back and forth from relative to relative, with the occasional family friend thrown into the mix. Some even say (although most refute) that the Young Street Bridge, spanning part of the Wishkah River near Kurt's childhood home, provided him with shelter, be it for an hour or for a day—a place that would loom large as a symbol in his story.

This pain inspired Nirvana's dark and emotive "Something in the Way," Kirk Canning's beautiful cello adding a haunting quality to the already gloomy song. But the Young Street Bridge has also become a symbol of hope. While dilapidated, it represents something enduring, much like Kurt did. After decades of exposure to weather and wear—and ongoing debate over its usefulness—the bridge remains standing, still designed to support others. In that way, it has come to represent tenacity. The parallels to Kurt's life are difficult to ignore.

The bridge holds deeply personal meaning for those who feel connected to Kurt, even as its role in his childhood is uncertain. It became synonymous with the instability he faced early in life, inspiring one of Nirvana's most haunting songs. Free and unpolished, it isn't something preserved behind museum glass. Its weathered reality—muddy banks and an unforgiving landscape—feels unmistakably Kurt.

The bridge is also a reminder that things are not always what they seem. Kurt was proof of this. And to those who understand its meaning, it holds great value outside a concrete abutment. To some, the bridge is erroneously portrayed as just a reminder of a man who battled addiction and died by suicide, but it's often misjudged, the same way Kurt was. Kurt was not defined by his addiction, and he should not be defined by his suicide.

No matter what Kurt experienced as a child, he found solace in music and art, his creativity on display from his early childhood. He was nothing if not predestined to fulfill something—anything—artistic. A quick Google search of "Kurt Cobain art" produces countless images of his childhood drawings and his adult artistic endeavors, the likes of which appeared on *Incesticide*.

Kurt's creative tendencies were cultivated in Aberdeen—a working-class lumber town separating the coast with the Olympic Peninsula known for its blue-collar grit and resilience. Despite his contempt for the town, Aberdeen played a crucial role in the man Kurt grew to be. Its overcast weather provided the perfect ambiance for brooding, thought-provoking art and music that was equal parts invigorating, dark, and twisted. Much of what Kurt witnessed growing up in the small town would also shape the way he viewed society, birthing a man with a heavy social conscience and a fierce desire to protect the marginalized at all costs.

I asked Mark Yarm, the author of *Everybody Loves Our Town: An Oral History of Grunge*, to weigh in:

> "In the liner notes to *Incesticide*, Kurt made it very clear if you're sexist or racist, we [Nirvana] don't want you listening to our music," Mark said. "Which, I think, was a very noble thing to say. But when the rest of the band wrote 'Smells Like Teen Spirit,' they saw their audience turn into the jocks who would've beat them up. Unfortunately, you can't gate-keep your music; you can't say, 'This is not for you.' (You can, obviously, but . . . it's not necessarily going to work.) Then Nirvana was fundraising for Bosnian rape victims and were aligned in a way with the Riot Grrrl music. Although, according to Krist, Kurt wasn't very political, he was very socially minded. He did speak to a lot of people who were in the LGBTQ+ community or who had fractured homes or other kinds of problems. He appealed to a wide stock of people, including the normies in the backward baseball caps. It was a pretty wide swath of appeal. Kurt did want to control the audience, but once you've reached that level of fame, you can't control who will adopt it, who will take it up, and who will love it. It's totally out of your hands."[5]

Kurt was sensitive, empathetic, and a protector of the vulnerable from an early age, making it impossible to ignore just how deeply his parents' divorce may have affected him. He was also part of a group of children suddenly navigating fractured home lives. His pain was personal, yet deeply relatable, and led to the soundtrack for broken generations to come.

Despite these challenges, Kurt recognized that his childhood wasn't all bad. To say Kurt had a happy childhood isn't fictitious. But at what point does childhood end? For some, it's eighteen years of age. For Kurt, childhood may have ended when his nuclear family did—before he even had the chance to reach double digits.

"I had a really good childhood up until I was nine years old," Kurt explained.[6] "Then a classic case of divorce really affected me, and I moved back and forth between relatives all the time. And I just became extremely depressed and withdrawn."

By nine, children have developed and begin to exercise critical thinking skills, learning to ruminate about the world around them as abstract concepts begin to take shape. Sadly, it's reported that children who experience a divorce in this age range are more likely to suffer from substance abuse.[7]

It's no secret that Kurt had a tumultuous relationship with his parents. During Jon Savage's 1993 interview, Kurt's parents' divorce was a topic of discussion.

> "I remember feeling ashamed, for some reason. I was ashamed of my parents. I couldn't face some of my friends at school anymore, because I desperately wanted to have the classic, you know, typical family. Mother, father. I wanted that security, so I resented my parents for quite a few years because of that."[8]

In a 1993 interview with Robert Hilburn, Kurt again spoke about his parents' divorce.

> "I was embarrassed, and I became really detached and quiet. My mom would take me to school, and I wouldn't even look kids in the eye. I knew everyone knew that I only had one parent. That probably isn't a big deal in a big town, but it is in a small town."

With divorce comes the promise (or threat) of new relationships and new parental figures. Before the legal shift to joint custody in the mid-seventies, a child's mother was customarily awarded sole custody. (Even after the change in custody laws occurred, it was and is still common for mothers to be the custodial parent in most cases.[9]) There were stories about instability in Kurt's home life after the divorce, but the reality may have been more complicated. The presence of his mother's boyfriend—and her dependence on him for housing and financial stability—may have played a role in Kurt being asked to leave the home. As he navigated a fractured family structure, moving between households at a time when he was already struggling to feel secure, he rebelled. His behavior worsened as the family he craved continued to slip further out of reach, contributing to an eventual shift in custody.

Kurt wanted attention—nothing out of the ordinary, considering all he'd been through, and at such a young age. Children of divorce are at an increased risk of struggling with adjustment issues, and Kurt was no different.[10] He was deeply affected by his parents' divorce, and the emotional trauma he sustained at an early age didn't mean he was broken; it just meant he needed compassion, understanding, and stability.

Kurt's mother eventually gave his father, Donald Cobain, full custody of their son. Donald remarried, and Kurt's stepmother was a point of contention, with disagreements ensuing. For a young Kurt, this proved problematic. As evidenced by her interview in Brett Morgen's *Kurt Cobain: Montage of Heck*, Kurt had a strained relationship with his stepmother, Jenny Cobain. She seemingly had regrets over the way he was treated, passed from home to home, from family member to member. Discussing Kurt's misbehavior growing up and lashing out against his parents and siblings, Jenny explained that "[i]t's almost like he [Kurt] didn't—he didn't feel worthy because he was rejected, basically. And I don't know how anybody deals with having your whole family reject you."[11]

Feeling like an outsider would become a recurring theme throughout Kurt's life, influencing both his worldview and the ways he chose to express himself. In a 1993 interview with journalist Kevin Allman, Kurt spoke about his childhood scuffles, and at one point Allman asked Kurt, "You actually got beat up?" Kurt's response: "Oh, yeah. Quite a few times." Kurt was asked about whether he spray-painted "GOD IS GAY" on trucks around Aberdeen. The Nirvana frontman was candid in his response:

"That was a lot of fun. The funniest thing about that was not actually the act but the next morning. I'd get up early in the morning to walk through the neighborhood that I'd terrorized to see the aftermath. That was the worst thing I could have spray-painted on their cars. Nothing else would have been more effective."[12]

Not surprisingly, Kurt would go on to become the unsung hero for many marginalized communities. The tragedy is that he never got a chance to see his lasting impact on society.

In an interview with Jon Savage, Kurt explained his life in the small Washington suburb, especially as he navigated adolescence.

"I became antisocial," he told Savage. "I started to understand the reality of my surroundings, which didn't have a lot to offer. Aberdeen was such a small town, and I couldn't find any friends that I was very fond of, or who were compatible with me, or liked to do the things that I liked. I liked to do artistic things and listen to music."[13]

Kurt harbored resentment toward his hometown, much of his anger stemming from the way he thought women were treated, so much so that he became one of rock's most vocal feminists. In the same interview with Savage, Kurt shared a no-holds-barred message about sexism:

> "I could never find any good male friends, so I ended up hanging out with the girls a lot, and I just felt they weren't

being threatened *[sic]* equally and they weren't treated with respect. I hated the way Aberdeen treated women in general, they were just totally oppressed. The words 'bitch' and 'cunt' were totally common, you'd hear them all the time. But it took me many years after the fact to realize those were the things that were bothering me. I was just starting to understand what was pissing me off so much, and in the last couple of years of high school, I found punk rock and it all came together."[14]

The things that bothered Kurt—the casual language he heard growing up in Aberdeen, the inhumanity of words like "bitch" and "cunt"—had to go somewhere. In *Montage of Heck*, we hear that frustration surface in the so-called "train tracks" story, which Kurt narrates as his first alleged suicide attempt in high school. Many have dismissed the story as fabricated, a fictional part of his musings. Whether true or not, it points to the same place: pain, confusion, and a young artist trying to make sense of what he felt. As Kurt says in his own voiceover, "And during that month happened to be the epitome of my mental abuse from my mother." Aberdeen remains central to Kurt's creativity because so many of those stories, true or not, take root there, even if he tried to distance himself from the town whenever he could.

In the late 1980s, after bouts of homelessness and dropping out of high school, Kurt eventually used music to retreat from Aberdeen, leaving the Washington hamlet altogether. Olympia promised more than he could have hoped for from his hometown. If you circle back to interviews with a young Kurt, you'd hear him say that Nirvana was from Olympia—not Aberdeen. Kurt would even respond to questions regarding his favorite things about Aberdeen with answers such as "Knowing that I don't live there anymore."[15]

Yet, despite his disdain, many Aberdonians still sought to honor his memory. In 2005, the town erected the famous "Come As You Are" sign, an homage to one of their own. They feel him beneath the Young Street Bridge, even if he never slept there. They see him in the murky depths of the Wishkah, mud and all. They sense his presence in his childhood house, even if it was a place that harbored a mixture of love and pain, both of which we can never fully understand.

At the same time, not everyone in Aberdeen agrees on the best way to remember Kurt, if they even should at all. Some resent the attention he brings to Aberdeen and reject the tourism. Some reduce him to a caricature they'd rather forget. This tension keeps Kurt's memory a source of debate, but before judging the town, it's worth considering Kurt's own words on judgment itself.

> "I always knew to question things. All my life, I never believed most things I read in history books and a lot of things I learned in school. But now I've found I don't have the right to make a judgment on someone based on something I've read. I don't have the right to judge anything. That's the lesson I've learned."[16]

Kurt's words.

In 2011, it was even reported that the local parks board recommended changing the bridge's name. But the town refused to rename it after their most famous resident, the same resident who literally ran screaming from town, directly into a microphone. They did, however, name a small piece of land adjacent to the Wishkah River after him. But the bridge would not be named after Kurt, and this decision was almost unanimous among council officials. A local pastor questioned if doing so was the legacy they wanted to leave their children. Part of the pushback came from critics who argued that because Kurt used drugs and died by suicide, naming a bridge after him somehow glorified those actions.[17] A representative for Aberdeen stated the town's preference to "[l]eave the [bridge] as it is and let old history live with new history." The council also rejected naming the bridge after another trailblazer, Alexander Young, so they weren't just rejecting Kurt.

Naming the bridge in honor of Kurt does not exalt his substance abuse and eventual suicide. This train of thought perpetuates the fallacy that a person is defined by their struggles and not by their achievements, of which Kurt had many. It also attempts to erase all the positivity Kurt set forth. We should celebrate him for his achievements. We should also recognize that, despite Kurt's unstable home life, he persevered. Naming a bridge after Kurt would not promote substance abuse and suicide; it would promote tenacity and determination.

Kurt lives on regardless of what they call the Young Street Bridge, and no matter what, it will always be "Kurt's Bridge," even if it's reduced to rubble. Tearing down a structure doesn't undo the impact he had, or the people he continues to reach. He struggled but still forged ahead, forming Nirvana, hell-bent on making a name for himself in the music industry. The persistence of building something meaningful out of very little is what the bridge represents. According to Nirvana bassist Krist Novoselic, "Kurt paid for that demo . . . he cleaned toilets to earn the money to make that record."[18] Anyone who's ever questioned where their next meal is coming from can understand the sentiment behind working odd jobs, especially a bright-eyed kid determined to have his band's demo heard, to have his voice experienced loud and clear in all its smoker-grit glory. And refusal to name a bridge after him—hell, tearing the whole thing down—won't change that in the least.

As fans visit the bridge, they look to connect with the man so often distorted by the narratives surrounding him. Some venture past his childhood home, hoping to understand a bit about the enigmatic musician. But as they look for ways to connect with him, staring into the abyss of a house that Kurt left decades ago, they should also consider the role that the hospital waiting room of Grays Harbor Community Hospital played in his youth, as he's rumored to have spent many a homeless night there. A trip to Olympia will provide a glimpse into the home Kurt made for himself with then-girlfriend Tracy Marander, even though he'd yet again find himself unhoused after tearing the music scene asunder. Admirers should look for couches that bear a piece of his soul, of which there are many. And if they look hard enough, they just might find him.

Kurt's struggles with being unhoused didn't end with *Bleach*. He struggled to afford his apartment in Olympia and, after recording the future certified gold, platinum, and diamond album *Nevermind*, he was evicted—an experience that remains widespread today, as roughly 4.2 million young people in the United States currently experience homelessness. Once again, the instability returned to Kurt's life.

Despite the uncertainty that marked much of his early life, perhaps the most meaningful lesson from Kurt's childhood is simply this: it happened. Beautiful childhood memories embroiled with teenage angst, a lack of stable housing, and pain. It all happened. We can learn from it and honor Kurt by acknowledging it. Kurt was a proponent of societal change, but that's not always how he's remembered, especially when the media deems sensationalism more important than honoring his complete memory. Kurt Cobain, like all human beings, had multiple descriptors: he struggled with substance abuse, but he was also a sensitive, socially conscious human being and a true artist.

One example of Kurt's empathetic ways was evidenced on Saturday, March 19, 1988, when Nirvana played the Community World Theater, with Dave Foster on drums. "Bring cans of food and ye's fee shall be reduced," read the flyer. Even as Kurt was struggling to find his next meal, he was taking time for others. Nirvana's talent was already being recognized in local pockets, a new band ready to annihilate the face of music. Interviews with Kurt that date back to 1989 exploded with palpable excitement, journalists aware that they were in the presence of burgeoning music royalty. In his article "On the Subs Bench: Nirvana," when he interviewed a young Kurt, John Robb stated that Nirvana could "find themselves at the vanguard of guitar pop noise at its best."[19]

During this early period of touring, one band Kurt particularly loved playing with was Sonic Youth. In an interview for *Hollywood Rocks* in February 1991, interviewer Chris Long said to Kurt: "I saw you play with Sonic Youth at the Hollywood Palladium, that was a great show. What's it like doing a show with a band like Sonic Youth that's so . . . abnormal, I guess is the word?"

Kurt replied, "It's a big thrill for me because they're one of my favorite bands, they always have been, so it was a really casual, fine experience . . . I'd prefer to tour with a band like Sonic Youth than any other type of band. I couldn't even think of another band I'd rather tour with."[20]

I asked Thurston Moore of Sonic Youth to share his own memories of Kurt: "My fondest, most lasting memory of Kurt is the slight, yet profound and intelligent smile he would share with you. He could be sullen, bedraggled, and troubled but that smile would always arise like a gentle ray through a thicket. It would even shine through his eyes like some holistic essence. It allowed you to feel his genuine kindness and concern for all the misfits of the world, those victimized by any aspect of injustice. Kurt exemplified their voice, a raging, heart-struck, beautiful tenor."[21]

This glimpse into Kurt's character helps us understand that, although he was eventually a celebrity, he was also one of us. His presence looms large in the hearts of those he affected, and he wasn't as misunderstood as some may think. To many, he is remembered for his empathy, and even while he was struggling, he had a way of making others feel seen—a true selflessness. He ate stolen food like so many Americans are forced to do. He was affected by the same systemic injustices that continue to plague society, yet he persevered. He wanted to leave Aberdeen and did. He wanted to become a musician just to afford some Kraft Mac & Cheese and wound up with craft service. He wanted a home and made one with his family, even if only for a short while.

But everything comes full circle to the Young Street Bridge and what it represents.

To remember Kurt, those who love him flock to the bridge, leaving with fistfuls of dirt in an attempt to connect with the inscrutable rocker. They look to feel his spirit and know that they, too, have a piece of something larger than themselves. Because Kurt's impact was that profound. A rusted bridge complete with graffiti and muddy banks is, at first glance, nothing out of the ordinary. It looks worse for wear, and the town agrees. It doesn't seem fit for a campfire, let alone as temporary housing for a blond-haired, blue-eyed boy.

And maybe it never was.

The Young Street Bridge symbolizes Kurt's internal and external struggles, but it also reflects his perseverance. He wasn't destined to die young; he was failed. Honoring him means learning from those failures—acknowledging that no one is immune to pain and working to remove the stigma around mental health so others don't meet the same fate.

I watched a video where Kurt was referred to as a "broken musician."[22] The comment was in reference to his battered and abused black Fender Stratocaster, signed by all three members of Nirvana (which fetched close to $600,000 at auction).[23] Calling him "broken" reduces a complicated human being to a foregone conclusion, as if his fate were sealed rather than something that might have changed with support. His death was not inevitable. He had options. People always do. There is always hope.

We have access to Kurt's baby pictures and home videos—a blond, bright-eyed toddler bouncing around with a toy guitar—but none of that meant his fate was sealed. His life could have taken many directions, and viewing him as "destined" ignores how pain, stigma, and untreated struggles converged over time. What matters now is recognizing where systems and support fell short so we can create new beginnings for those who suffer in silence.

I spoke with Jimmy Drescher, lead singer of New York City's notable and esteemed hardcore punk band, Murphy's Law. During our conversation, Jimmy commented on Kurt and what could have been done on his behalf. "You can't save a person from themselves," he explained. "It's the point in your life where you're alone—you go into the bathroom, you're sitting on the toilet, you're alone—you're alone with yourself. It's the moments when you're alone with yourself that you're the most dangerous to yourself when you're in that head state. They should have put him [Kurt] somewhere and put him there for a long time until he changed. That's when you need to be monitored. And there was plenty of money for people to do that for him. But he was making too many other people money, so you keep the machine working because once the machine stops working, other people stop profiting."[24]

Kurt changed the landscape of music as we know it. He was simultaneously the antithesis and definition of a rock star. He was an introvert, a dreamer. And his legacy lives on today, albeit unquantifiably. Kurt's seen in some circles as the unsung hero of gay rights. He was a vocal feminist. He pushed for racial equality and in no uncertain terms told racists, misogynists, and homophobes to fuck off, not buy his music, and avoid his shows like the plague. His bottom line was to make an impact. And an impact he made.

I spoke with Rebecca Sevrin of Frightwig, the iconic all-female punk band Kurt had a deep appreciation for, about her take on his legacy.

"I like how Kurt was championing the underdogs," Rebecca explained. "He wasn't sexist. He liked weirdness, outcasts, and underdogs. Kurt saw beauty in places others couldn't and was able to channel his off-beat taste into music that moved a lot of people."[25]

Aberdeen may have felt stagnant for a young Kurt, but it still offered a boy from a broken home chances to explore his creativity. Smaller towns offer familiarity but less diversity, and for Kurt, this proved limiting—Olympia simply had more to offer. Yet something good still came from his time in Aberdeen. He turned those turbulent experiences into beautiful, prolific art that connected people from all walks of life and helped shape a man who would champion the marginalized. His lyrics may be indecipherable at times, but they carried ideas, values, and music born from real pain. Kurt could have done anything with his fame—bought cars, lived lavishly—but he remained a humble, bohemian artist who used his life experiences as his medium. The tragedy is that he couldn't see how important his words were, or that his life was worth living.

Despite everything Kurt endured as a child and young adult, his life ended far too soon. In the years that followed, alternative narratives grew out of the public's struggle to process such a devastating loss.

Mark Yarm, who has studied Kurt and the era extensively, and I discussed mental health and how people explain away uncomfortable truths.

"People can't really understand why he took his own life," Mark told me. "That's where it's created a vacuum where all these conspiracies come in . . . Obviously, in this day and age, there are so many outlandish conspiracy theories. But I've had people say to me or have heard people say, 'Why would he do it? He had a young daughter who he loved,' which is true. I'm sure he loved his daughter more than anything. But they ignore the fact that he was a depressive with real mental health issues. He was a heavy heroin user, and his marriage, by all accounts, was not in very good shape. There were the crushing demands of fame. All these things together, it makes a lot of sense . . . So, as someone who suffers from depression, I'm exhausted sometimes. But I think anyone who has experienced depression, it doesn't matter how much love you have for other people. Ultimately, you want the pain to be over . . . I did talk to Courtney Love. She is not innocent by any means, but there was a lot of sexism, blaming her for his death or saying she killed him, which is as ridiculous as it gets. But people are willing to believe that. I know why people make up conspiracy theories, and it's to make sense of a nonsensical world. I just thought that should be addressed. I think it's pretty pernicious. I did watch that *Soaked in Bleach* movie, and I thought it was just selling a false narrative . . . I understand the obsession with it, but it can get gross . . . Courtney Love is no angel, but blaming her and saying she's a murderess is just beyond the pale. The thing about Kurt is we did know that he was depressed and suicidal. We know an immense amount about his life that would point to why he would do it. It's not a big mystery, but people want a conspiracy. It's probably human nature to try and explain away an unpleasant truth."[26]

Regardless of the theories that circulate, the narrative that paints Kurt as tragic and broken ignores what he truly stood for. His struggles with depression, addiction, and fame were real, human experiences—not fodder for sensationalism. Acknowledging that complexity honors him far more than any one-sided story ever could.

Kurt chose to speak out about the societal issues that disgusted him. Even if he never meant to be the voice of a generation, his words resonated—and Aberdeen played a role in that. Maybe it was the overcast surroundings or the homeless nights that shaped him, but Kurt is still felt in Aberdeen, whatever becomes of the Young Street Bridge. He battled addiction and died devastatingly young, but his life still mattered. Acknowledging his struggles isn't shameful—it's how we learn, grow, and do better for those who need support.

Renaming—or saving—the Young Street Bridge doesn't promote addiction or suicide. It honors expression and resilience. And even if the bridge is torn down, what it represents endures: not despair, but hope.

Kurt Donald Cobain died at just twenty-seven years old in a greenhouse above the garage of his Lake Washington home. And he lives forever in the lives he's affected. He stood for equality. He stood for compassion. He stood for those the rest of the world forced to sit. If that isn't something to celebrate, then I don't know what is.

Chapter 2

"NEGATIVE CREEP"

As I researched Kurt's childhood in Aberdeen, I connected with some of his friends—people who prefer to remain anonymous and are wary of the attention. Past experiences with fans crossing boundaries had made privacy essential.

A few months before Kurt passed away, one friend ran into him in front of Linda's Tavern in Seattle. Kurt was happy, smiling. He had recently shared the stage with one of his favorite bands—the Meat Puppets—and was on cloud nine. No matter how famous he got, the real Kurt Cobain was still just a starstruck fan at heart. I think this detail speaks to his humility that I kept encountering throughout my research for this book.

While interviewing and working extensively with those who knew Kurt personally, I managed to gain access to images, insights, observations—and soon Kurt was no longer a stranger from the cover of *Rolling Stone*; he was someone's friend, son, grandson, father, brother, hero. He was, in some intangible way, becoming *my* friend—across time and space. And my admiration for him grew exponentially. As I listened to stories, I could feel the excitement for a time and place when a bunch of angsty kids were gearing up to start something revolutionary—when Nirvana was nothing more than an idea.

That idea became something more tangible when a friend of Kurt's sent me a series of photos—one of which showed a dilapidated, boarded-up home; another showed a vacant lot after the town tore down the otherwise historic location: 1000 ½ E. Second St. in Aberdeen. Another photo pictured a bathroom in squalid condition before the home's demolition. It was explained to me that the state of this bathroom probably wasn't much better when Kurt lived there. People question why the township didn't preserve this landmark. But if Kurt had crashed in as many places as it's reported, there would be countless buildings the township would have to maintain as they fell into disrepair.

Among the photos were shots of Kurt's grandfather, Leland Cobain. The love he had for Kurt was palpable in the images. Some captured him holding various electric guitars, or standing in front of the historic Melvan and Kurt's KISS mural, brimming with pride at his grandson's artwork. The real gut punch was a photo of Leland, smiling, proudly displaying a T-shirt with pictures of a young Kurt on the front. To him, these weren't pictures of Nirvana's lead singer; they simply were of his grandchild, and you could tell how much he missed Kurt. He outlived his grandson, and it didn't have to be that way.

Leland's home featured a gallery of photos dedicated to preserving his grandson's memory. He often welcomed Kurt's supporters to his house, and understood they were eager to learn more about their fallen hero; some wanted to touch a piece of his history, while others wanted to feel Kurt's presence.

Sadly, not everyone visited Leland with pure intentions. I learned about the time he was robbed after giving a visitor a ride into town. Even so, it didn't stop him from carrying on in his grandson's honor, writing back to Kurt's admirers whenever possible. I suppose it was equally comforting for him.

Over the years, Kurt's supporters—and harshest critics—sent Leland countless letters, often upward of thirty a day. They missed Kurt, and Leland offered a way back in—a way to feel connected to him again. Some simply needed a place to express something darker, one letter claiming Kurt was in an "everlasting lake of fire." It couldn't all be fan mail, after all; proof that cruelty still reaches the people left behind.

Leland did his best to answer every letter, although it became increasingly difficult as he aged. At one point, a template was created to help him streamline communication, keeping up with his beloved grandson's fan mail as best he could. When he finished reading letters, he felt uncomfortable discarding such personal correspondence. People bared their souls in these letters, and Leland felt that the onus to uphold their privacy was on him. What if someone went through his trash? So he asked a friend of Kurt's to dispose of them securely, ensuring the names and stories entrusted to him remained confidential.

Sadly, Leland joined Kurt in 2013, passing away at the same hospital where his grandson was born. But he celebrated Kurt up until the time of his passing. In addition to the private letters Leland received, the Aberdeen Museum of History once held memorabilia from Kurt's life and contained letters from admirers across the globe, a literal display of love and public remembrance for Nirvana's late frontman. A devastating fire in 2018 destroyed much of the collection, though some objects were reclaimed. A new museum has since opened in Aberdeen, providing another place for fans to connect with his legacy.

The rest of the photos were snippets of Kurt's life, from 17 Nussbaum Road (widely regarded as the site of Nirvana's first show) to Kurt's Memorial Park and the Young Street Bridge—"Kurt's Bridge." These photos conceal the raw and powerful statements scribbled by those who felt Kurt on a deeply profound level. Some comments were on the bridge itself; others were written on battered and bruised guitars, in true Kurt style.

One woman even flew from Spain to Aberdeen after losing her brother in a car crash. His final wish was to have his ashes scattered in the Wishkah River beside Kurt. Kurt's friends explained to her that he had never actually been scattered there, but in McLane Creek in Olympia. Even so, she chose to honor her brother's wishes, scattering his ashes in the Wishkah, a gesture that shows how deeply Kurt resonates across the world.

That same stretch of the Wishkah hasn't remained unchanged. In recent years, its muddy banks beneath it have visibly eroded. The reason isn't mysterious—the bridge's concrete foundation has become more exposed due to erosion and visitors leaving with fistfuls of dirt, wanting to carry home a piece of the Nirvana frontman. But for every ounce of mud they ride home with, they leave something in return—tangible offerings, from tennis sneakers and flowers to guitars smashed to bits.

There's a visible shared grief—something that's somehow universal. They may not have known Kurt, but that doesn't mean they don't feel an inexplicable connection, be it through similar upbringings or even shared hardships. To better understand the harsh realities behind Kurt's experiences and why this makes so many people feel seen, I reached out to Nick Soulsby, author of popular titles such as *I Found My Friends: The Oral History of Nirvana* and *Cobain on Cobain: Interviews and Encounters*. His honesty and devotion made him a trusted name in Kurt Cobain literature.

His words were sobering: "There's a homeless guy I've known some six to seven years called Darren. Each day, he pays to get a spare carrier bag from a shop. He shits in the bag at night because he doesn't want to shit in the street as if he was some animal, he doesn't want the indignity of fearing being seen or actually being seen, he doesn't want to be arrested or attacked, not to mention the basic discomfort of the cold night. So, every night he endures the indignity of sleeping by a bag of his own shit. Four years ago, someone called my name and I turned to see some happy guy I didn't recognize. It was Darren! Except his skin wasn't grey-blue and his eyes weren't looking into the abyss. He'd found a small job, they had a shower he could use, and he'd built up enough—he'd rented a room so he could sleep properly for the first time in years, which allowed him to look after himself, and he looked alive, drugs or no drugs, he was alive. Then COVID hit and it all went away and now he's in his thirties and he looks like a corpse. He's so scared of hospitals that he's been told by a doctor that he may have cancer, and he needs serious tests, but he simply won't go.

"The tenacity involved in surviving even brief periods of homelessness defies comprehension. The tiredness, the vulnerability, the loss of control, the feelings of failure and irrelevance. From the time of his parents' divorce in 1976, over the next ten years Cobain lived in a dozen homes, always temporary and unwanted, as well as enduring three spells of homelessness starting at age fifteen and involving sleeping in cars, on porches, in hospital waiting rooms, and in hallways. He loses a critical time in teenage life, one that embeds thinking that lasts a lifetime.

"I don't believe survival has much to do with determination. That would suggest it's something the individual has control over when it's just grasping at whatever might pull one up out of it. Cobain finds friends willing to take him in for brief periods so he can afford to pay rent prior to finding a girlfriend who has income stability and can give him a refuge to start creating. Some things do require a community to care, and at a particular moment, Cobain had just enough people around willing to care: that's what gave him the base to make his unique journey. Even after he breaks up with Tracy Marander, he continues to live at the same address, giving him the stability that gets him all the way from Nirvana not existing to *Nevermind* being recorded."

Nick then emphasized the urgent steps we must take as a society to support one another and break the stigma surrounding mental health and suffering—lessons that feel especially resonant when we consider Kurt's own life and challenges.

"It's very positive living in an era where the dialogue feels far less 'inside out' than it used to be, but it can still feel like people contemplating a broken machine and poking at it wondering, 'How do we fix this? How do we make it productive again?'" Nick explained. "There are so many complicated feelings, secret shames, critical internal voices, and unfathomable anxieties that can stop people seeking help at least to get through one day at a time. I can only hope that it's possible to make information visible and available, in as many different places and as many different formats as possible, so that the maximum number of people can find a channel or a helping hand at the right moment. It is sad so much of it is bound up with money to help those who can't afford to pour money into healing, or the time it can take to step away from sources of stress. And, in more cases than many people might wish to recognize, what we're speaking to is not an injury to be healed, it's a lifelong wound that will reopen and require coping mechanisms and support."[27]

Hearing Nick's reflections on lifelong wounds and the necessity of support systems made me reflect on the ways people learn to survive. His explanation of what it truly means to be unhoused—without shelter, without access to basic medical care, forced to rely on sheer survival instincts—reminded me how easy it is to romanticize these experiences in art or music. The tenacity we admire in Kurt is often the result of survival instincts kicking in, not a glamorous choice, and much of what we think we understand about his early life in Aberdeen ignores the real hardships he endured. And as Nick shared, Kurt wasn't the only one—many in his orbit faced the same unforgiving realities of being unhoused.

These hardships are reflected even in the stories that persist about his youth. One centered on his arrests and the time he spray-painted "AiNtGoTnOhoWwHaTcHaMaCaLlIt." During that time, Kurt lived with LaMont Schillinger, a teacher at Aberdeen High School. He was friends with his sons. While staying there, Kurt was arrested—but the well-worn mugshot isn't from that act of vandalism. It stems from a drunk and disorderly rooftop encounter. He and one of LaMont's sons were arrested together. When Schillinger went to bail out his boy, Kurt asked if he could be bailed out, too. LaMont refused, leaving Kurt to figure it out on his own.

According to those who knew him, Kurt's parents never checked on him while he was living with the Schillingers, making the arrest story that much more heartbreaking in how alone he often was. Decades later, the contrast is palpable: people from around the world flock to Aberdeen, looking to pay homage to Kurt. For a man who so often felt isolated, he ultimately touched the lives of millions.

While his message was universal, it's felt intimately from one person to the next, the sentiments on a graffiti-covered cement abutment offering a candid reminder. Beneath the bridge lies hallowed ground, a place where reflections weather the storm, just as a young Kurt Cobain once did. Thanks to Tori and Marcia Kovach and Denny Jackson, the Kurt Cobain Memorial Park—built beside this landmark—continues to honor his memory.

Chapter 3

"STAY AWAY"

Curtis Van Roland Thorfinson

Kurt Cobain had vitriol for Aberdeen, and at times the feeling was mutual. Yet plenty of people in town still choose to honor his memory. From shop owners to musicians and artists, there's no shortage of Aberdonians who take pride in the fact that Kurt came from their town. One of them is Curtis Van Roland Thorfinson, a longtime music photographer and owner of the Tangerine Tree, a record store in Aberdeen. He regularly hears stories about Kurt—from locals who knew him to visitors who come searching for traces of the musician who once called the town home.[28]

Some of these people share stories and anecdotes, adding to the legend that surrounds Kurt Cobain. Someone who grew up with Kurt once came into Curtis's shop, telling him about the two of them flipping through records as teenagers in Kurt's sister's bedroom before sneaking out for a smoke and wandering down beneath the Young Street Bridge. According to this man, it was the first time they had ever gotten high—the bridge, once again, becoming part of Kurt's story.

Curtis hears stories about the bridge regularly, but he believes they overshadow the truth. He pushes back, explaining that much of what's said about the bridge is often at odds with reality, especially when it comes to how significant it really was in Kurt's life. While he can imagine Kurt going down there to smoke cigarettes or spend time with friends, Curtis questions the idea that Kurt ever slept beneath it—one of the most persistent stories attached to the bridge.

"It's a really cold, rainy area," he says. "I can't imagine it's a good place to sleep . . . There's better, let's put it that way."

City officials have proposed replacing the aging bridge, with serious structural problems driving the conversation. The project would cost over $23 million, and while many residents understand that its demolition is largely about safety, others hope part of the bridge will be preserved. Curtis understands the need to keep a piece of the structure in Aberdeen, if only as a reminder of what it represents—Kurt, and a space to grieve and reflect.

"It's time to invest money and get things built—and I understand that—but they can always save a portion, take the opportunity to save that area underneath the bridge where it says, 'From the Muddy Banks of the Wishkah,' and make that for vendors and other people to still use . . . I don't know if it'll be there in the future. It's kind of sad."

Not everyone in Aberdeen regards the bridge as a piece of failing infrastructure. Many see it as one of the last tethers to the town's most famous son.

I ask Curtis how people in town talk about Kurt today.

"You live in Aberdeen; you met Kurt. You're friends with some of his old friends. How do you feel when people in town say that he was just this drug addict who committed suicide? What do you think about the town not renaming the bridge in his honor?"

Curtis is thoughtful in his response: "Well, I feel that there's been that kind of feeling from the folks here, up until recently. It still exists here. For the bridge, I think the people in Aberdeen felt that there were more suitable names to name an Aberdeen landmark, so they offered other names besides Kurt's."

Regardless of how people in town feel about Kurt, people keep visiting Aberdeen in search of Cobain's roots.

"Do you feel that when people come into your store looking for records, you get a lot of out-of-towners in search of Cobain lore?" I ask.

Curtis laughs. "Oh, I can't keep the albums in stock, so yes. I get the *Bleach* record, and I'll buy ten copies for every other album's three copies. So, yeah, they sell. The shirts sell. The albums sell. I think that anything that is a copy of a flyer . . . anything like that, they sell, too."

Nirvana's—Kurt Cobain's in particular—fame continues to grow exponentially. Consider the *In Utero* 30th Anniversary 8LP Super Deluxe, fetching an astounding $324.98 at the time of writing this,[29] or the fact that 2023 alone saw two of Kurt's guitars go to auction, one yielding close to $600,000[30] and the other selling for over $1.5 million.[31] So, no, Nirvana and its infectious lead singer's popularity are showing zero signs of slowing down.

For all the astronomical figures attached to his name now, Kurt was still once just a guy standing in line at a movie theater.

Curtis recalls his first meeting with the Nirvana frontman. "My friend Jay and I were standing in line smoking Camel cigarettes, waiting to get into *The Unbearable Lightness of Being*, which is a Milan Kundera film, and I got a tap on my shoulder. Because I grew up in Ballard, I knew of Reciprocal Recording studio, and I knew who Jack Endino was [producer, *Bleach*] . . . It was Kurt. So, we sat there and smoked cigarettes and basically talked about what he was doing. He was recording at that point in time; he was traveling over to Smart Studios with Butch Vig [producer, *Nevermind*] in Wisconsin. And he was in a quiet, kind of giggly mood, which continued when we went into the movie. He and the lady that was with him were sitting behind us, Kurt with his shoes up on the seat next to me . . . I could hear them giggling throughout the movie. I wondered what was so funny . . . And then it was over and we departed. But when he first tapped me on the shoulder, he just wanted a cigarette, and then he wanted another. I think he had about three while we were sitting there talking. He was such a prolific smoker. I felt that Kurt was quiet and really soft-spoken. And my friend Jay, who's the opposite, was kind of overshadowing and out-talking everybody. . . . It was definitely before things went a little bit . . . crazy and big with *Nevermind*. I feel like this was the calm before the thunder of Nirvana."

"Did anybody else recognize Kurt, or was this before the band was really recognizable?"

"Yeah, I don't think anybody else recognized him," Curtis says. "I recognized him. Everybody's always like, 'Did you get his autograph? Did you get his picture?' I was like, 'It was 1991 . . . I didn't have a phone.' What's funny is that I'm a photographer, and I didn't even have my camera with me."

What I love about this story is its simplicity—a reminder that Kurt was a real person. And, of course, the movie fits him. *The Unbearable Lightness of Being* wrestles with the tension between freedom and emotional weight—the same kind of searching Kurt gravitated toward in books like *Perfume*, a book about beauty, alienation, and people trying to make sense of a world that often feels designed to isolate them.

"I know there's a lot of back and forth with how Aberdeen residents see Kurt," I note. "But the people who choose to honor him—what are some local goings-on in his honor? There's February 20th . . . Kurt Cobain Day, right?"

"Yeah, there are a lot of different characters here. I think a lot of people are upset that certain places have gotten torn down. When Kurt was in a band called Fecal Matter, they used to practice around Aberdeen—one spot was at Rita's, Greg Hokanson's [drummer, Fecal Matter] mother's place—with Kurt, Dale [Crover, Melvins], and sometimes others. They also had a gig in Moclips at the Spot Tavern . . . but the town tore it down. Locally, there was a place called The Pourhouse where I've heard Kurt and Krist played Beatles songs drunkenly after a show that took place in Hoquiam Eagles. We're talking about very early . . . right after high school."

"So that probably would have been around '85, right?" I ask.

"I would say that's about right. So, a lot of people look at the township taking away the things that the bands played in—that Kurt played in—and I think that makes a lot of people really upset. But those people that tore it down . . . they knew what they were doing. They're part of what I'd say is that group of people who want to develop Aberdeen into this attractive place for people to move to. I think that a lot of people here could care less. But you have certain people here in town who are investing lots of money into making places for the flocks of thousands of people who visit, so not only will you have record stores, but you'll also have a future museum that you could go to, and find books, and do all kinds of stuff like that."

"There are people still working to preserve his memory, despite those who really don't want to associate him with the town," I say. "There are things going on to keep Kurt alive in Aberdeen."

"Exactly. I bought a guitar that belonged to Warren Mason, who was Kurt's guitar teacher. And I haven't decided what to do with that, but I thought if there ever was a museum that this could live in . . . And other people have said that they have artifacts."

I consider how these fragments of Kurt's life still circulate, pointing out that, even thirty years after his death, Kurt's memory is honored worldwide. Curtis agrees, explaining that even in his travels, he hears people across the globe talking about Kurt, placing him among the greats.

I ask Curtis what it was about Kurt that made him stand out—why so many people found him relatable.

"It's such a good question because I think that a lot of the movements, let's say in punk rock music, have not always been the same, meaning that there are movements that were about or against misogyny," Curtis explains. "There were movements that were against being homophobic. There was a very powerful punk rock movement at the famous 924 Gilman that came out of California, and I know that Kurt was somebody who subscribed to punk rock music. He really enjoyed that music."

Curtis explains that a similar sense of authenticity carried over into how people experienced Nirvana. That kind of honesty has a way of putting words to emotions, making people stop and think, *this feels different*. They sense the music is coming from a place of brutal honesty—the same way many first connected with *Bleach*. It was an album that felt like it was made just for them.

"I do think that if Kurt wasn't attractive, he probably would not have been as popular," Curtis says. "If he wasn't poor and didn't come from a little tiny logging town, he probably wouldn't have been as popular. The fact is that he was from a rough part of the world, and I heard things—stories—about him being pulled off stage by assholes and beaten up. I've heard stories about him being teased.

"In the existing punk rock community here—there are a lot of people who tend to take jiu-jitsu for self-defense. But I do feel that, at this point, if Kurt Cobain saw Aberdeen, he'd say, 'Hey, it's come a long way. The LGBTQ+ community has its own parade with the rest of the town. They have their own rainbow flags in their stores.' That would have never happened if Kurt Cobain hadn't paved the way thirty years ago. It just never would have."

Kurt's impact on the small town of Aberdeen didn't stop at advocacy for the marginalized or oppressed groups. The ripple effect of Kurt's life and Nirvana's music has had profound life-changing effects on individuals from Aberdeen, and people from far and wide who visit the small town to pay homage to a man that quite literally saved them.

"There are people who come into my record store and tell me how Kurt changed their lives. People talk about how Nirvana kept them from killing themselves. People who tattooed artwork on their arms. It goes on and on and on. It's more than just a click in time. It's a movement, and I think it's becoming legend. That's the best way to put it. It's becoming bigger than Kurt."

"I've heard [that] from the people he directly affected, too. . . . from the people he saved from themselves, so to speak," I replied.

While Kurt was moving in between Aberdeen and Olympia, Curtis explained that Tracy, Kurt's former girlfriend, worked so that Kurt could stay home and write songs. Buzz Osborne (of the Melvins) also helped Kurt by bringing him along as a roadie, giving him a deeper connection to music and performance. Through music, Curtis notes Kurt "found his family," who enabled him to do what he did.

"A lot of people are determined, but they also need people around them to help and support them and get them to where they want to be. I think Kurt had loving people around him through different parts of his life. . . . He found his ability to say, 'Hey, I'll give you myself, and not have to acclimate to my surroundings.' That part is important to the story. He was allowed to be himself."

When you're forced to rely on yourself early, there isn't much room to be anything but who you are. Kurt's early life wasn't stable. He was passed from relative to relative, sometimes with nowhere permanent to land. In a way, that kind of uncertainty forces resilience early. Sadly, it's something many young people learn before they should.

"Is anything being done to assist residents who may be unsheltered?" I ask, thinking about the uncertainty Kurt experienced growing up.

"Yes," Curtis says. "How do you differentiate between who's the problem and who the people are who really need a place to sleep? But it's like, 'Hey, get sleeping bags, get meals, and go down there and help these people in need.' Multiple groups are going down there giving away food in packets. There are libraries. There are food banks. Aberdeen is number one in all the areas. They bring all the people in need of housing to Aberdeen. All those individuals come here because Aberdeen has the facilities to help them. So, yes. Aberdeen has a lot of unhoused residents. Aberdeen has a lot of people that need help . . . It's kind of become that people are purposefully putting themselves on the street, purposefully going out and stealing stuff; but then there are other people . . . The houses, the economy, and everything is pushing people out of their homes, and now you're seeing your neighbors pushing shopping carts as a result."

Aberdeen continues to draw people who feel a connection to Nirvana and to Kurt Cobain in particular. Some arrive simply to see the town Kurt voiced opinions about, but others end up staying, drawn to a place that feels like him while embracing an emerging arts scene.

Emerging musicians play open mic nights, many of them first inspired by Nirvana at a young age. Others come hoping to channel that same restless creativity into their own work, the overcast skies the soundtrack to their inner musings—writing, creating, or finding their place in a town Kurt once inhabited. People like Curtis also work to encourage that next generation, helping disadvantaged kids get a fair chance to explore music and creativity for themselves.

"It's all because of Nirvana," Curtis says. "You have that kind of small-town commitment that supports local artists because they appreciate how Nirvana put Aberdeen on the map."

"Do you think that local people in Aberdeen took something positive away from Kurt and his life?" I ask Curtis.

He thinks about this. "I would like to think so, but I feel that . . . I don't know. More and more, we're becoming selfish. I don't know how much we think about each other anymore. A lot of those people who spoke up against the wrongs that happened to innocent people, you don't have those people doing that anymore . . . If you speak up, you become a black sheep, and you have to be able to wear that title. You have to be able to be tough enough to get through it. There was supposed to be a Kurt Cobain youth center. Never saw it happen. There was supposed to be a place for kids to go other than the YMCA. That's what made it special to me, my record store . . . I could hand these kids a guitar or a keyboard for them to play, ask them to file some records or teach them a trade. I was really able to help the youth of Aberdeen. Who knows, maybe one of the kids that comes shopping in my store is going to be the next Cobain. You never know. But the proposed youth center, I haven't seen it happen yet. And I'm like, 'Well, it should. We should have a place that helps kids,' just like I try to help them. We need to help them to understand that there's value in who they are. But instead, these kids are missing out on childhood due to societal issues that plague them."

What Curtis says sounds familiar to Kurt's experience.

"Do you feel Kurt in Aberdeen?" I ask. "I know how that sounds."

"It's interesting," Curtis begins. "If you listen to the music and live here, you do feel where Kurt is coming from; you do understand it a lot better than if you lived somewhere else."

When he moved to Aberdeen from Seattle, Curtis noticed, "there's a rough exterior; there's a way of thinking. There's a way of understanding things."

"I feel that it's a very lonely place in a lot of ways," he adds. "It's not a place where you're finding you have a lot of friends everywhere. It's isolating. It's not for everybody. . . . This is the soundtrack of [Kurt's] life. This is the way that he wrote his lyrics. Did he think, *I'm going to write a song about Aberdeen*? I wonder if a lot of his angst and his anger—if it wouldn't have been there if he hadn't been mistreated.

"And that's the thing. I think that the environment makes us who we are. Aberdeen is shaping people, including Cobain way back when, and I find that I see kids that look to have his haircut. And it's such an important thing. Kurt's inspired generations of kids who just want to be tough enough and have a voice . . . There are bands everywhere that are starting up. Some people want to have the same guitar as Kurt. I find that owning a record store here, I wouldn't want to have it anywhere else because there are real people—real music fans—and I think they're very proud of their poet who came from Aberdeen. He's a pretty important guy to a lot of people here, and I think that it's nice to live among people who appreciate him, versus what I felt when I first got here. I felt that there was just a lot of animosity."

Aberdeen's poet. I couldn't have said it better myself. After speaking with Curtis, I understood more about Kurt's Aberdeen roots, the way the town remembers him, and his indelible legacy, his flaws as widely celebrated as his successes. Curtis' perspective evoked a young Kurt—ambitious, unapologetic, and determined to be heard beyond Aberdeen.

As one rabbit hole led to another, I found myself digging deeper into the first bloom of Nirvana, the early days of "Kurdt." My journey to learn more about Aberdeen's most famous son continued, sifting through various lore and distinguishing—to the best of my ability—fact from fiction, gathering information straight from the tap.

In my research, Nirvana landmarks that were long demolished, torn down but not forgotten, painted vivid scenes of the band's inception. I wondered what Kurt's life looked like then, including late-night jam sessions and Nirvana's first show. My next stop was clear: The Green House.

Chapter 4

"SCHOOL"

Tony Poukkula

THE AIR WAS THICK WITH SWEAT, FEEDBACK, AND NERVOUS ANTICIPAtion—most of it radiating from the band. Kurt Cobain leaned into his guitar, hair obscuring his face as he played with a kind of raw urgency. In the cramped living room, something electric hung in the air, a mixture of excitement and uncertainty. The band was barely Nirvana, yet they were already beginning to write history—even if no one in the room knew it at the time. It was a Saturday in March 1987; the address was 17 Nussbaum Road in Raymond, Washington, affectionately referred to as "The Green House." To some, it was just an ordinary house party. But in the not-so-distant future, it would become the site of a historic event: Nirvana's first show.

They didn't even have an official name at this point.

To learn about The Green House, I took my questions to the source: Tony Poukkula.[32] This was his home, and he jammed with the band—a legendary badge of honor if ever there was one.

★★★

"The show was in my front room," Tony begins. "Kurt, Krist, and I went to the same high school. I was very good friends with Ryan Aigner [Nirvana's first unofficial manager]—he was like a brother to me. Ryan also managed my band, Black Ice, for a couple of years. I've always been good friends with him and his wife. One day, while visiting Ryan's home, we started chatting, and he mentioned Nirvana. He said, 'Hey, Kurt and Krist have a band together. I know that you guys have jam sessions all the time and have parties on the weekends. They need to get out and do something. Could they come down and play at your house sometime?' I said, 'Yeah, we're always open.'

"Nirvana came around that Friday—I had a PA, drums, my amp—everything—already set up. But Kurt brought his own amp, and Krist played with all his own gear, as well. I actually still have the microphone Kurt sang with.

"Keep in mind that I was thinking this would just be a jam session, so I was playing along with them for the first song. This was when they gave us 'Heartbreaker.' But Ryan came over and said, 'Hey, they don't really jam with people.' He was whispering in my ear while I still had my guitar on. He said, 'They don't really jam with people, do you mind sitting out?' and I said, 'No problem.' I went and grabbed a Michelob, and I just sat and listened to them. They were a little rough, but I thought the songs were great. I remember standing in the kitchen with my roommate talking about how good the songs were."

"That's amazing." I try to picture cracking open a beer as Nirvana plays their first-ever show in my house. The concept seems unreal.

I tell Tony that I researched Aberdeen extensively—studying Kurt's own interviews, combing through old newspaper articles, speaking with people connected to the town and Kurt's early life, and reaching out to locals working to preserve the area's history—in an effort to better understand his roots.

"Aberdeen was pretty depressed," Tony tells me. "It was a cedar mill town. And Raymond was even more of a cedar mill town. I think it was a population of four thousand in Raymond. I think, at that time, Aberdeen had a population of eighteen thousand. And the band drove out to Raymond for this show; it was their first time out as Nirvana. It was great music. This was when they had Aaron Burckhard on drums. I actually used to jam with Dale Crover all the time, and then with Dave Foster. He was one of their drummers, too. We always had a lot of fun."

"That must have been wild, to put on their first show."

"I didn't think about it at all until I came home from work one day and my wife turned MTV on," Tony says. "I was watching and I said, 'I think I know these guys.' That was a really weird time. I mean, it was crazy. But I was pretty pumped for them. Growing up, we all started playing in bands at a young age. A lot of guys would gravitate towards being in bands; they wanted to start playing instruments early on. Kurt was one of them . . . he was always interested in what we had going on musically. My singer, John, used to say that he saw Kurt on our front porch, standing there, looking through our front window, watching us practice. I always had my back to him, so I didn't see him, but John said he ran him off a few times."

I can see a young boy, dirty-blond hair erratic across his face, hands cupped around piercing blue eyes, staring in wonder as he dreamed about his own band. Kurt's home life left much to be desired, and music was his reprieve. So naturally, he immersed himself in it to escape—the candor in his creations offering a tether to something bigger than himself.

Once upon a time, Kurt was simply a dreamer—like so many of us.

It's no secret that his parents' divorce stripped Kurt from the only stability he knew, leaving him craving something constant. Music gave him a way to process his feelings, his creativity showing up across different artistic outlets. He gravitated toward expression as a way of understanding his role in what must have felt like a confusing world.

Kurt wasn't alone in trying to make sense of an unforgiving place, imagining a future that pushed back against what Aberdeen had to offer. Music offered him that possibility; it offered him a life where his imagination knew no bounds, existing outside the confines and isolation of the only town he had ever called home. Maybe somewhere he could find people whose values aligned more closely with his own. He eventually left Aberdeen, connecting with others who shared that same restless energy and the desire to build something that was truly his.

"He was just a punk kid, you know?" Tony says, laughing. He even recalls Kurt once asking if he would teach him guitar, though nothing ultimately came of it.

"What was he like in high school?" I ask. "Was he introverted?"

"He was very quiet," Tony tells me. "I remember this one art class he was in. There was all this killer—just killer—artwork hanging up that Kurt did. Like artwork of Jimi Hendrix and other incredible people. I remember his Jimi Hendrix artwork, and it was phenomenal."

Kurt's artwork, scribbled across his bedroom walls or scrawled inside his Mead notebooks, carried the same urgency to create—another language that allowed him to express what he struggled to say out loud. Whatever space was available became a canvas. Those same Mead notebooks held his private musings—thoughts and sketches that would eventually be made commercially available to the public. From sheetrock to paper, Kurt was never without the need to create, to purge what marked his soul—or what tainted it.

The drawings themselves were raw and unfiltered, littered with morbid, darkly humorous images, intensely personal in a way that offered a glimpse into the restless and relentless mind behind them. In many ways, Kurt's artwork was a portal into another time and place, long before fame entered the picture. The urge to create had been there since the beginning—his voice and imagination later resonating with millions.

That reflection leads us to a different subject: the way Kurt's story has been told over the years.

"There's something I want to comment on. There have been a few authors from our area who wrote about Nirvana and Kurt, but they never reached out to me," Tony begins. "I was involved in that music scene, especially when Nirvana was starting out, and I have many fond memories. But these authors never contacted me. Suffice it to say, some people are trying to ride Kurt's coattails by retelling his story. But if these people really wanted to do their research, they would have gotten a hold of me."

So much of Kurt's life has been cherry-picked, it seems—the most sensationalized parts shoved to the foreground, while perspectives like Tony's are sometimes glossed over. Kurt's life was a mixture of beauty and pain; it becomes difficult to separate the good from the bad, tragedy taking center stage. Unfortunately, Kurt's upbringing in a bleak Aberdeen only reinforces darker narratives, the lighter memories dismissed as less compelling.

"I think that's why we have so many musicians from Aberdeen and some of the surrounding areas; because everyone needed to dive into something," Tony tells me.

"People would say how they weren't surprised when he took his life or that he was someone they knew was going to die young," I reply, considering his point.

Tony doesn't hesitate. "That's kind of a bullshit attitude."

"It is."

Our conversation gave me a glimpse into a less familiar part of Nirvana's history—the same history that birthed one of the greatest musicians of all time. Whether you played in a band or simply hung out with kids who did, you know the palpable excitement that went into these shows. Back rooms and basements were packed with secondhand furniture, while beer bottles decorated every conceivable surface. Cigarette smoke hung thick in the air as kids congregated for one reason: to find their people. The band wasn't just there to perform; they were there to help everyone escape, if only for a few minutes or a few hours. Complicated home lives didn't exist—they simply faded to gray. The only thing that mattered in the room was the energy, the camaraderie, and the thought that something better wavered on the horizon.

I thought about the music that shaped Kurt and how—like many musicians—The Beatles impacted him. On October 27, 1989, while being interviewed by Mimmo Caccamo on his early musical influences, Kurt said:

> "I would say the biggest influence I've ever had would be The Beatles, because I listened to The Beatles since I was five years old up until I was in fourth grade—the same three records over and over every night! I sang the songs, and I wanted to see The Beatles. It was about 1973 when I heard on the radio that they'd been broken up for three years, I was totally devastated! Then I was introduced to hard rock, such as Aerosmith and Led Zeppelin, and I got into that. It kinda meshed together when I started playing guitar, it kinda intertwined—The Beatles melodic style and hooks with heavy raunchy guitars. I would say that's probably how our style started."[33]

I could only glean so much about Kurt from old interviews. When speaking with those who knew him, I found that I was offered a more intimate piece of the confounding—and intricate—puzzle that is Kurt Cobain.

After Tony and I spoke, I reached out to Ryan Aigner. Ryan is incorrectly regarded as Nirvana's first official manager. He assumed the responsibilities, but the title was not one he sought out.

Ryan knew Kurt Cobain and Krist Novoselic before the world did. He understood the underpinnings of Nirvana and what went into the band's inception. I couldn't create a complete picture of Kurt without talking to Ryan, so I reached out, my intentions clear from the outset. I knew there was more to Kurt than depression; there were pockets of pure happiness, and Ryan shared with me honest reflections about Kurt Cobain, the human being.

Chapter 5

"IN BLOOM"

Ryan Aigner

When I reached out to Ryan Aigner, I was expecting a brief interview. Instead, we had numerous conversations, and he became an invaluable part of this book. Not only did Ryan help me understand more about Kurt, but he shone a light on Nirvana's early years, dating back to when Krist and Kurt were still in high school. I could have used other books as research, but I wanted to hear stories firsthand from Ryan, knowing he would be essential to this process. However, not every story is recounted here, as I felt that certain pieces of Kurt Cobain's illustrious history deserved privacy. Instead, I stuck to what showcased Kurt's unwavering tenacity and originality.

Throughout this project, Ryan was incredibly humble and gracious, although initially hesitant to share his experiences about Kurt and Nirvana. There had been previous liberties taken with some of his stories, but after a thoughtful conversation where I explained my intentions behind this book, he agreed to a formal interview.

Our meeting would be the first of several pivotal conversations. Thanks to Ryan, I was able to understand more about Kurt—where he came from and the experiences that shaped the person he would become.[34]

★★★

"After Kurt passed away, I was kind of broken up about it—as you can imagine—for about ten years," Ryan tells me.

He's open and honest, and I know this is a difficult subject for him to discuss.

"I really didn't know how to handle it. I mean, we're [Ryan and Kurt] only about a year apart, so I was twenty-eight when he died . . . Right before Kurt passed, I thought that I'd been wanting to reach out to Kurt and Krist for a while, as I was certainly proud of them and all the things that were going on. And I wasn't sure about all the media hoopla that was going on, the rumors, and all that.

"And then Kurt was dead. I thought, *I'm never going to question myself about reaching out to an old acquaintance again*."

I don't take Ryan's words lightly. He understands the loss behind this book, the reason Walter brought me here. We speak briefly about the project and my plans for using it to assist various organizations before shifting to how he originally connected with Nirvana.

"The confusion is over how I got involved with the band," Ryan explains. "But I was involved with them before they *were* a band."

I tell Ryan about my conversation with Tony Poukkula, specifically Nirvana's show at his home.

"When Tony and his band started rehearsing up the street, I was attracted to that," Ryan begins. "My parents were out of the house working on call all the time. So I was allowed to go up the street to where Tony was playing. Tony and all the guys he was with were a year or two older than me. And I showed up day after day after day and became good friends with all of them. That's when I started understanding about this thing where you can just be a musician. The members of Tony's band—Black Ice—were my doorway through. I talked myself into not only being their sort of roadie/production manager, but I was also running sound for them. I even recorded a couple of mixtapes live. And years later, various members of the group said, 'You know, the way you captured sounds, it's the greatest.' But I did all this because I loved it and loved all these people, and that's how I got interested in music, progressing into playing an instrument. I wanted to learn from Tony, who is extremely talented."

As Ryan's passion for music grew, so did his involvement. Nothing about those early days was glamorous—getting to rehearsals meant loading gear onto a local transit bus for the trek over to the Novoselic house.

One day, they were loudly rehearsing in Krist's bedroom when his father, Kristo, came home and burst in, demanding to know what was happening. The group was scared to death, but Krist calmed him down, and as they were leaving, his father said, "Why don't you sell those goddamn guitars and buy shovels or something useful?" Years later, when Nirvana was ready to press their first single, "Love Buzz/ Big Cheese," they etched that line into the record's runout groove, which became infamous and widely remembered.

In Nirvana's earliest years, even the smallest steps forward felt significant. For a group of young musicians coming from a struggling logging community like Aberdeen, the idea that anyone in Seattle might take their music seriously was almost unbelievable.

"The minute we were recording anything, it was a huge, huge success," Ryan tells me. "We went from this poor, depressing, no-future community to having people in Seattle who were willing to put us out."

At the same time, the band's confidence was still fragile. They were young musicians watching other groups begin carving out space in the regional scene, trying to imagine whether something similar might be possible for them.

Despite his closeness with Krist Novoselic and Tony Poukkula, Ryan had yet to really connect with Kurt.

"But that's when all this started, back in '81 with the individuals in this very small community. We all knew each other in one way or another. You know, Krist was Mr. Popular and Kurt was the wallflower. He was this individual whose family was in disarray . . . I didn't live very far away from them, so I got to go over there a couple of times and he [Kurt] was like, 'I don't want to mess this up for my mom. Because she needs it.' But we all understood each other because of our families, and we tended to sympathize with each other, but we didn't really talk about these things.

"The very first time Nirvana ever played anywhere was at Tony Poukkula's rental house that he was sharing with Jeff [Franks] in Raymond, Washington. Jeff was the drummer in Tony's band."

I assume he's referring to the show at Tony Poukkula's house in March 1987, which he confirms, and then explains what the band had in store for them in the weeks following the show.

A few weeks later, on May 6, 1987, the band performed a radio broadcast at Evergreen State College's KAOS station in Olympia. At that point, they still had not settled on the name Nirvana. For a time, Kurt had been calling the group Skid Row, until discovering another band had already claimed the name.

Ryan remembers this period slightly differently from Tony. In his recollection, Aaron Burckhard had already left the band before they began performing under the name Nirvana.

"Aaron B. was out of the band before they formally became—and performed—anywhere as Nirvana," he says. "Dave Foster was 'the' actual first drummer of the actual band Nirvana. . . . I started hanging out a lot at this house where Kurt and Matt [Lukin] had lived, but Matt had recently moved out because the place was pretty primitive. There was a hole in the floor, and Kurt had moved this big clawfoot bathtub into the kitchen so he could raise his turtles in it. He didn't really have food there either, so he'd come over to my house to get something to eat.

"I don't think the stove even worked. The whole place was tiny, and the living room was packed with band gear. It was so dingy that

I'd usually go back home just to use the bathroom. That's the problem with poverty—you get these slumlords who keep the rent low but never fix anything."

"Did Tracy [Kurt's girlfriend at the time] live there?" I ask.

"Tracy came down on weekends," Ryan says.

He recalls that she, along with Shelli Dilley, who was formerly married to Krist Novoselic, and several others from the local scene, were all there at the Raymond show.

"The night of the Raymond show—they finished their set at the end of the tape, and Tony hadn't had an opportunity to play," Ryan explains. "So the whole point was them [Tony and Jeff] hosting and drinking and having these jam sessions, basically. And when they [Nirvana] were done playing, everyone's guitars were still there. I was a right-handed guitar player so I ended up picking up Krist's bass, and Kurt stopped playing and we went on and played 'Breaking the Law' for a couple of bars. One of the things Krist was still interested in was singing and playing, so we went into a twenty-minute version of 'Sex Bomb' by Flipper. That's when Krist went into the bathroom, took his shirt off, squirted himself with fake blood, and we went back to playing."

After speaking with Tony and Ryan, I noticed some conflicting information about Nirvana's first show. I was curious to see if Kurt spoke about this show and came across an interview he did with Rick Hankey and Jennifer Carr for MTV on December 13, 1993 (*Live and Loud*).[35]

"Do you have any memories of the first couple of gigs you did?" they asked.

Kurt responded:

> "Let's see . . . the very first one was a party, I think. If we played together in the house for a couple of hours and two people stopped by, we considered that a gig. So, I mean, that was good enough. We had an audience of two people. Locals who hated our guts and thought it was terrible music. But the first

> official show we actually played was at a party. It was way out in the woods. I can't even remember what town it was. It was somewhere in between Montesano and Aberdeen and, it was, you know, a typical kegger type of thing. It was pretty amazing. That was a fun night. I think it was Halloween night. We were really drunk, and we had some fake Halloween blood, and we smeared it all over ourselves and played our seven songs off the tape. And we alienated the entire crowd. The entire party moved into the kitchen and left the band, just left us there in the front room playing our songs."

What caught my attention was that the party at Tony's house was in March of 1987, but Kurt said their first show was most likely on Halloween. Research from LiveNirvana.com shows that on October 30, 1988, Nirvana played at the Evergreen State College in Olympia. More specifically, in Dorm K208. In the pictures from this show, Kurt and Krist are covered in fake blood. According to Ryan, there was also fake blood at the Raymond house party. Kurt said that the band was left to play alone in the front room while the party moved to the kitchen; in our interview, Tony explained that the band played in the front room of his house. Ryan and Tony both agree the band's first show was in Raymond in March 1987. Since Kurt said he was inebriated at the Halloween show, I suspect he melded these two memories.

Ryan was around for several of Nirvana's early rehearsals, watching the band work through songs in cramped living rooms long before they ever played larger venues. He had spent years around other local musicians, including Tony Poukkula and his band, so he already had a sense of what most aspiring groups sounded like at the time. Kurt, however, approached music a little differently, and it caught Ryan's attention.

"I had been to only a dozen of these rehearsals, and after Kurt would quit for the night or the song, he would say, 'What do you think?' And I was pretty blown away by all of it, you know?

"So, here's the thing. When I was working with Tony, he was learning Van Halen songs. And I was used to working with him and running sound for the entire band, watching him night after night after night. But also, Tony and I lived together for a little while when he was in between situations and my house was just sort of like an 'everybody-was-welcome-there' kind of place when I was with my mom. And that's how I got to know all these people. But Tony could just whip out these eruptions like 'Hot for Teacher,' 'Panama,' and 'Mean Streets,' you know? It was like, 'Holy crap, dude.'

"And Kurt was writing these songs that were way, way simpler. But they sounded sonically—especially with the vocals and the bass and the drums, the whole thing compressed, and there's just literally three of you in the room—it just sounded like this huge orchestration. Like the same kind of orchestration that I'd just experienced with this [Tony's] band, Black Ice . . . I mean, [Kurt's] just playing through this tiny little Fender Champ amplifier, and he's got this really silly Hi-Flier. It's got [string] action on it that's like three feet off the fretboard, and I don't even understand how he's getting the sound.

"Because I came out of this previous experience [with Black Ice] where it's all about how you have to have all the parts and pieces, and it's got to be just exactly the right parts and pieces. And then it takes all this finesse, and then you've got it. But with Kurt, there was never finesse. You just look at him and it's like: no finesse.

"But he was the first person that made me say, 'Oh, maybe I could do this,' and when I said that he was like, 'Oh, absolutely.' Whereas Tony never said that to me. Tony humored me by saying, 'Okay, do this or do that.' And Krist—when I was down in Arizona with him, riding around in the back of the Zebra Van, practicing—he would teach me an A chord or an E chord and basically say, 'Just play that and go to the G and then go back to the A and keep doing that.' It was a little condescending.

"But Kurt was the one who gave a couple of pieces of advice that I actually followed through with. He said, 'Well, you know, show me a particular riff or a couple of notes or whatever it is that you're currently playing.' So, I showed him, and he said, 'Well, that's a song right there.' And I honestly didn't expect [him] to say it, and I was like, 'Oh, come on. Quit BS-ing me.' And he was just completely sincere. He said, 'You see the things that I'm creating, they're less complicated than that.' He was literally the first person to ever give me that kind of confidence, ever."

The gratitude in Ryan's voice is unmistakable.

"And then he [Kurt] said one other little piece of advice that ended up being really useful. He said, 'You just get some guys and start a band. It doesn't matter if you know how to play or not. You work it all out. And that's all you got to do.' And that was a very different message."

"So Kurt kind of encouraged you and made you aware of the fact that you could do that—start a band and write songs—too?" I ask.

"Yeah, that's it exactly," Ryan says. "That's really where [Kurt] sort of gave me the license to step away from them [him and Krist] . . . And because he also said that what you do is you just find four musicians and find a room and start playing what you can. And it will come later. It will begin to take shape and form as you apply your aesthetic knowledge. He didn't say those exact words, specifically. But he was absolutely right. That's exactly what we did. And that's where the foundation of the Psychlodds [Ryan's band] began. And I mean, the first two concerts that my band played, we opened for Nirvana. They were dinky little shows that nobody knew about, nobody came to, nobody made any money, it was all out of pocket, and equipment broke down. I think it's nuts what we did in order to not go to a football game."

Despite everything he was going through personally, Kurt often seemed to encourage and lift those around him. He told Ryan: "You know, it's about one percent talent and about ninety-nine percent creativity."

"And that's the exact opposite of what Tony would have said at the time," Ryan says. "I mean, that was the whole argument with why I was not working with Black Ice anymore. I was saying, 'You know, you need to write original songs,' but they wanted to be a cover band.

They said that the only way they got gigs was to play what people wanted to hear. But the thing with Kurt was that he was like, 'Yeah, no, I don't even know how to do that [play covers]. So I have to write my own stuff.' And that's the thing about the difference between creativity and artistry.

"In your opinion, do you know or have you ever heard of somebody who just has to get it out—creativity? They're compelled to do whatever artistic expression, whether anybody's interested in it or not. That was Kurt. That's who Kurt was."

I tell Ryan about a band I played in during my twenties where our bassist didn't know how to play at first. He bought a bass anyway and learned as he went.

"This is the birth of Nirvana," Ryan explains. "And that's how Kurt was. He had to get it [his creativity] out there. Yes, he was a student of The Beatles. Yes, he was a student of Led Zeppelin. Yes, he loved music. Yes, he studied it intensely and intently because he had nothing else in his life to do that was positive. He had no active, interested girlfriend in high school when he became a teenager. He had no success with sports. Yes, in Montesano, he was on the wrestling team and the baseball team, only because his father, Don, wanted him to. And he was so pissed off about Don and Wendy splitting up. I mean, he was a juvenile with those kinds of emotions, and no one was saying, 'You know what? We're sorry. We need to spend time with you. We're going to quit being so stupid and selfish and "it's all about me" and just sit down and let you be a kid for a second.' And I was experiencing the same thing and Krist was experiencing it, and all of us were experiencing the same thing. The adults that were raising us—no one said, 'My job is to be a stay-at-home parent.' No one did that for us in our lives, ever."

Ryan touches on some pain points. The lack of stability he describes—the emotional kind—naturally bled into the physical instability Kurt faced later on. I tell him that the bigger picture isn't whether Kurt slept beneath a bridge—it was the fact that he was unhoused and that so many other people experience the same housing crisis he did.

"Does it really matter where he slept?" I ask. "Does it matter if he was couch-surfing or sleeping in his car? The takeaway is that he was unhoused. And he's not the only one."

"Geographical insecurity," Ryan says. "And that is a trauma—it's a generational trauma. And you can go, 'Oh, he slept under the bridge, he didn't sleep under the bridge.' And it's exactly what you're saying. It's the fact that he didn't know where he was going to sleep from one day to the next. That's the thing. And as a society, we're not interested in it."

Ryan and I decide to connect again several weeks after our first conversation to ensure all the details of our first interview were correct and to cover a few topics that weren't previously discussed. Like our last conversation, I give him space to speak—I don't ask questions or react. I let Ryan remember Kurt.

"If Kurt had lived another year and just thought about the consequences . . ." Ryan trails off. I know this is difficult for him to discuss, and I know our conversation is dredging up painful memories. He knows, however, that his recollections could help others who feel a connection to Kurt, flaws and all.

"I mean, here he has just created this child [Frances Bean]," he continues. "And he has nothing of value that he sees in his life, so much so that he's trying to anesthetize himself—literally—daily. And yet he has now brought little Frances into the world. Can you imagine the emotional chaos? The emotional turmoil? The emotional guilt? 'Thanks, Dad. You've done it again. Yeah, you did the same thing that Grandma Wendy and Grandpa Don did to you and your sister.'

"I think about whether Kurt could articulate that at the time or not because he was only in his twenties. I mean, five days ago, I probably couldn't have articulated all this now. But he was so young—so young. Twenty-seven, you know? Do you remember what you were doing when you were twenty-seven years old? I mean, I can't picture being twenty-seven and the whole freaking world knowing who you are. And they've got these statistics out there now that say the prefrontal cortex in most males doesn't even—on average—completely develop until twenty-six. That's not even considering when and where he started his drug addiction. So, if you're cooking your brains with heroin for a dozen or so years, how does that affect your development? Because you're still developing.

"But the whole time I was around, Kurt was the one who wasn't taking drugs. I was bombed and stoned out of my mind all the time. But he was the sober one, and of course, this is the kind of thing that gets left out of the books. I never saw him drink. And part of that was this stomach issue thing . . . I didn't know him until he was like nineteen or twenty, and that's when I thought it [Kurt's stomach issues] started, like right around that age, because that's when he became homeless."

"I read somewhere that it may have been psychosomatic," I add.

"It very well could have been," Ryan explains. "But Kurt said he had scoliosis, and it's not like back then he could have just Googled what the symptoms were. I guess people were saying maybe it was Irritable Bowel Syndrome or something . . . I mean, I could see nerves or stress doing something like that, and I could see it being anxiety related . . . He just needed that downtime, just two weeks to heal. But when you've lived with it for that long, it becomes psychosomatic."

After spending time discussing some of the more difficult parts of Kurt's life, we take a short break from the interview. Conversations like this can be heavy, and sometimes it's best to step away for a moment. We talk off the record for a bit, and the conversation eventually drifts to Kurt's profound impact and how many young people still flock to Nirvana in droves, similar to when the band first hit it big.

"What drew people to Kurt and the music?" I ask. "I mean, you hear kids everywhere listening to them."

Ryan doesn't even have to think about this.

"Nirvana is more popular right now than they have ever been," he says. "And this is the source of the problem because it was always such a huge contradiction. If Kurt had continued to struggle, he'd probably still be alive."

"Struggle?" I want to make sure I understand correctly.

"Had he struggled to create his art. That happens all the time. People are excellent musicians, excellent songwriters, excellent singers, and excellent guitar players. I mean, Tony Poukkula is a great example. And Kurt isn't; [he] self-admitted. But this thing where he wrote these songs, which are incredibly unique—that strike a chord with so many people—that was the problem with the whole thing. He wanted to be liked, he wanted approval, he wanted love . . . But he was also mad about [his whole problem with Wendy and Don] and frustrated about that, angry about that, full of rage about that; oh, and don't worry, you're gonna be on the cover of *Rolling Stone* magazine because you have the number-one record in the world for being frustrated. And not [be] able to talk about how you composed your song. It's so many contradictions, and then, of course, all the people that you're pissed off about—the bullies in high school, the jocks—they're coming to your shows, they're buying your product. And that's why you're . . . successful. It's not because the punk rockers bought it. It's because the mass media bought it. The mass public bought it. They loved you, and they're the last people you want. You just want Mom and Dad to love you. That's it."

What Ryan is getting at goes deeper than creative struggle alone—and whether it would have changed Kurt's fate. Kurt's struggle was different. He ultimately received approval from a massive audience, and that audience included many of the same people he had once felt alienated from—the bullies, the jocks, the crowd he often railed against. Fans cheering Nirvana on in arenas weren't always the people Kurt seemed to want approval from in the first place. His music allowed him to express that frustration, and when it reached millions of listeners it also reached the very audience it was meant to challenge. That was the paradox. The success his music needed to survive also meant it was embraced en masse by many of the same people he often pushed back against.

One of the band's clearest declarations of disdain for the establishment and certain audience members came in "Smells Like Teen Spirit," though its meaning has often been misconstrued.

"That ['Smells Like Teen Spirit' video] gets so misinterpreted thirty-five years later," Ryan begins. "You see the big anarchy signs on the chests of all the cheerleaders, and they're not cheerleaders. They look like . . . not the girls you'd want to bring home to Mom. And part of that is the director and the people involved—Kurt said 'Yes' to all of that. And, of course, MTV ran it constantly. It was such a contradiction and a problematic thing for him because he wanted to be loved and he wanted to be accepted and he wanted success, then all of sudden you've got to explain yourself. You can't walk down the street anymore. You can't—you're no longer anonymous and everyone listens to . . . You can't pass gas anywhere without somebody . . . You talk about how much you crave your anonymity, and the thing about it is . . . he's human. He's us. He's the average American child product of the working class. Which is your story. It's my story. Basically, any Gen Xer—it's their entire life story.

"We were all latchkey kids. We were all left alone by the time we were eight because our parents couldn't afford a babysitter anymore. And we had to grow up and be self-monitored. And part of Nirvana's success and popularity is appealing to millennials. But why, I couldn't even answer that.

"Kurt was so far down in his depression and his marriage and his drug abuse. And now he had procreated. If you can imagine the horror that must have been . . . Can you imagine being Kurt Cobain now, having been tossed around between Wendy and Don and Grandpa Leland and all the insecurities that go along with that from a financial point of view, a geographical point of view, a nutritional point of view, an emotional point of view?

"People, if they don't already know, will feel the impact of an individual like Kurt who was willing to go against the institutions. And it was these particular things that he said or did that helped create where we are today."

Kurt lambasted Aberdeen at every conceivable opportunity, and his refusal to bend—to accept what he knew was wrong—gave others permission to be themselves. But that kind of defiance came at a cost, especially in a hostile environment. Ryan saw that firsthand and recalls how Aberdeen could be at the time.

In one incident, the lead singer of Ryan's band was duct-taped to a telephone pole just off school property by a group of students who targeted him for being someone who refused to conform to the social norms of the community.

"Someone else was with him, and a mob—mostly men—was spitting on them, because this particular guy [Ryan's singer] was too obstinate."

Ryan notes that although Washington is often viewed as politically liberal, towns like Aberdeen were deeply homophobic when he and Kurt were growing up. His singer wasn't gay, but the hostility in Aberdeen often had little to do with sexuality at all. Instead, it reflected how rigid the social environment there could be during that time.

"The school was also predominantly white back then," he says. "And I'm talking about my senior class, which was over three hundred people, so pretty a lot of people for a rural community. And that's where Kurt was going to school and ultimately dropped out from."

Earlier in the interview, Ryan told me he "was the one that had long hair in high school, and [he] had it before they had hair policies in wood shop when people got scalped because of it.

"People would come up to me and go, 'What kind of a faggot are you?' That's when you could say shit like that. And so this is why Kurt, as a human being, was attracted to me. It was because I was already in conflict with society, particularly in Grays Harbor County. These kids were misfits but were like, 'Well, I'd rather be with you,' because I was running into all this [adversity] everywhere."

I asked what Aberdeen was like in high school.

"Well, there was the group of people that lived there who were largely our parents—working-class people—that were working lower-paying jobs, and they weren't incredibly well-educated. And those were the people that we were running into on a regular basis. Does that mean there wasn't a liberal faction at the time? Of course there was. Unlike today, there was no arts program at all. But my wife, for example, grew up in Northern California, where all she did during high school was liberal arts. But that did not exist [in Aberdeen]. And if it did, it was hanging on by a thread. I mean, you basically had band and you had print shop. I had three periods of wood shop and an auto shop class and English and Contemporary World Problems. And I took late arrival and skipped as much as possible, so I didn't have to be there. And Kurt just dropped out . . . Shelli dropped out . . . Krist graduated, but he was battling this European 'honor your parents' kind of thing."

Despite the fact that Kurt eventually left school, Ryan remembers that art was one of the few outlets available to him there. He also acknowledges Kurt's artistic ability, but notes that there weren't many paths available to him in a place like Aberdeen.

"There weren't a lot of other opportunities for him [Kurt]."

Others who attended school with Kurt remember his artistic talent as well. Brett Walker, who had an art class after Kurt's, recalls seeing him draw frequently.

"Kurt drew Eddie [the mascot from Iron Maiden] a lot," Brett explains. "Kurt had the art class before mine when I was a senior in high school. When I would come in, I would usually see him drawing Eddie. When I came into art class, Kurt seemed very quiet and kept to himself."[36]

I'm curious about the underpinnings of Nirvana and what drove both Kurt's creativity and his urge to rebel against established institutions. Ryan had just described how Kurt often resisted the expectations placed on him growing up in Aberdeen, so I ask him about the familial struggles Kurt may have experienced at home: "It seems like there were issues with a guy his mom was dating, where he was shuffled from house to house. It also seemed like Kurt had issues with his stepmother, which led to him being shuffled around again."

"That's absolutely true," says Ryan. "I can speak about that a little bit because we [he and Kurt] went over there to go pick up some laundry—clean laundry, or dirty laundry—or something. I can't remember exactly the specifics of it. And we went to that house [1210 E 1st St in

Aberdeen] apparently where the fella was and she [Wendy] was living and into the room where that famous picture was taken—the one that you see all the time of Kurt up in the bedroom playing his Hi-Flier, you know? We were in that room. But this wasn't the day that photo was taken. And the whole time we were there, Kurt was just like, 'We gotta get out of here before anybody comes home.' I was in that room having a conversation with him, like, 'Why do we need to hurry?' And he was telling me the story about why."

"Was it the boyfriend?" I ask.

"Yeah," Ryan answers. "You know, she [Wendy] didn't really have a way to support Kurt and the household without him [the boyfriend]. And Kurt in no uncertain words had been told, 'Please leave.'"

"By her?" I ask.

"Yeah. Because she was afraid she'd . . . lose the boyfriend. Lose the economic power of this boyfriend, in spite of the fact that he wasn't a pleasant person."

Ryan explains that it isn't uncommon for single men to meet women with children—children who want a father figure the men may not be prepared to become. Eventually, conflict can arise between the children and the significant other, leaving the mother in a difficult position: choosing between protecting her child or preserving the relationship.

Ryan says that, in this situation, the mother has to make a choice.

"You side with the kid like a mama bear and say, 'Sorry, buddy.' Especially today, that's way more common," Ryan explains. "But in the eighties, when all this stuff was going down for Kurt—for Wendy—that was a very, very different world."

With Kurt's younger sister Kim still at home and the possibility of losing the financial stability the boyfriend provided, the situation may have left Wendy in a similar dilemma and Kurt searching for somewhere else to stay.

"And he [Kurt] just wants Don and, of course, Don didn't want him, and Kurt's horribly insulted," Ryan says. "It's just a cluster, you know?"

★★★

It's getting late, so we decide to pick up our conversation another day. I still have questions—particularly about why Ryan eventually parted ways with the band and whether there were tensions behind that decision.

When we speak again, we pick up on band dynamics. Ryan recalls suggesting that Kurt show up earlier to gigs, bring spare equipment, or help cover travel costs. He wanted the band to be a bit more professional, but it ultimately put him and Kurt at odds.

"We had this sort of conflict where I was like, 'Maybe we should try harder to be professional,' but Kurt was like, 'That's not punk rock,'" Ryan tells me. "He [Kurt] was still not convinced that he would ever be anything. It was like an exercise in futility from his point of view. Can you imagine a world where nobody [in Nirvana] broke through? We're looking back through the lens after Nirvana happened, and it's hard to picture a world before that. But that's the world I'm talking about, where he [Kurt] was in such conflict with me. I thought they sounded cool and thought they should be on the radio, but he thought I was full of shit. We were just always arguing about manifesting positivity, and he had one foot in 'I'm never going to amount to anything.' So we were just arguing constantly. Part of that gets brought out when you read his journals or read Azerrad's book where Krist said, 'Ryan's Republican work ethic,' which I was offended by since I don't consider myself a Republican at all. I'm really liberal. But Krist certainly did [consider me that way]. He was the smartest, most globally informed person I ever met. And I looked up to these guys because Kurt was teaching me how to play guitar and Krist was teaching me how to play guitar and allowing me to be in this place that gave me access to other bigger acts, like the Butthole Surfers, Danzig, and Soundgarden. And I didn't mind carrying heavy shit or borrowing my boss's work van and lying to him to use it."

Ryan says he often went out of his way to help the band get to shows, sometimes improvising solutions when they lacked transportation.

"The thing about the Raymond show [Tony Poukkula's house]—I borrowed this huge panel van from my boss, concocted this whole lie about moving a friend from one apartment to another, and brought the van from Ocean Shores to Kurt's house in Aberdeen and then drove to Raymond."

It was more than a favor—if anything, it was a constant hustle.

"But it was this fight of how to make all these different things happen," Ryan says, reflecting on his efforts to help the band in their early days. "And because I had a job, didn't have a significant other, had my own apartment, had access to work vans, had money and accessibility, and didn't have a lot of conflicts with other people, I could BS my way into things [for the band]. The thing about Kurt is he was shy. He was busy just trying to figure out music . . . I was in conflict with lots of people."

Ryan remembers one show in particular: Nirvana's February 25, 1989, performance at the Hub Ballroom at the University of Washington with Chad Channing on drums. The last show he worked with the band. It was a huge bill that included Girl Trouble, Skin Yard, and The Fluid. Photographer Alice Wheeler captured some iconic photos from the show. Around that time Nirvana was beginning to evolve, even offering Jason Everman the position of second guitarist as they prepared to tour. For Ryan, it was a moment when things were clearly changing.

"This show was part of the reason why I left," Ryan tells me. "My motivation was that they were successful from an artistic point of view—they were players, and I wanted to be a player. The band asked me for money because I had a job. They couldn't even pay for the production cost of the *Bleach* album, and they asked me for a loan, and I said 'No.' Next thing I know, Jason is in the band. We weren't meeting eye-to-eye on what we should or shouldn't do because they never saw themselves as being economically successful. So, it was never 'I'll give you a percentage or I'll pay you.' But . . . backstage at this show was loaded [with alcohol]. There was so much alcohol back there . . . So I get them [Nirvana] to the show and get them set up and did the sound check. And then you're back there with nothing to do, so you drink. I drove home that night, blitzed out of my mind still, and realized I couldn't believe I even made it home and hadn't killed anybody. And I thought, *How much longer am I gonna be lucky?* And I decided I was done. I knew I needed to settle down and get married and get out of this whole lifestyle thing. It was just too stressful for me."

Before I started writing this book, I was only familiar with one version of Kurt Cobain: the wildly famous rock star who claimed an unprecedented amount of success in a wickedly short amount of time. But Ryan helped me understand a time and place when the world had yet to experience "Kurdt." I gained a deeper understanding of Kurt's childhood, his tenacity, and the band's extraordinary journey to international stardom—learning it from someone who was there—but I also saw a young man molded by a troubled home and bouts of homelessness. Pain was the foundation that bound this young group of musicians from a small logging town, who created shared experiences that gave birth to something revolutionary: Nirvana.

Ryan is part of Nirvana's incredible history, and his stories helped me understand more about the man, not the myth, separating the Kurt Cobain he knew from the version engineered to entertain.

Through our discussions, Ryan and Tony provided me with great insight into Kurt's early years in Nirvana. But my quest to understand the enigmatic musician was far from over. I had more interviews to conduct and more people to connect with to learn about Kurt's life in Aberdeen. One of these people wasn't old enough to fully grasp what he experienced as a budding musician. Yet Kurt lived with her and her family, and I knew speaking with Misty Kuhl, sister of Greg Hokanson (Kurt's first drummer for Fecal Matter), would be another avenue I needed to venture down before leaving Aberdeen.

Chapter 6

"WHERE DID YOU SLEEP LAST NIGHT?"

Misty Kuhl

THE INTERNET IS A VERITABLE TREASURE TROVE OF STORIES, MOST LOOKing to sensationalize every aspect of Kurt's life for the sake of clicks. From the start of this book, I've tried to go a different direction. I didn't want to create something redundant. So, I connected with people who might have a different vantage point on Kurt before Nirvana, including those who had yet to be interviewed and might offer the keenest insight into his character.

This led me to Misty Kuhl, someone who remembers Kurt for being a kind, decent human being.[37] She recalls a young man of humble beginnings, marked by trials, tribulations, and undeniable determination. How she knew Kurt is the missing puzzle piece.

There was a time when Kurt lived with Greg Hokanson and his family. Greg had previously been pressed for interviews by other writers, and I wanted him involved in a way that felt comfortable. He endorsed this book before his passing, which means more to me than he knew. But it was his sister, Misty, who spoke with me. She remembered when Kurt lived with them, and I valued the chance to learn about a young Kurt from someone who had never given an interview before.

★★★

"Kurt had about three friends, and everybody else treated him as poorly as possible," Misty tells me. "I mean, he was not a popular guy. He was not somebody that had a ton of friends in a big social circle. He was a victim of child abuse and neglect, and that was a big part of what made him who he was."

It's not easy hearing someone say that Kurt—or any child—was a victim of abuse. What was disregarded in the seventies and eighties would now be recognized as abandonment and neglect, and if Kurt was forced out of his home while still a minor, that meets today's legal definition of child abuse—regardless of perception at the time.[38] But Misty says it best—what Kurt experienced and endured made him who he was.

Misty attributes much of what Kurt experienced to being a generational issue.

"That's just part of being a Gen Xer," she says. "In my household, it was very much the same. Abuse and neglect were the norm. I mean, our parents were partying or at the bars and drinking. And the kids were just left to do their own thing and figure things out on their own. There were a lot of us that grew up in the Harbor that, by the time you were fourteen or fifteen, you were basically leaving home, couch surfing, and staying with other people. Sadly, you could do better for yourself living this way than what your parents were doing for you."

This makes me think of the bridge.

"I mention the Young Street Bridge a lot in my book," I tell Misty. "It seems as if you can't sleep beneath it, due to unforgiving natural elements. But people are missing the bigger picture. It doesn't matter if Kurt slept beneath the bridge . . ."

"He wasn't sleeping in his house because he wasn't welcome there," Misty says. "That's the bigger picture."

In a joint interview Courtney Love and Kurt had with Jonathan Poneman, Courtney said, "But he was a boy and so he would go and live under the bridge or he'd go live in a fort. I mean, he really did." Kurt added, "I always wanted to experience the street life because my teenage life in Aberdeen was so boring. But I was never really independent enough to do it. I applied for food stamps, lived under the bridge, and built a fort at the cedar mill."[39]

Before becoming a writer, I worked as a special education teacher with at-risk students, many of whom were considered unhoused—often misunderstood because they had somewhere to sleep, just not a stable or permanent home. But lacking a permanent residence is still being unsheltered—and Kurt may not have slept beneath the Young Street Bridge, but he did know what it was like to be without a home.

"I understand the bridge is more of a sentimental value connected to Kurt and the song 'Something in the Way,'" I say. "But I think people need to really reflect on the determination of a young man whose parents bounced him back and forth from relative to relative—look what he still achieved."

"I never heard Kurt's parents mentioned once," Misty tells me. "I've only heard them mentioned by writers or people who are doing stories. Kurt never mentioned his mom or his dad ever. Or any family member, for that matter. He was alone. When I talk about the Harbor—just that really dark, depressed feeling—it was common. I mean, I hate to say it. It's . . . absolutely awful."

Hearing Misty speak about the Harbor makes it easier to understand the environment Kurt grew up in—a working-class community with economic hardships and families stretched thin, kids left to navigate life on their own terms. It became clear how Kurt was able to wage war against the world, brandishing his guitar and a series of journals. He grew up experiencing one of the greatest challenges a young person can face, and that's homelessness. And he faced it alone. Did anyone remind him that his efforts were worthwhile, or that his talent would pay off? He was alone in his determination, which makes his journey to meteoric fame that much more incredible.

Misty tells me Kurt lived with her and Greg after a period of time with LaMont Schillinger and his family.

"Kurt lived with us for a few months. I was so young. I don't really know what the exact timeline was, but I know that he was living with us for a long time. It was a while before my mom even found out that he was living with us because my brother hid him up in his room. We had a two-story house, and my mom was a bartender at the nicest restaurant in Aberdeen for about twenty years . . . she would go to work as soon as we got out of school, and she'd be there until two in the morning. My brother would essentially be in charge of me. And then, of course, because we had an open house with no parental supervision, all the parties were always at our home. So, Kurt and some other guys would always be drinking beer and smoking pot and playing music. It was just an everyday thing."

"And then your brother hid him upstairs?" I ask.

"Well, Kurt was so quiet that you wouldn't even know he was there," she says. "My brother would get his plate of food and then go back down and act like he was getting seconds and take another plate to Kurt. He would also wash his clothes and other things like that. You would see Kurt slipping out of my brother's room into the bathroom and slipping back in really quiet, and I was sworn to secrecy. My brother made it very clear, 'You will be beaten if you say anything.' And I knew that was true. So I kept Kurt's secret. Later down the road, I found out that, once my mom discovered Kurt was staying in Greg's room, my brother made him pay rent to sleep in our broken-down car in the driveway. But it was just boys being boys."

I ask when all this happened.

"I'm trying to think of how old they must have been," Misty says. "I think it was after high school to be honest. I must have been ten or twelve. Greg was eight years older than me, and Kurt was nine years older than me, so they were probably late teens, early twenties. Probably nineteen to twenty, if I had to guess. And it was winter and it was cold. I didn't know that Kurt was sleeping in the car until later when I heard . . . I had heard things before, but I didn't realize what I was hearing. And one time I actually saw him crawling into the car, and I felt terrible because it was freezing cold outside. I remember asking my brother, 'Did you give him any blankets or any pillows? Does he have anything?' and my brother said, 'He doesn't need anything. He's got all that. He doesn't want any of it.' Insinuating Kurt didn't want or need anything . . . which I found to be very strange. And I remember being concerned about Kurt in that sense, but I was pretty much just told to mind my own business."

Misty told me Kurt would quietly exchange a few of Greg's clean clothes for his own, something their mom never caught on to.

"They shared clothes," Misty explains. "Kurt didn't have much, you know? He just had what he carried around in a bag. He didn't have much to his name."

"How long do you think he probably slept at your house and in the car?" I ask.

"I would say probably three months."

"That's tough in the winter."

While Misty couldn't recall exact dates, she remembered a particularly cold stretch when Kurt stayed with them.

"Well, I want to say that he probably was sleeping inside our home in the fall time," she tells me. "That's when my mom found out that he was in our house. However, I don't know if she thought that he had somewhere else to go and that he was just being dramatic."

This isn't the first time I've heard this. Some people feel that Kurt wanted to be homeless. He had relatives he could have stayed with, but instead chose the path that felt harder, less stable. For him, the opposite may have been true. By then, Kurt knew what he wanted to do. He wanted to play music—wherever he could, however he could—and staying with family may have meant more structure and less freedom to come and go as he pleased. If a battered and broken-down car gave him shelter from the proverbial storm without asking for much in return, then I can see why he'd choose it over an unwelcome couch, exposed in the middle of a relative's living room.

Misty was young when Kurt lived with them, but she remembers it clearly: being dragged from one garage to the next while he played.

"I sat on cement floors, listening to them play music and drink and get high," she tells me. "And then he'd hurry up and rush me home and put me to bed before two a.m. It was just the way it was."

"I heard that Kurt was always the sober one," I say. "That's what I was told. He wasn't much of a drinker. He was usually the one that was not doing too much."

Misty expands on this. "I don't remember him ever being wasted or belligerent or acting foolish. But they definitely drank beer and smoked pot, that was for sure."

As we talk, our conversation turns to the many stories I heard about where Kurt supposedly slept growing up—stories that often contradicted one another and seemed designed more for attention than accuracy.

"Everybody has fabricated stories about Kurt," Misty tells me. "But from what I know is that Kurt did not have a permanent residence from the time he was very young . . . Sadly, you have a lot of people posthumously looking to cash in on Kurt, laying claim to his 'childhood home.' But just because he lived with someone for two months doesn't make their home his childhood home, especially when he was only to be shipped off to someone else."

"I heard Kurt used to sleep in the Grays Harbor Community Hospital where he was born," I say. "He would sleep in the waiting room."

"I've never heard that," Misty says. "There was Grays Harbor Community Hospital and then there was St. Joseph's Hospital. And I might be prone to think that it was St. Joe's because that hospital was right up on the hill above our neighborhood, making it a short walk. And they didn't have any type of security or anything whatsoever. As a kid, I went and roamed around there with my friends. So I think that it might have been St. Joe's where he would have been sleeping. St. Joe's is now a recovery rehab place."

Maybe Kurt didn't care where he slept, as long as he had the freedom to play music. It felt like the most crucial part of his personality—music first, shelter second. But internalizing everything going on around him isn't the same as actually rolling with it, and I wanted to know how this looked on the surface.

"Kurt was a slow-moving person," Misty tells me. "When I think of him, I remember his slender, slight frame—he was always hunched over, very ho-hum, if you will. Just kind of always meandering around, never in a rush to get anywhere. And he wasn't the type of person who was easily excited."

"Do you think he was excited when his record was signed?" I ask.

"Maybe once his record was signed, he became excited. I don't know. I mean, most people would be excited, but Kurt just wasn't that type of person."

I tell Misty that I heard Kurt was a difficult person to truly understand, to know intimately.

"I keep circling back to my sentiment about those who eagerly say they knew Kurt so well," Misty says. "Kurt was not a person that people knew well. I don't care if you spent every day with him. He was very reserved and to himself. Kurt was around our family right up until he became a worldwide rock star. He was still hanging out with my brother. I mean, he was around for quite a few years. I was in the background, watching and observing, and it meant nothing at the time. But when I look back on these memories, I can definitely see just how withdrawn Kurt was. He wasn't like everyone else. He was different. He was so different from all of my brother's other friends. And I mean that in a positive way.

"Growing up, I always knew who to trust—and who to steer clear of. And I always felt safe around Kurt. I knew he would never harm a hair on anyone's head, human or animal. He was a good person. He was a kind person. I mean, he was a wild boy doing wild things with his friends. And, sure, they could be invasive."

To Misty, Kurt was different from her brother's other friends. As someone she trusted, she still protects his image decades after his passing.

"Naturally, I'm very defensive of Kurt's memory, especially when people erroneously badmouth him on social media or in

Aberdeen—especially those who never knew him," Misty says. "He put Aberdeen on the map, yet some people have the audacity to speak ill of him. 'Oh, he's famous for being a drug addict. We don't want to idolize people and put them up on pedestals. What does that do for our kids?' But these comments show how misunderstood Kurt was and still is."

So much of Kurt is up for discussion, even the personal musings in his journals. Riddled with complex thoughts, they reflect a man steeped in his own mind, working tirelessly to express himself. More often than not, they were misinterpreted.

Misty remembers a different side of that expression:

"The thing about my brother and Kurt—that I remember—is that they would have these little sessions where they would just ramble stupid, perverted, disgusting, weird things," Misty begins. "They would try to outdo each other with how outrageous it could be. And they would think it was so funny and they would crack up laughing. I just remember them saying racist, misogynistic, and grotesque things . . . just as outrageous as they could be. They would think that it was hysterically funny. And, you know, in hindsight, they were probably drunk or stoned. But it goes to show you how misunderstood Kurt was, and that his musings were just an artistic expression and not a reflection of the person he was. He was an artist. He used his drawings to vent his frustrations with life. I would see Kurt journaling and drawing a lot of pictures of really grotesque images. From this art, Greg and Kurt would write song lyrics with all of these really grotesque mental images. They would doodle and write, just knowing that they were being completely . . . out there. It was the goal to be as offensive as possible. So if somebody has come across that type of content and thinks that this is how Kurt lived his life, that's really not what was happening. That was really just Kurt expressing himself in a place he felt safe—his journals."

After he left Misty's family's home, Kurt climbed to an untouchable plane of international fame. From what I've learned, however, he was still the same fundamentally decent person, despite his struggles.

"He was just a really normal guy," Misty says. "He found an outlet for his pain and found a way to express himself. And, more importantly, growing up, he was just a good human being. And I'm pretty sure he grew up to be an amazing man."

Misty recalls a time Kurt helped her make a little bed for her cat when it went into labor. They bonded over their love of animals, even if he'd end up ignoring her to hang out with her cats instead. She didn't mind—it simply reinforced how much he cared about all living creatures.

"I was home alone, and it must have been nine or ten o'clock at night. I was trying to get to bed, but something was wrong with one of my cats . . . Kurt was always so sweet and gentle with them, and he loved spending time with them. . . . One night, my brother and his friends were drinking and partying, but Kurt was home. And my cat was bleeding and clearly in distress. I had no idea what was going on but was extremely worried because she wouldn't lay down and was in visible pain. But Kurt immediately knew what was wrong. 'Well, she's going to have kittens,' he said. 'She's pregnant.' I had no idea she was pregnant. So he said, 'Yeah, so get a box and put some blankets in it and put her in a nice safe place, and she'll have her kittens.' And that's exactly what happened. He helped me get a box together, and I remember him cutting it with a box knife so that she could get in and out of it, and then I filled it with a bunch of blankets and other things to keep her warm and comfortable. Then I took her upstairs and put her in my room, and she had kittens that night. Kurt would come back and would check on the kittens and hold them and play with them. We even ended up keeping two of the kittens. But Kurt was there when no one else was. No one was around to tell me what to do. I had no idea what was going on or what was wrong with my cat, but Kurt did. And his sensitivity towards animals was apparent—he truly loved them."

Stories like these say more about Kurt than any interview ever could.

I think of the photos of Kurt with his feline friends. A quiet calm appeared on his face in these pictures, his happiness no longer eclipsed by the pitfalls of fame or the relentless and often inhuman demands imposed on him. These photos endearingly display Kurt's humanity. But analyzing a life filled with promise yet cut devastatingly short is a double-edged sword. Kurt harbored such a bright light but never saw it; the real tragedy is that the rest of the world did.

"Can you tell me about the last time you saw Kurt?" I ask.

Misty pauses for a moment.

"The last time I saw him he was working at the YMCA, outside pulling weeds. I was running around with my friends and didn't even notice him at first. I remember that he was leaning over in a garden bed. I ran by, and he said, 'Hi, Misty.' I didn't know who said my name and, looking around, saw that it was Kurt. I remember asking, 'Oh, what are you doing?' and he said, 'I work here.' And I said, 'Oh, okay,' to him. And that's my last memory of Kurt. I know he hung around with Greg still, but that is the last encounter I personally had with him.

"For Martin Luther King Day, my conservation district [the Grays Harbor Conservation District] went to the river bank by the Kurt Cobain Memorial Park and planted trees to preserve that embankment," Misty tells me. "That project meant a lot to me because of my connection to Kurt. . . . it was the project that they were launching right when I started working for them—I knew I was meant to be a part of it."

This was her spiritual awakening in a sense.

"That was my sign."

She isn't the only one who has experienced something like that—a sense of connection, or of being guided toward certain moments tied to Kurt, even decades later. But Misty saw a part of Kurt that not many people experienced, even if she was young. She was able to see Kurt for who he was and not what the world needed him to be.

After the interview, Misty and I became fast friends, and she quickly became someone I cherish, introducing me to the Grays Harbor Conservation District and all the incredible work they do. This book now supports their mission to help the Harbor, and in return, they've vowed to keep preserving and maintaining Kurt's Memorial Park. It's not an easy task, as the park sees a good deal of foot traffic, graffiti, and vandalism, but the Conservation District is committed to its safeguarding.

Because Kurt's Memorial Park runs alongside the Young Street Bridge, my involvement with the Conservation District led me into the discussions about the bridge's future, with several local historians asking me to assist them with an initiative to "Save Kurt's Bridge." I agreed, provided that it could be done safely.

There were several options for preserving it, from turning it into a pedestrian-only bridge to demolishing it and moving a piece of it to Kurt's Memorial Park, which runs adjacent to the structure. Trusting that engineers would make the appropriate call, I started a petition to inform Kurt's supporters of the town's plans and to show support for saving the bridge—even just a piece, if that's all that could be done. I was surprised when the petition gained traction and even more surprised when Matthew Wells, a celebrated journalist for Aberdeen's newspaper, *The Daily World*, reached out for an interview. It was humbling to see the front page of the paper with the headline, KURT COBAIN BOOK AUTHOR WANTS TO SAVE NORTH ABERDEEN BRIDGE, my words mentioned throughout.[40]

It was the first time I appeared in print in connection with Kurt, and it affected me. The experience reinforced why I wrote this book. More often than not, Kurt is flattened by assumptions or shorthand about who he was and what he represents—defined by his depression, or treated as someone destined to die young. There's this idea of a tortured genius that tends to overshadow everything else. But he was more than that. He was complex, not defined by his struggles. It also made it clear how important it is to explain what the bridge means to so many people. Misty and the Grays Harbor Conservation District will continue to care for Kurt's Memorial Park, and even if the bridge is torn down, it won't erase what the space represents or the gentle boy who put Aberdeen on the map. It won't erase "Kurdt."

In Memory of Gregory Steven Hokanson
September 26, 1968–September 4, 2024

Chapter 7

"COME AS YOU ARE"

Antony Hodgkinson, aka Tony the Interpretive Dancer

DURING MANY OF NIRVANA'S CONCERTS, THE AUDIENCE WATCHED IN awe as someone danced on stage with the band. But this someone wasn't just a lucky fan—he was an interpretive dancer who accompanied Nirvana during numerous performances. The most notable of these shows was Reading '92. Everything around Kurt was spiraling—nonstop media scrutiny about the band and rumors that he was too unwell to perform. At a certain point, the only thing left to do was throw two middle fingers in the air and take back control of his own narrative.

For those closest to Kurt, this wasn't just an epic performance to read about later or hear about in a tabloid—it was something they were part of. Antony Hodgkinson, affectionately known as "Tony the Interpretive Dancer," was onstage, watching his friend go from being a punching bag to hitting back, and he was right there with him.

We set a time to talk—I have a million questions—and from the first hello, he's warm and welcoming.[41]

★★★

"Thank you for inviting me." Tony smiles, and I'm immediately put at ease. I see why Kurt gravitated toward him.

"I'm honored to have you be a part of this. Writing about the Reading '92 concert is this massive chapter in my book," I begin. "Kurt's been portrayed as the tortured artist caricature, and I think it's been done to death."

"It's sensationalism," Tony begins. "It's that tabloid mentality; it's just sensationalism. People—they sort of love that, really. I guess we're all guilty of that. You know, I love the whole rock drama, rock documentary: sex, drugs, rock and roll. But, sadly, some people just focus on a conservative viewpoint of drugs. So many people have such a misunderstanding about drugs and why people do them."

I agree and tell Tony I'm focused on the positive, not the clickbait.

"I think you'll be surprised at how many people appreciate a positive angle and viewpoint on Kurt and Nirvana," Tony tells me. "Did you see the *When Nirvana Came to Britain* documentary? It's a BBC documentary that came out two years ago, maybe. It's from the viewpoint of when they came to Britain initially because they were bigger here than anywhere else. . . . You should watch it; I did a couple of interviews for it. Some people have said, 'When did the documentary become about you, Tony?' It's just my viewpoint on the whole thing in Britain. I was a massive part of that. . . . it's got a lot of positive spin on the whole thing."

I set out trying to understand why so much about Kurt bears a maudlin façade.

"Here was this beautiful person, and most people don't realize he stood for so much more than what the media highlights," I say.

"Well, yeah, they portray him as some crass drug addict, basically," Tony says. "That was just not true at all."

"It's terrible, and I hope this book can achieve the opposite."

"Yeah, positivity is the key."

We circle back to Reading '92 and how it's arguably one of Nirvana's biggest shows.

"Reading is the huge one, really," Tony says.

During the Reading '92 concert, Tony is on stage with Nirvana, physically experiencing their music as he dances.

"I love watching you on stage," I say. "You're showing how music is art and you're interpreting it; you're interpreting this living art right then and there. And you're just one of the band. I thought it was amazing."

"I sort of became Kurt's stage familiar," Tony explains. "It was about not repeating moves as well, trying to do as much as I could. And basically not making it look too professional. Because, to me, music and dance is an all-inclusive thing. If I was too professional, it wouldn't be inclusive. People quote me all the time on it. People would come up to me sometimes, saying, 'Hey Tony, what are you doing? That's shit, I could do that.' And I go, 'Yeah, that's the whole point! You can do it.' It's all-inclusive, you know? I was just—I guess, in a way—a lucky fan over the years. And I got to dance for Nirvana and everybody else was into that because they could probably see themselves doing it. If I could be on stage doing it, yeah, you could, too! There is that possibility. You know, you're included, it's about getting people involved."

"That's amazing."

"Yeah, it was an amazing show," Tony continues. "But it's—you know—it's obviously over the progress of time where, sadly, Kurt leaving us and him becoming a mythological rock star like Jimi Hendrix, Keith Moon, Janis Joplin. And then, over the years, the shows just became massive. My partner a while back showed me viewing numbers on the particular live songs of Reading. We were going down it, just going down the first page of half of the setlist, or just over half the setlist. And it was into the hundreds of millions of views. And if I'm not mistaken, when they released the '92 concert on DVD, I'm sure it was broadcast in the US on some network to like, I don't know, thirty-odd million people, anyway. So it has become this big, mythical, all-encompassing show.

"But the thing is, after—not the day after, maybe a couple of days after—I'd left Kurt and [bandmate] Dave [Grohl] in London, I was back in my house, wherever it was, in Derby, on a rainy September day, and I could talk to people about the show. 'Who's Nirvana?' . . . Because they were just like a headliner at a festival among many other festivals, you know? Nobody really knew the band that I knew, and you just sink back into normal life. It was quite a massive juxtaposition, you know? People think it would have been all glitter, glamour, champagne, sunshine, or whatever. And it wasn't. It was just back to rainy Britain without anybody knowing anything I'd done. It was like, 'Yeah, so what?' But now it's like, 'Oh God, you didn't tell me that you did that.' I was like, 'Yeah, I don't really self-promote myself that much.' And then in a way, I wouldn't discuss it because they'd go, 'Nirvana? Never heard of them,' so there's no point having the conversation. Or I'd say it and they'd just go, 'Oh yeah.'"

"But now you're synonymous with Reading," I say. "How did you come to meet Nirvana, then?"

"Well, basically, it was through a really dear old friend of mine, Russell Warby," Tony explains. "He was a booking agent, and we met. He came up to Nottingham in the late eighties—'86, '87, I think it was. And I met him at a club in Nottingham. I was wearing a T-shirt from a festival I'd been to, and he said, 'Oh, I went there,' and we just got on like a house on fire there. And he set up a booking agency called Nomad. And he ended up bringing a lot of Amphetamine Reptiles, SST, Shimmy-Disc, Sub Pop [record labels] bands from the US, alternative rock, I'd say. You know, The Jesus Lizard, TAD, and Screaming Trees.

"And then Russell asked me to do a bit of driving. I'd had quite a life-threatening illness. And through that, I'd become quite damaged physically. I had physical scars, and then I was quite psychologically damaged because it's like an infinite cycle sometimes that you have to break out of. . . . I was quite socially awkward, lacking confidence. So, Russell would get me out and about and say, 'Come and drive, I've got some bands that need picking up from the airport.' And we'd pick up whoever it was, like Bongwater or Screaming Trees, TAD, Mudhoney, the Tar Babies, SNFU, loads of the old bands . . . Actually, I didn't pick up the Tar Babies, we met them on a tour . . . I think it was 1989. It was called the Lame Fest tour, and it was Mudhoney, TAD, and Nirvana. I think they were doing a rotational headline. . . . it was when Chad [Channing] was still playing for Nirvana. I picked them up from the airport . . . I don't think around that time I'd really hung out with—or met—many, if any, American musicians. So, it was quite an exotic sort of scenario, really. Because I was intrigued about their life and where they'd come from, and they were intrigued about the same. I don't think Nirvana had been to the UK, either, not to my knowledge.

"I just got on with them [Nirvana]. Helped out on the tour. A year later, David joined the band, and then we started to get closer; it was . . . because Dave's just a really good egg. He's a really nice guy, dead friendly. What you see is what you get. There's no real front. So we got on really well . . . I think it was a London show. Kurt actually wanted me to go on stage and sweep the stage in between songs, like a janitor. I'm not entirely sure; I can't remember his thinking behind it. So he was saying, 'Yeah, you can do this and that.' I was like, 'You know, I've already been the driver. I'm not gonna be the janitor.'

"And then it came around to a dare of dancing for them—Russell's girlfriend at the time, Lorna—they dared me, 'Why don't you pick something out of Lorna's wardrobe and dance in her clothes?' So it was like, yeah, why not? I'm not machoistic in any sense that I'd say, 'I'm not doing that.' That's what I did in Leeds for the first time. I had leggings. Lorna's leggings, Lorna's dress, and I can't remember, I think it might have been L7's makeup and lipstick just daubed all over me because they were supporting at the time. It was Victims Family and L7. And I did it [danced], and Kurt just went, 'Yeah, man, when do you wanna do it again?' So I did it two or three times more on that tour, and then, when they were back in the UK, if I was in the UK—because I ended up touring in my band as well, then—I'd just meet up. They'd phone up, I'd speak to them, speak to Kurt or Dave, and then do the shows that I could do."

"That's awesome," I say, but my words aren't doing my thoughts justice. As he talks, I'm transported to a time and place when Nirvana is still climbing the ranks to international stardom while Tony dances on stage. What a wild ride.

"How many shows did you play with them?"

Tony pauses and ruminates for a moment, as if he is rifling through a catalog made up of countless unforgettable shows.

"Maybe up to about ten over the years. From like 1990 to 1992. The thing is, I was asked at one point—I think Dave asked me at one point in '92 maybe, could have been '91—about going on tour permanently with them. And I turned it down because I'm creative in my own right. I said to him, 'At the end of the day, I'm probably gonna get bored of dancing to somebody else's music all the time. I'm sort of compelled to be creative myself.' I turned that down. I know many people would go, 'Why?' So I turned that down because I was touring with my band, Bivouac."

Tony has been a musician for most of his life, and an incredibly talented one. In many ways, his love of music paved the way for a friendship between him and Kurt, and I'm curious to learn more.

"Tell me about your music. How did you become a musician?"

"I'll have to sort of go forward a little bit to track back," Tony begins. "Basically, I didn't go to university or college or anything like that. When I went to school, I was a bit of a troublemaker. I used to fight a lot. I used to be extremely aggressive. I got expelled from my, what we'd call comprehensive school. So, I ended up being expelled. Basically, I got expelled for taking my dad's advice. I used to get bullied quite a bit because I was quite small. And I strangled the school bully in front of the assembly line. I think he was unconscious. So I got expelled for this. But it was on my dad's advice! They had me in the headmaster's office going, 'You know, Antony's done this.' And I'm just looking at him [Tony's father] going, 'Well, you know, you told me to do this! If somebody picks on me, you make it known they've tried to pick on you and they've lost or, you know, you've defended yourself.' So, anyway, I got expelled. The behavior sort of continued."

Tony's bullying is a disturbing reminder of how common this practice is, especially in schools. While writing this, I came across numerous forums—and even had interviews—where people described how Kurt helped countless others overcome obstacles such as bullying, to one degree or another. His words, antics, and general persona taught others how to cope with adversity.

Tony continues, "When I was in my mid-thirties, I did go back to college to retrain in music technology. And when I went there, they found that I had learning difficulties. I didn't read very well; sometimes it's hard to understand the written word. I did what was called the Educational Psychologist Test, and I was very heavily dyslexic. Quite hyperactive, all over the place. I've obviously had this for most of my life and not realized it. My behavior, when I was younger, was born out of frustration. So, I was heavily dyslexic, and I needed to express myself in an alternative medium to the, I guess, the average person. So, I left school and got involved with firms. These are football firms, basically gangs or whatever. Quite aggressive, violent. Used to get into a lot of fights. And then I think the start of the process was one night I ended up punching out one of my best friends because I was just out of control. And then one of my friends punched me out, knocked me out. And basically, overnight, I lost all my friends. I was ostracized from the group. And I guess some people would carry on and go, 'It's their fucking problem, you can't accept me?' But I sort of went the other way, thinking, 'Oh, right, okay, there's something not right.' Not long after, I thought, 'I want to start drumming.' This was the start of me playing music . . . As soon as I started drumming, all the aggression went. I wasn't fighting any longer. I was just into drumming. And I just kept doing it, practicing for a few years. And I ended up getting in a band in around 1991-ish. Something like that. Bivouac. And then I was with them for maybe three years. Toured the UK, Europe, and America.

"So that's how I got into making music. Through a very, I guess . . . I don't know what it was. I see some people who have a self-conscious spark where you actually think, 'I can't behave like that, I need to change something.' Rather than, 'It's everybody else's fault.'

It was, 'It's my fault, I needed to make changes.' Sometimes you've got the spark to be able to do that and become chameleonic in life, too, you know? To get through it. And it was like, 'Okay, I need to do this.'"

Tony's transformation is not uncommon and shows the importance of music and how it can completely change a person. It's easy to see why he hit it off with Kurt.

"A thing I was gonna say about Kurt, if he didn't particularly agree with you, he'd still listen to you," Tony shares with me. "It wouldn't be, 'No, shut that down,' all the time. He'd listen to a different viewpoint. You have to because you never know. It isn't black and white. There are other things in between that can make a difference. He'd always listen rather than shutting it down. And this is the problem, isn't it? Shutting it down before you've even read or listened . . . Reading about Stonewall and whatever scenes there were. It's like, 'I don't like that.' You don't like that? Okay, because you've experienced it in one way or another? You've read about it or seen a documentary or whatever? Fair enough. But don't just put it in the 'bad pile.' That doesn't do anything for anybody's critical thinking at all, really. It just makes people dumber."

That's part of what made Kurt stand out. He didn't shy away from topics simply because he disagreed. He took the time to educate himself about opposing viewpoints. In many ways, this worked to shape his music. Kurt had steadfast beliefs, and he came armed with the knowledge to support his social stance—whether that meant openly condemning racism, homophobia, and misogyny, championing women in punk, or rejecting the hypermasculinity he saw growing up.

As Tony and I continue our conversation, I ask if he has any stories or sentiments he'd like to share about Kurt.

"Some people, probably quite a lot of people, would see me as a liability, could be embarrassing, blah, blah. The whole gamut, really. But he had the faith to put me on fucking stage with them. And he loved what I did, and I performed with them. He was a lovely guy. He could be very quiet, quite shy. He'd be reading the room, you could go in and, you know, I could talk to him like I'm talking to you. You could have a laugh. He'd understand, I'd understand his ways, they'd

[Nirvana] understand our ways, sarcasm, sense of humor, banter, and whatever. Like I said before, he was . . . Even if he didn't agree with you, he'd still listen. For instance, I was mortified when they'd smash their equipment up. If you wanna do that, you do that. But I couldn't do that because I've always been very precious about [my equipment], I've got a really . . . My mum bought me a really horrible drum set. (Sorry, Mum!) . . . we couldn't afford anything else. And I evolved from that; I kept buying other little bits and making it a lot better. So I've seen what it was like, and I valued it—not that they didn't value their instruments. And I'd sit down with Kurt sometimes and go, 'Why are you smashing equipment up?' I'd tell him my story, and he'd listen, and then you'd go, 'Great, I've accomplished something,' and then the next night, he'd just smash it again! And I thought, *Yeah, fair enough, he's listened to me. And he's been a sweetheart about it, but he's gonna exact whatever energy he wants in a performance and smash stuff up at the end.* And I was like, 'Yeah, great, we'll agree to disagree.' He took me under his wing, and a lot of people wouldn't have done that. The condition of my mind at the time—they just wouldn't have done it. He was sort of like 'live and let live.'"

That same energy followed him onto the stage, but it wasn't as reckless as it looked. Tony elaborates.

"There are bits where he's getting into it as well; he's dancing with me. I don't know how much that happened at other shows. He just got into it as I got into it. The attraction on stage, there weren't rules. Sometimes the only rules—or rule—before the show . . . They'd [Nirvana] probably go, 'We really want you to dance to X, Y, and Z.' And I'd be like 'Yep, okay.' And I did do that; I'd set myself boundaries, because . . . I didn't wanna punch Kurt out from flailing around. But now and again, we had interactions on stage, just having a little chat as he's doing a solo or whatever. I had to avoid Krist's bass because he was very . . . Yeah, you don't wanna get hit by that bass. I didn't wanna knock Kurt out or anything like that. There were boundaries on stage, but anything else was just, it was a punk rock show. Let's go and perform, can you perform to this?

"I don't know if it was Reading '92 or '91 where they [Nirvana] did go, 'Oh, we want you to perform to this song,' and I'm like, 'I've not heard this one before.' And David goes, 'It goes like this *[imitates drumming],*' and I had to think of how I was dancing to the song. I was thinking, 'Yeah, Dave's going *[imitates drumming].*' And I'm like, 'Oh God, I'm doing that in front of tens of thousands of people.'"

"Reading, to me, is like this unicorn kind of concert," I say, transitioning to my next point. "It seemed like Kurt was getting beaten up pretty badly by the tabloids. You know, rumors about this and rumors about that. That was why he was brought out in the wheelchair and had the hospital gown on. I thought that was great how he kind of clapped back and was making fun of some of these accusations."

"Yeah, sticking two fingers up the tabloids," Tony says. "It was getting to the point of . . . It seemed to be like everybody and everything wanted a piece of him. And he was, in a way, an accidental mega-rock figure. There was no intention to be like that. Obviously, he felt it difficult to navigate. It was just two fingers up to the media."

"Yeah, and I thought that was great," I say.

Tony agrees. "Aw yeah, definitely. *[Speaking as Kurt:]* I'm still here, it's like, who gives a fuck what you think?"

"Is there anything you can speak to about mental health?" I ask, shifting the focus to an essential part of this book, considering what Reading represented at the time. "I'm one voice. I don't know if this book is going to be able to undo countless other voices."

Tony understands that I'm referencing the kind of coverage that keeps circling back to Kurt's death—where the tragedy becomes the headline. My goal is simple: stop romanticizing his suicide and steer clear of the "27 Club"[42] rhetoric that exalts it, inadvertently or otherwise.

"Yeah, but it's a step in the right direction," he says.

"That's what I'm hoping," I explain. "Do you think there's anything we [friends, family, collaborators] could have done to have helped Kurt? Or things we can do to help other people who might be struggling the way he was?"

"The Reading show was the last time I saw Kurt in person," Tony recalls. "I may have spoken to him on the phone maybe a couple of times after that. I was touring myself. I wasn't at home. As I said, I was touring a lot in the US and Europe. I wasn't really within the new inner circle of Nirvana or the touring group or whatever. So I wasn't really aware of how bad things were getting until . . . Was it the Rome incident? Which was earlier that year, February that year, maybe. I've had friends, unfortunately, commit suicide. But . . . sometimes people can hide it really well . . . Then there's also the aspect of helping somebody. I've had this through people, myself, with addictions. If you're not willing to help yourself, it doesn't matter—any, whatever intervention—you're not gonna help. If a person can't help themselves or doesn't have that realization, there's nothing you can do. You've got the aspect of them not having the realization and wanting help or it becoming a critical mass. Something breaks. You do look back and you think, 'Well, you know, how would I have dealt with everybody wanting a piece of me?' All the time, at any given time. You can't go out, you can't go doing standard things, you know? It must have been really dreadful for him. But he had time for everybody."

Despite Kurt not having time for the millions of people who "wanted a piece of him," as Tony explains, there was still a widespread connection to him. He gave people permission to be exactly who they were, rejecting macho culture and refusing to conform to expectations.

"What do you think it was about Kurt that was so different or unique or just resonated with people?" I ask.

"Because he was talking from experience," says Tony. "A crummy childhood, homeless, being angry about misogynistic views, homophobic views, racist views. You know, I guess he was like a people's champion. He laid it down with rock music that had a different groove to it at the time. That energy was obviously danceable. People could lose themselves to it and go, 'I can relate to this.' What better than somebody helping you solve a psychological conundrum while you're dancing to the music in the club? Or you're feeling better about yourself because of some things he's quoted. And you go, 'Yeah, it really just helps people. It therapizes.' He was always championing the underdog, so to speak."

We shift the conversation to Kurt's positive impact since it's the way Tony remembers his friend.

"I will talk about it [his time with Kurt] in a positive sense," Tony explains. "It's been positive for me for my whole life. When I'd been lacking confidence or feeling worthless in an artistic sense, I just think back to the days of Kurt and how he gave me a chance to do the dancing. Okay, shrug this off, and let's move forward. He's prevented me from going into a lot of dark places, really. He was a sweetheart. You know the ways of the US press and media are just insane. It just angers me that some say he was just some destructive, disrespectful drug addict. He wasn't. You can't get any further from the truth.

"It's made me more accepting of people as well. Because I hear in a local friend group or the mainstream media where they go, 'Aw, Kurt was just this X, Y, Z.' And he wasn't. I'm more accepting now of other people when people are portrayed to me . . . as such and such. Were they really? Let's investigate further . . . I was privileged to cross paths with him. One of those serendipitous . . . what would you call it? Happenstance. We'll go with serendipitous. It was a serendipitous occasion."

Watching them on stage, it's easy to see why it felt bigger than that—why it felt like more than just crossing paths. They just clicked. There was a kind of harmony to it—Kurt screaming into the microphone, and Tony using his body to convey that same emotion. You didn't have to understand the lyrics to feel it. Tony brought that out physically, face paint and all. I ask him about his stage aesthetic and the makeup that went along with it.

"Well, it's like warpaint, because of my inner aggression . . . which is still there—but it's controlled."

Tony likens this to when he's drumming or gigging, going in as "precisely and hard and heavy and groove-oriented" as possible, something that showed up on stage with Nirvana.

As for the face paint, he explained that "It's like warpaint. But it's also like a clown, a mascot, for instance. Like I said, I was like Kurt's live familiar. The mascot. People . . . did they know who this was? They sort of knew who I was a little bit by then. So it was like a combination of warpaint and clown makeup. And then I'd have a formal shirt on with a tie just to keep it formal because it was a formal event. And then, I'd have Lorna's crocheted trousers that I wore generally quite a lot over those days."

He wore Converse that matched his lipstick, and at one point had an upside-down Satan patch safety-pinned to the back of his shirt. It wasn't about taking a side—it was more this mix of punk elements he pulled together.

"Kurt was saying, 'Yeah, Tony, just keep it weird,' you know?" Tony tells me. "So I would do weird things, and it does wind people up, and if you're doing something with your art—and people love it and people hate it—and it's like, 'Wow. I'm doing the right thing.' I wouldn't want people just to like it all the time. People have to hate on it. And if they do, it's like, 'I'm doing the right thing here.'"

"I think it's incredible," I say. "Did you plan the dances before you came out? Or you just kind of felt the music and felt the energy when you came on stage?"

"When I initially did them [the shows] in 1990, backstage we'd [Nirvana and Tony] just get ready," Tony says. "I'd have a few drinks and we'd just go out and do whatever came into our heads and just be weird about it. Some of the kids used to really, really hate it. And hate that I was wearing women's clothes. Nowadays, it's like, so fucking what? If I wanna wear women's clothes, I'll wear women's clothes . . . I can be supercritical of myself. Sometimes I'd watch the earlier performances and think, 'Well, I need to change it around a little bit,' and then by '92, late '91, I sort of changed it around. I would rehearse a little bit. And sort of warm-up and I'd have visualizations of what I'd do for each sort of song and sometimes try and mirror what Kurt was saying. Not that I really listened to the words.

"The thing is, with me, with music, I'm very much a rhythm-and-melody person. You could play me the most world-beating, lyrical song, poetic or whatever, and I wouldn't understand the context of it. I might read the lyrics afterwards. I don't really listen to the words. But I'd listen to Kurt and what he was saying and what he was expressing and just try to mimic that, really. But sometimes I'd just do too much. I've got a bad neck. I've had a bad neck for most of this year. And I'm almost certain it stems from the '92 concert. Because I overdid it. I ended up getting whiplash because I got just so carried away.

"That was another thing at the end of the show [Reading '92]. They [Nirvana] wanted me to dance to the Wipers, D7, and 'Territorial Pissings.' After a two-hour set that I've danced for most of, I needed to go out and do these really high-octane [songs] . . . It was like, yeah, just do it. I was in a quaint escapist world myself then."

I ask Tony if the band rehearsed before the show.

"No. I think they did . . . maybe one rehearsal," he clarifies. "I wasn't there. I don't even remember or know where it was. I wasn't involved. I just turned up the day before."

"They were just on point, they were just . . . It was great," I say.

"Well, that's what happens when you've got Dave behind the kit as well," Tony adds.

"Yeah. They were all amazing," I say. "I'm trying not to gloss over Dave or Krist. Those would be two other totally separate books; that's why I'm trying to focus on how the three of them really gelled together. You have Dave, who I call the pace car. He's keeping this incredible beat. Then you've got Krist who, no matter what, he's got some funny anecdote or he's always smiling. And then you've got Kurt that's so focused and staring out into the audience with that razor-sharp precision. They each did their own thing, but it just worked so well together."

"Or Krist's singing," Tony chimes in. "You know the thing he does? Is it the start of 'Territorial Pissings'? Well, that is his singing voice."

I laugh. "I didn't know. I was like, 'Is he being funny? Is that a joke?'"

"No, no!" Tony laughs, too. "That's Krist. That's his singing voice! Russell was saying he went to Dave's fiftieth and they were doing karaoke. And he had Krist as his partner to sing, and he's going, 'His singing voice is like that.'"

"It was just funny," I add. "The whole show was just . . ."

Tony finishes my thought. "It was punk rock. The whole show was just totally relaxed. The energy, let's just fucking go. To analyze it, there were some odd notes here, and some odd notes there. Tune in here, tune in there. But who gives a fuck? It was just, 'Let's go. We're doing it. The energy's there.' If the energy's there, you're committed, you've got great songs, you're a great band. That's what creates a legendary performance, really. Obviously, they've got a great dancer, as well." He laughs.

"Absolutely, one hundred percent," I agree.

Tony is wonderful to watch as he performs on stage with Nirvana, even thirty years later. It's surreal talking to him after watching the concert and makes me feel like I was there.

Tony explains how people perceive his role in Reading '92.

"Well, I've had people say that they've witnessed the show as I would have done because I guess they move into the show through me by proxy. That's the great thing because I'm dancing as you dance . . . A lot of people were going, 'I don't think I could have done this for as long as you did. I'd need to stop five minutes in.' But the thing is, it's coming from that performance background where you turn up and you do the job. If you don't do it, you're out of a job. It's plain and simple. You can't turn up to the gig and go, 'I don't fancy playing tonight,' or, 'I'm not dancing tonight.' It's like, 'We're doing this.' It's take no prisoners, we're going."

I comment on his solos and Kurt's raw, candid performances—thinking beyond Reading, especially *Top of the Pops*. Kurt was unapologetically himself and wasn't going to conform wholeheartedly to any parameters he disagreed with, intentionally butchering his performance on the British TV music show.

"The 'Smells Like Teen Spirit' one," Tony says. "That's brilliant."

It wasn't just about pushing back for the sake of it. When Kurt disrupted performances that threatened his creativity or cheapened the music, it came from a place of caring about his art. But it didn't stop there—he was just as aware of the people around him. I then mention Kurt wishing a happy birthday to Dave's mother on stage at Reading '92—a small gesture that showed he was aware of those around him.

"Yes, to Virginia," Tony tells me. "Sadly, we lost her last year. She was lovely . . . She was very much accepting. Dave's very much a mold of his mother, really."

"He seems very down to earth."

"Oh yeah, he's brilliant," Tony says. "Fantastic."

Kurt was a vocal feminist—Nirvana played Rock for Choice, a concert supporting women's reproductive rights. The band also staunchly opposed homophobia, performing at the No on 9 benefit show for gay rights. They didn't do it for the accolades; they believed in the values that inspired some of their biggest songs. And when those values came under fire, Kurt was often the first one screaming about it.

"Yeah . . . empowering the underdog," Tony says. "These marginalized groups shouldn't be marginalized . . . I will hate somebody on a personal level but . . . the trigger will not be sexuality, race, sex. That's never the trigger point. People really let themselves down and really need to think about it when they're being racist and misogynistic, homophobic . . . You're allowing something in that shouldn't be there naturally. We're not born racist, we're not born misogynistic, we're not born homophobic. It's learned behaviors, isn't it? Kurt stood for a lot, for those causes. Ironically, as well, he stood for these marginalized groups and certain youth movements. He was part of one of the last youth movements that happened. From '94 to '99—the internet—everything becomes everywhere, you are seeing it a lot more nowadays. But that was the whole joy of 'scenes.' Like Kurt writing letters to Mark Lanegan [lead singer for Screaming Trees]. I used to write to fan clubs, and you'd see articles in magazines, and it'd all be part of a scene. It was marginalized, these youth movements. It was part of one of the last ones."

Our conversation shifts to the unhoused crisis and Kurt's sleeping arrangements, possibly beneath the Young Street Bridge.

"Well, maybe not under the bridge," Tony weighs in. "But in his car. He had those experiences . . . that informed him of his position on these sorts of affairs. And, you know, it's a problem. I think there are a lot of people . . . a lot of people don't show enough humility. I've been humbled a couple of times in my life; one of the times was before I met

Kurt when I was really ill and I was scarred up internally, externally. And I learned from that experience. I learned humility. I was humbled and . . . you need to think about things a bit differently . . . and sometimes you're pushed to the extremes and you either show it or you just carry on down the same path of, 'It's not me, blame, blame, blame.' But Kurt experienced [being unhoused], and when they recorded *Nevermind*, they [Nirvana] had no money. They had no money, and it was probably like all of them sleeping in the same room."

Tony then reflects on Kurt and his desire to leave his hometown of Aberdeen, watching and absorbing the world around him, fully aware and finding his calm in the middle of a raging music scene.

"He was a sensitive soul," Tony says. "He just had to get out. He was sleeping in his car. There's actually a story from a while ago, when I met Slash through Russell. He was fascinated with the stories of our early Nirvana outings and things like that. One that we had a laugh about—Kurt, he'd been sleeping in cars, but when he came over here, they'd have hotels, and me and Russell would be sleeping in the van or the car outside their hotel!"

He laughs as he recalls this interaction, then focuses on the documentary *When Nirvana Came to Britain*.

"It's such a positive documentary about Kurt. It's about early days. You know, having fun, being dicks."

People want more positivity tied to Kurt's name, but for Tony, suicide complicates that. It's not just about navigating a friend's passing—it's deflecting comments that undermine what Kurt was going through.

"Just his lasting legacy of . . . I dunno," Tony says. "Suicide is a weird thing, and for it to end like that . . . I've got into many arguments, people going, 'It's the cowardly way out.' I don't think it is because I couldn't do it. I couldn't imagine being in that headspace to do that thing . . . And obviously, Kurt had an ego, didn't he? And your ego keeps you alive, doesn't it? It's very hard. But that happened, and it's happened to my friends. And it's like . . . It's not a cowardly way out at all."

Tony has one more sentiment about his friend, another memory to share.

"Kurt was a lovely, sweet, kind guy that you could take around to your mother's house for tea and cakes. He was absolutely lovely. He had time for everybody."

We chat for a few more minutes, and Tony tells me about what he has on the horizon. His band, Island Apes, has an upcoming album, and he's working with his partner on a collaborative project called Great Raven. Tony's always creating, always finding new avenues to express himself musically and artistically. This reminds me of Kurt and, in many ways, reflects the underpinnings of their time together. Kurt and Tony were two musicians—two artists—born to create, their friendship that of mutual respect and unequivocal admiration.

Our conversation helped me understand a time and place where Kurt was a commanding presence on festival stages, his energy as infectious as the music itself. Although entertaining, grainy recordings of Reading '92 offer limited insight into what was happening behind the scenes. But speaking with those who lived it offers a palpable vibrancy that captures the thrill of Nirvana; it captures Kurt, contradictions and all.

More than anything, it reinforces something simpler—how important it is to focus on the positive. You can't just remember Kurt for how it ended. You have to remember the good, too.

Understanding Kurt's paradox—his craving for success while also desiring privacy—made me even more curious about how it all came together on stage at Reading '92 and in the time leading up to that show when Kurt was pushing back against everything surrounding him. I thought of who to contact next—someone who could help me understand the emotionally charged Seattle music scene, still burgeoning, with fame already taking hold. That someone was the celebrated photographer Charles Peterson, who captured Kurt's essence in a way that can only be described as transcendental, Reading '92 included.

Chapter 8

"FRANCES FARMER WILL HAVE HER REVENGE ON SEATTLE"

Charles Peterson

ONE PHOTOGRAPH—TAKEN BY CHARLES PETERSON ON AUGUST 30, 1992—captures Reading Festival and its chaotic intensity in a single frame. Kurt bored a hole into the camera's lens, unconcerned as the breeze pressed his white hospital gown taut against his legs. The crowd was ravenous, but for that moment, he gave the camera his full attention. No flying kicks, no thrashing antics. Just Kurt.

This single snapshot, etched into music history, is how so many remember Kurt—locked in on the music, everything else fading into background noise.

I reached out to Charles to learn more about that moment. We connected, and I explained this project.[43]

★★★

"This book focuses on Kurt's legacy," I tell him, wanting to hear his perspective.

"I guess we can start at the beginning," Charles begins. "I was photographing the Seattle music scene from '82, '83. And then all of a sudden, somebody's talking about this new band from Aberdeen. Bob [Whittaker, Sub Pop Records] would bring them up and have them play closing on a Sunday night at The Vogue at one of their showcases. I actually went to photograph Blood Circus because, whoa—Blood Circus is going to be huge, you know? And I didn't photograph Nirvana that night. I wasn't particularly impressed with this kind of dark, moody dude up front who really didn't even move around at all. I think I left halfway through the show; it was a Sunday night, after all. I was saying to Jonathan [Poneman, Sub Pop Records], 'Are you sure you want to sign these guys?'" Charles laughs. "Which is why I wasn't running the record label. And he says, 'Yeah, yeah, yeah. I'll send you a demo tape.'

"Then *Bleach* came out, and I was just totally blown away. The next time I saw them, they had a new drummer and a second guitar player—Jason Everman—for a short period. And they were just—Kurt was doing jumps and on his knees and just all over the place. I thought, *Okay, these guys are amazing.* Then I remember Jonathan saying to me, 'Dude, whatever you do, just don't read the lyrics, okay?'" Charles laughs again. "He said, 'It's kind of nonsensical [the lyrics]. But the way Kurt delivers them is amazing' . . . I agreed. We can get to that later on—the power of Nirvana, Kurt's lyricism, and sort of what it means.

"I was tasked to go take a group photo of them over on Bainbridge Island, and we ran around for an afternoon. They were great guys. At the time, Kurt was super shy. Krist was gregarious. The first time I met Krist was actually out at Bobby Whittaker's family cabin. La Push [Beach] on the Washington coast. The ocean. It was at night, and we were all out there, around a bonfire, on the beach, and all of a sudden we just hear this wild howling off in the distance. We look and this six-foot-seven dude [Krist] is running down the beach, stripping his clothes off as he's running towards us. He jumps over the fire and then continues running down the beach until you can't see him anymore, and it was like, 'Oh my God, what was that?' And then he comes back, and that was kind of my introduction to Nirvana.

"I remember Kurt coming over to the loft one time when The Fluid was there. I had a loft on Second Avenue around the corner from the Sub Pop offices. We were all partying, and Kurt pretty much just sat on the sofa by himself. Then we were dragging him along to the Re-bar and to The Vogue later that night. I actually have a snapshot of him there, just all spotty-faced. I was like, 'Oh man, that guy is pretty shy.' Believe it or not, I'm actually quite the introvert as well. Which is a really crazy thing to become known as a people photographer, while also being an introvert.

"And I think that, at times, Kurt and I, when we were together—this is often the way with two introverts—we sort of became like magnets, repelling each other a little bit. Chris Cornell [Soundgarden] was quite the wallflower as well. But I think what happened is Kurt would get on stage—I'd get there—and that's when he opened up and became this thing that was beyond him in his regular life. And that's also at the same time when I was comfortable to really open up and just become . . . almost practically trying to become part of the band, in a way."

"Your photos are wild," I say. "You really knew how to capture Nirvana and the setting; you're time-stamping these incredible moments in music history. You can look at your photos, and you feel the energy in the room."

"That was really my intention from early on," Charles begins. "I didn't want to just make another press photo of the singer standing at the microphone. I was in art school as well. I went to study photography at the University of Washington and got my BFA in '87. So I approached it from an art school direction. I was aware of all the great photographers and knew what to pull out of all that to make it my own."

"Well, you did an amazing job. I look at some of the photos and wonder how you captured them. Like the ones where Kurt is upside down, guitar in hand."

"Well, you know, it took two, that's for sure," Charles says. "But I've always had really, really fast reflexes."

No matter what Nirvana show you watch—Kurt could be standing at the microphone, still, one moment, and thrashing about on the floor the next—Nirvana's audience was always prepped and ready to go. Charles captured the scene so vividly that you can practically taste the sweat and feel the latent angst when you see his photos of Kurt.

"Can you describe how the audience responded to Nirvana?" I ask. "Nirvana really knew how to enrapture their audience."

"Yeah. I mean, they weren't alone in the Seattle scene that way, certainly," Charles explains. "But I think the audience actually came before Nirvana. Seattle was really well known for its crazy audiences; traveling bands knew about Seattle at that point. And bands like Scratch Acid and Dinosaur Jr. would come through and audiences would go crazy. I remember seeing a show in New York or LA around the mid-eighties and everyone was just sort of standing there with their arms folded. And I was like, 'What the fuck? Why even bother coming out here to the show?' Everyone was kind of standing around as if they were doing it with a critical eye instead of just losing themselves in the music.

"Nirvana was able to really—in the footsteps of Green River and Soundgarden and Mudhoney and TAD—just step into those shoes and then make their own whole freaking outfit at that point. They really—there was just something about them that was different than what was going on before. People ask me this all the time. It's really kind of hard to nail down.

"I mean, obviously, it's been written about *ad nauseam*—the sort of influences of Kurt, everything from hardcore punk to The Beatles. But I think that there was an underlying melody and sensitivity that wasn't in some of the other bands. And Kurt was really good at sort of shape-shifting his voice without it being too obvious and weird or cliché. So, to me, a lot of the Nirvana songs—even on *Bleach*—each one sounds a little different from the other, whereas some of the other bands—well, obviously they had different songs—but a lot of Soundgarden songs sound really similar, to a degree. And it's [Kurt's vocals] not a classical singing style at all, in the same way that Chris Cornell or Eddie Vedder or someone would do. And it's not an in-your-face kind of singing, like Mark Arm or Tad [Doyle] or somebody would do. It kind of—it cuts that balance.

"To me, when you come back to the lyrics . . . what I think is the staying power of Nirvana and Kurt's songwriting is what's called the transmutational aspect of it. Transmutational essentially means you can take it and make it anything you want, the meaning. For the most part—especially towards the end—his songs started to have more storytelling to them or some sort of thing to hook on to. But early on it just seemed like sort of rambling diary entries, almost of these weird, mundane experiences that really don't make any sense. And a lot of the words—when he sings them—are somewhat indecipherable. But you can take it and shout along whatever words you want to it that are close, you know? Nonsense words even, and then still feel all this emotion. And you can use thc music when you're happy, when you're sad, when you're angry, whatever. It's like—you can kind of transform it into what you are experiencing emotionally inside of yourself."

"A couple of people I talked to had called him kind of like a chameleon," I say. "And I guess, you know, I never really looked at it like that. But whatever mood I'm in, I can put on Nirvana, and it amplifies that mood or makes me feel a certain way. Do you, as a photographer and in capturing Nirvana—specifically Kurt on stage—feel that his onstage persona changed throughout his career? Do you think he was kind of similar in how he behaved? I think of all the shows where Kurt's jumping about and then it was just amazing seeing *Unplugged* where he was just sitting there, this portrait of a musician, you know? I was just wondering what that looks like from a photographer's lens."

"Yeah, I mean, certainly, there's a lot of other access and physicality aspects to it," Charles answers. "As a photographer, there's obviously a great big difference between photographing him two or three feet away, on the floor or a small stage, versus someplace like Reading where the front of the stage is a fifteen-foot drop kind of thing. I think he sometimes struggled to sort of fill the stage, in a way. I think he may have been more comfortable if there was a way that he could have played a giant show, but at the same time made it intimate for himself. If that makes any sense."

It does.

Charles continues, "I mean, probably my favorite photo of Kurt and favorite moment of the whole Nirvana experience was at Reading ['92]. I'm on the side of the stage sitting next to Mark Arm, watching him. And suddenly, in between songs, Kurt stops, and he looks over at me and Mark, and he's mouthing something like, 'How am I doing?' or 'How's it going?' or 'How are you guys?'—something to that degree. And we're waving at him and we're like, 'It's great. We're fine.' I mean, we're just mouthing these things back and forth to each other, and then he's just looking at us with this kind of impish grin on his face. Then Mark and I start waving like, 'Dude, you've got forty-five thousand people out there waiting on you,' and sort of wave back at him as if to say, 'Go do your thing.'" Charles laughs.

"I think he really—in that moment—it was really important for him to sort of look to the side of the stage and see his old friends and peers there, in this environment."

"Kind of like that comfort," I chime in. "Like, okay, he's in this new environment, but he's got his people there—the people that he knows are still there waiting in the wings."

"Yeah, which is in some ways why I think—well, there's a number of reasons—but why the Rio shows were so awful: because it just was not the right environment for him. Not to mention most likely being drug-sick and all that. But I think that Nirvana . . . I think they were really going to be happy if they were as big as Sonic Youth. I think that was their goal initially. Like, 'Wow, if we can sell one hundred thousand records like Sonic Youth, that's going to be amazing,' and play these shows to fifteen hundred people versus five hundred. And then it just . . . as we all know, it totally blew up."

"To be a part of the height of this big buildup and watching this band catapult to fame . . . that must have been really amazing," I say.

"Honestly, yes and no," Charles clarifies. "I know you want to keep this positive, but let's get a little dark . . . I really didn't photograph or even go see the band towards the end. The last few times I saw Kurt, he just looked terrible."

Charles had already seen addiction up close, and he couldn't be around it again.

"I just couldn't deal with it anymore," he explains. "I understand addiction, and it was not a matter of blaming a victim or anything like that. It was just like . . . you just can't. I mean, the person is constantly disappearing into the bathroom for periods of time. It's just ugly, you know? Nothing really matters beyond the drug. And we had some issues that got ugly at one point, and then we made up, and it had to do with these English journalists that had come to town. It turned out they were being weird and then that made Kurt and Courtney weird. Plus, you're in your twenties, and everything just seems so heightened and important. You make factions."

Charles continues, "I think a lot of us—boy, if we could turn that clock back . . . We would do things so differently. I mean, some things, yes, we would do the same, but other things would be like, 'Oh, man.' I mean, I was actually one of the last people—other than his little drug posse—I was one of the last people to run into Kurt when he was alive. This must have been about two or three weeks beforehand, maybe a month. But anyway, at that point, he was pretty much just . . . They just spent their time out in the cabin doing drugs mostly, I think. My memory is mixed in with those bittersweet things. And, of course, all the tragedies with other people that have happened since.

"The whole thing is cursed in some ways. I mean, it's blessed and it's cursed. And I say that, but in life, we have shadow and light, we have dark, and it is all part of it. I think that maybe some of the lasting power of it is that it wasn't all just this positive experience, but it wasn't all just this negative experience, either. So it does kind of run that gamut in life."

Most of my conversations about Kurt toggle between shadow and light, as Charles puts it. There are times where conversations flow freely, stories about Kurt's dedication to his art at the helm of each discussion. Other times, there are uncomfortable pauses, my interviewees and I both unsure of how to broach the subject of Kurt's suicide. It also feels as if so much of Kurt's empathy and compassion can be attributed to the pain he endured at such a young age. It's something to mourn and celebrate simultaneously, especially since Kurt made one hell of an impact on those he touched—even those he never met.

"In fact, in the book [Charles Peterson's *Nirvana*], the photos that I'm putting out . . . I wanted it to stay very positive as well and just be about the energy of the music more than anything else," Charles tells me. "The book itself is composed of about twelve different shows that are jumbled together into one big show. And then sections are broken up with song titles—just sort of ambiguously broken up with song titles to give it some pacing. But what I decided, in the end, was that the last section, of course, would be them destroying their instruments and all that. The song I put to that is 'Endless, Nameless.' Then I was like, you know what? I don't want this finality. I want it to come full circle. So, I put in a section after that called 'On a Plain,' which is sort of like, not an epilogue . . . I wanted for them to essentially play the encore that they never got to play. So the book actually begins with a photo of them at the Commodore Ballroom, plugging in their instruments, and then the very last photo in the main section is them also at the Commodore playing, still playing, so you can kind of put it on a loop, in a way . . . I just didn't want the finality of that ending.

"One of the reasons this book has taken so long to come out is that I have said 'no' to various publishers that have approached me over the years. And not because they were necessarily fishing for any sort of dirt, which I don't really have. I've got a couple of pictures of Kurt nodding off; you may or may not know that even looking at the picture. But what they always wanted, I think, was what we've come to call a 'band book.' And I don't make band books. I did not want to make a band book. I want to make an artistic statement. I suffer from imposter syndrome. And I think Kurt did as well. So I didn't actually believe that I had enough material to make just a Nirvana book . . . I'm supposed to make a history of these guys, and I feel like I don't have their history. I wasn't there for much of it. I was there for some of that, maybe there for more of it than some other photographer . . . But then it was a year and a half ago, and my family went out of town for the summer, and I just was like, 'Okay, how can I do this?' And I just printed out hundreds of pictures . . . and for two weeks just took over the house while they were gone, put Nirvana on shuffle, and laid these out. It's the music that sort of drove the edit and how I was going to sequence this and put it together. And then, of course, my editor really fine-tuned it . . . She's a small fine art imprint . . . I didn't want words; I wanted photos . . . an emotional and visceral experience versus your intellectual train-spotting experience."

There's a ton of demand for Charles's book, as Nirvana's unwavering prominence is felt everywhere.

"It feels like Nirvana is more popular than ever," I say. "You can't turn a street corner without seeing people in a Nirvana shirt."

"Well, as my eleven-year-old daughter and a few friends at her school say, 'Oh yeah, Nirvana is my favorite *brand*.'" He laughs. "But it's true; they have no clue who the band is, but they love the merch."

"Do you think it was the whole 'I can have a beer with this guy' persona of Kurt's that added to his appeal?" I ask.

"Well, there are a number of factors," Charles tells me. "One, there's the finiteness of it. He never went on to make lousy solo albums. Sub Pop always joked about the whole 'loser' thing, and it's kind of a tongue-in-cheek thing. But Kurt, in a sense, really kind of does represent the loser . . . Again, that's the tongue-in-cheek thing. By 'loser,' they [Sub Pop] meant it more like the outsider. Because we were called 'losers,' it's sort of like accepting the word and making it your own kind of thing. So that was kind of the joke. I do think that he and his music—or the band—appeal to that outsider sense. And again, like I said earlier, it's that transmutational aspect of it.

"We had a New Year's Eve party, and we started having a dance party, and I was just kind of DJing on the fly from my phone. I dropped

'Smells Like Teen Spirit,' and I think at that point the fourteen- and fifteen-year-olds outnumbered the adults in the house, my son's friends. And they're all into hip hop, that's their thing. All of a sudden, they went nuts and were screaming and shouting.

"They [Nirvana] were really just that iconic last of a . . . Grunge was sort of the last great musical movement before everything was immediately accessible via the internet. So, there's that mystery of the finiteness. What could it have been? But it wasn't, and so this is what we have. It is fascinating to see the younger generations pick up on it."

Charles continues, "But I think there's one important thing that has been a constant in my life and was an aspect of Kurt's life, which is chronic pain. I've had migraines since I was . . . I don't know, two, three, and I don't think I've ever had a single day in my life where I've actually felt well. Whether I have a migraine or not—most days I do—I think that that was something that Kurt really struggled with and has not actually been talked about enough: his stomach issues. Which we now, of course, know that stomach issues can affect just your entire systemic body. And I think that he really struggled, and unfortunately, he discovered that opioids—for him at least—took care of a lot of those issues and cleared it up. And at first, it probably allowed him to do a lot more than he would have been able to do otherwise, particularly with the way things accelerated and the grueling tour schedules and press schedules and all of that. You know, that sort of 'be careful what you wish for.' I always emphasize that I always had empathy with him for that just because of my own issues through life. Oh, and it's so obvious that he had scoliosis, as well. I mean, that famous photo of mine of him just alone with all the black around him from the back. I mean, you can just see it in his stature that he's got some issues going on. And then, of course, throwing himself on drum kits and whatnot. It didn't help. And at the time we had no clue about diet or all that. God, even if we did, we probably wouldn't have done anything about it. It would have been far too much of a pain in the ass to be gluten-free or dairy-free . . . at that time, especially . . . Fortunately, I never turned to opioids."

We sit in the weight of what he's just shared—the physical struggles of Kurt, the private battles fans never witness. Charles and I take a break from our interview, each running a few errands. During this interlude, we reflect on Kurt, knowing that when he calls me back, he'll have another story to share.

"I had a real vivid memory of—I guess it would have been the second to last time I ran into Kurt," Charles begins. "I've been thinking about various artifacts that we could potentially use for this museum show, and I remembered, *Oh, I have this camera that Kurt came by the house and left with me.* It was a vintage stereoscope camera. And he was like, 'Can you figure out how to . . . source film for this and use it?' I said, 'Yeah, sure, I'll give it a shot.' I never did. This was early March [1994] sometime; it was kind of unseasonably nice weather, very similar to what we're having today. He dropped by the house in his Falcon, and I just remember we met outside; he seemed in a bit of a hurry, but we chatted for ten minutes or so while he showed me the camera, and we caught up on this and that. I just remember—it struck me—I just remember his piercing blue eyes, like that late winter bright, bright day. It was just beautiful. I stupidly—I should have gone and grabbed the camera and said, 'Hey, can you take a picture?' but I was never like that around him. I was never like that around a lot of the guys. At that point, you knew when they went on the road, they got it all the time. It was just my own imposter syndrome, as well—I don't think Kurt would have cared . . . I don't know if I would have the same memory per se if I had taken photos. Does that make any sense? It might have turned into something else or would just be this thing I have to constantly try and relive, the story. But now I'm thinking, 'Wow, what an interesting thing to have at the end of the show, this camera that he bought and handed off to me.'

"It's fun bringing back those positive moments . . . I think that sometimes what's gotten lost—and I think it's being reclaimed to a degree, with retrospect—it's the insouciance of the players and of the scene. We really weren't taking ourselves very seriously. I mean, it's sad, it's tragic, that non-seriousness . . . a time that had to have a very serious end. You can't avoid that. But it was a really pretty funny time, no matter how heavy or angsty you might think the music is. The Soundgarden guys were some of the goofiest of all, you know? I think that listening to their music . . . I mean, the first time I met Chris Cornell must have been 1984, maybe '85. Some random house party out near the University District and Wallingford. I was there with Mark Arm and just our gang that we rode with, and here was this young, beautiful-looking guy that they introduced me to who was like, 'Oh, yeah, I'm playing music here.' We were getting drunk, and there were a few girls and we were talking to them. I'm just like, 'Jesus, any party you go to with this guy, don't even think about it.' Then the lights are out and we're all drunk and wrestling on the floor.

"We were just young dudes—some of us—in or out of college, others just coming together, making music. You know, starting up a record label. No real expectations. I mean, everybody wanted to make a living at music. And boy, you had to suffer to do it, too. I think that the unheralded chapter was when Kurt and Krist and Dave went to Olympia, lived in Olympia. You know, before *Nevermind.* And just practiced the hell out of it [their songs], like lived on peanut butter sandwiches and Top Ramen and slept in cold warehouses and shitty apartments with mold on the walls and just practiced the hell out of their songs. They lived like monks to perfect their craft, and it totally paid off. They were very driven. Kurt especially was very, very driven in that way."

It was April 17, 1991. Nirvana played the OK Hotel in Seattle, where they debuted "Smells Like Teen Spirit" for an enraptured audience. It's safe to say the world was never the same, and even harder to believe that three years later, Kurt would be gone.[44]

Since then, various museums and exhibits dedicated to Nirvana—especially Kurt—have been established, and Charles and I speculate on what he might have thought about the ways people choose to honor his legacy.

"I see things all the time, and I would just be like, 'He would so detest [that]' and/or find funny, like weird tattoos," Charles says. "But he might find a lot of it hilarious as well. He was a very funny person and a prankster. I do think sometimes he took some stuff maybe too seriously. It was a crazy, crazy two years there."

This leads Charles to recall when Frances Bean Cobain was born.

"I was just flabbergasted when they [Kurt and Courtney] had a child. I was like, 'Oh my God, on top of everything else.' Maybe that's just a sign of my own immaturity at the time. I don't know, but I was like, 'Oh man, I can't imagine . . .' They were fortunate to have money and be able to have a nanny and all that. I mean, at Frances's first birthday party, I went and there were a number of people there, and we all knew each other. What I did, actually, is I brought an SX-70 with me and took a bunch of Polaroids, a huge stack of Polaroids, and then just handed them to Kurt at the end of the night. A couple of those surfaced, I think one or two in his journals. The tricycle with the anarchy on it. And everybody brought gifts, and it was really kind of an overkill. I think Kurt—I was sitting there afterward, and I think he was just kind of embarrassed, and he just looked at me and was like, 'Oh, man.' Like kind of shook his head and disappeared into the bathroom. It was a lot for him to deal with.

"I think it was in just too short a time . . . You become a business, your art and your likeness and your ability to play and get up out of bed and get on an airplane and go here and do this. There are several hundred people depending on you and at least fifty to a hundred core people depending on you, for you to perform, and if you look at the lyrics of *In Utero*, he takes that on. I think the performer that took that on recently the most, too, is Billie Eilish, with her last album. It was brilliant, and it's a lot of the same, similar themes that Kurt kind of toys with in *In Utero*, that early fame and being something that you're not."

As our conversation winds down, Charles and I talk a bit more about my book's driving force—namely Walter, and how his suicide propelled me to learn more about the way we, as a society, handle the stigma surrounding mental health. At first, I was hesitant to incorporate him into this book. He was, after all, the reason I wrote it, but I didn't know how much to include about him. Charles's advice is simple: Be honest with readers. So that's what I did.

"The best work brings it personal," Charles says. "For example, with the Tacoma Art Museum show, I'm toying with this idea: I've got a little family snapshot from 1969 of me with my dad, my mom, and my mom's younger sister standing in front of the Buick and the house in Longview, Washington. Two years later, my father went through Western, which was the same hospital that Frances Farmer went through, that Kurt would then famously sing about twenty-two years later.

"I had to find out how to talk about that briefly as kind of an introduction to the show. I'm not just somebody that's parachuting in here because, 'Oh, I heard this band out in Seattle that's getting famous,' you know? Where does it connect with me and what I did through the art and with Kurt and what he did with his art? Kurt, and Krist, and everyone. We all can have that same experience of growing up. If it wasn't one weird thing from the sixties or seventies, it was another.

"Without being overwrought or too depressing—you've got to figure that out—where does that impetus start? Just looking at that photo [Charles's family photo] is like, wow—we had that same lived experience, and that's why the music resonated with me so much. And maybe that's why it resonates with people today . . . This is giving you the allowance to look deeper into why this music is emotional and why these photos convey that power."

We got off the phone, and I thought about our conversation. Parts were challenging—there are no two ways around it—but there's something special about imagining the early days of Nirvana. More than anything, I liked the concept of keeping things on a loop, like Charles does with his book. In many ways, this mirrors each interview: we start hopeful, but the reality of Kurt's suicide looms large. Still, I was excited about where this journey would take me next, each conversation unraveling more of the mystery surrounding Kurt Cobain.

Through Nirvana's music, Charles's photos, and the stories I was grateful to learn firsthand, I felt ready to take what I'd learned and continue honoring Kurt and Walter. I didn't want to psychoanalyze Kurt, but I did want to understand what made him tick and what made his music the extraordinary success that it was. With that in mind, I decided to write about some of the most iconic Nirvana performances, letting Kurt speak through the moments themselves rather than through my speculation.

Although not their first show, I started with Nirvana's Reading '92 concert, which only made sense after speaking with Charles and Tony the Interpretive Dancer. Kurt, at the time, was nothing more than a tabloid punching bag, yet he gave the performance of a lifetime, enduring undue abuse from the media. The energy, the erratic strobe lights dancing off his slight frame—even if you weren't there, you can watch recordings and feel the power and permanence.

I revisited this concert while reading some of Kurt's interviews, his words helping to guide the tale of what went into that iconic show—and what he experienced off the stage. Together with recollections from those who were there—some on stage dancing, others capturing what would become some of the most celebrated concert photos in music history—a portrait of this revolutionary performance took shape.

Reading, England, was the physical setting, but a backdrop of media theatrics threw all it had at an already overwhelmed Kurt. This became the public theme surrounding the inscrutable lead singer, with one of the band's most seminal shows proving just how fed up he was with the media's obsession with his personal life. Although we can only fractionally understand what Kurt faced at this juncture in his life and career, Reading '92 offers a glimpse into the mind of a musical genius.

Chapter 9

"SCENTLESS APPRENTICE"

Reading, 1992

"And just maybe I'm to blame for all I've heard
But I'm not sure"
—Kurt Cobain, "Lithium"

THERE WAS A CHILL IN THE AIR, NOT UNCOMMON FOR BRITISH WEATHER, even in the summer. The sky was pitch black, and the stage was cast in a faded, ghostly pallor. The crowd was massive, their excitement impossible to contain. As the festival drew to a close, concertgoers wondered if they'd witnessed the last act or if the finale was yet to come. Fans held their breath, questioning if Nirvana would make an appearance. The weight of everything—Kurt's health, minimal rehearsal, and whether the band could hold it together—loomed in the air.

Suddenly, the stage was aglow with an eerie green light. A figure in a white hospital gown, hanging dejectedly over his legs, was wheeled onto the stage. It was Kurt.

Leading up to the show, no one knew if Kurt would even make it. Depending on the coverage, he had been in and out of rehab, the band had split, or both. As the wheelchair dragged Kurt downstage, the roar of fifty thousand screaming fans cheered him on, begging him—imploring him—to rise.

Krist waited at the microphone, his slick leather jacket luminescent beneath the jade lights. Finally, he spoke, motioning toward Kurt, who sat slumped forward in the chair, his face obscured beneath the ragged edges of a long bleach-blond wig strewn across it, his frame so unsteady it looked like he might fall out at any moment.

"It's so—I can't say—it's too painful. This is too painful."

Kurt was wheeled to him, slumped in his wheelchair.

"You're gonna make it, man," Krist said, leaning down to address his friend before returning to the microphone. "With the support of his friends and family, he's gonna make it."

The audience erupted into a fit of frenzy as Kurt—their dauntless leader—rose to his feet. Slowly, gingerly, he approached the microphone. Would he make it? There was a pregnant pause as spectators wondered if he'd have the strength to lift his guitar, let alone belt out his trademark gritty vocals.

And then he sang. Bette Midler's "The Rose."

Only a few bars into the song, Kurt collapsed to the ground, a mess of gangly legs protruding beneath the pallid hospital gown, arms splayed out, garish Halloween wig still attached and scattered over his motionless face. A moment later he was up, ambling across the stage in search of his 1965 Fender Jaguar. He returned to the microphone, his guitar strapped securely around his shoulders, ready to punish the fretboard. A thunderous roar exploded from the audience; their demigod was alive and kicking, his wheelchair a giant "fuck you" to all the cynics and critics that insinuated Icarus finally flew too close to the sun.

As Kurt rocked back and forth, entrenched in "Breed," the band united in focus and energy. The house lights and Tony the Interpretive Dancer gyrating about on stage matched the chaos fans had just witnessed. Kurt's entrance gave way to his typical raucous onstage energy, no longer teetering on the precipice of death. The guitar came in sharp and heavy. His body jerked forward, locked into the rhythm, fully awake and revived.

Krist moved beside him, loose and fully in the groove, Dave crashing through the beat, Tony spinning in total chaos—but Kurt never broke. He was completely present and fully engaged in the performance, playing with concentration and control that suggested the media attacks only sharpened his focus.

It was messy. It was loud. It was Nirvana.

During a conversation I had with Gary Lee Conner of Screaming Trees, he talked about the first time he saw Kurt perform live, saying, "I thought, *Man, he's really got something. He's like a total natural performer.*"[45]

"Breed" dropped off, engulfing the stage in darkness with a faint red glow. A moment later, the lights illuminated the trio, Kurt's wig now discarded. Psychedelic strobes bathed the stage in constantly changing rainbow hues as the band ripped into "Drain You." The chemistry within the band was unmistakable. Dave played with fearless intensity while Krist jumped about the stage, the group moving as a single unit. Kurt was steady, shoulders set, and focused, but there was still a playfulness as he surged with the music. There was no excess to it, no distraction. He delivered every note straight, devoting everything to this singular performance. Kurt mesmerized and hypnotized the crowd in a manner that seemed effortless, contrary to the previous decade of hair metal bands that jumped about in skintight leather in all their self-aggrandizing glory. That was the key to his power—he was unassuming, even while screaming his face off.

At the time of the show, Kurt had just become a father—Courtney Love gave birth to Frances Bean Cobain on August 18, 1992, less than two weeks before the festival. In an interview with writer Pleasant Gehman, Kurt reflected on family, fame, and his role in Nirvana.

> "It's amazing the shit people can get away with. I don't understand. If I had known about all this crap, I would've

> thought twice about putting myself in the public eye so much. I had no idea people could abuse you so much. I don't even care about the band as much as I used to. I know that sounds shitty, but the band used to be the only thing that was important to me in my life, and now, I have a wife and a child. I still love the band, but it isn't the only thing I'm living for."[46]

Rumors about his family, his personal activities, and the band were frequently contradictory and seemed engineered to break down one rumor to spite the other. Privacy was a thing of the past—nothing was sacred in Kurt's orbit once *Nevermind* hit the airwaves.

He had a complicated relationship with fame, as evidenced in multiple interviews throughout his brief watershed of a career. He even rocked one of his own rough-hewn creations for Nirvana's cover photoshoot with *Rolling Stone* in April 1992, the words on his stark white T-shirt crisp, clean, and intentional: CORPORATE MAGAZINES STILL SUCK. It was one of his many jabs at the industry he catered to while simultaneously loathing it. Kurt's irreverent humor and refusal to be publicly torn apart carried over into his live performances, and those who watched Reading '92 will attest,[47] as made evident in his wheelchair stunt and triumphant rise after the collapse.

In an interview with Nick Chiericozzi, founding member and guitarist for the Brooklyn-based punk band The Men, I asked just what he thought of this iconic concert. "'Live at Reading' is really cool," Nick said. "The confidence and humor of that particular set are really there. Man, things just work out sometimes when you play a set, and for them to be on, at that show, on that night . . . That's what you hope to achieve each time you play, even if it's for seven people."[48]

This was not the first time Kurt's deliberately unhinged, high-wire demeanor was on full display. His antics were alive and well a year prior, when Nirvana originally played the Reading Festival in '91.

In an interview with Wm. Ferguson, Dave Grohl shed light on Kurt's erratic, albeit entertaining, behavior that day, referencing an image of the rock trio taken some time before Kurt's shocking swan dive into the drums. The band had just finished "Endless, Nameless" when Kurt made his way downstage. Inexplicably, he ran headfirst into Dave's drums, guitar and all, then sprang to his feet, triumphant despite a serious shoulder injury, waving at the audience. It was a moment time-stamped in Nirvana lore.

In the photo, Kurt is grinning, arm outstretched, brandishing a bottle of extra-strong cough syrup.

"There were thirty thousand, maybe thirty-five thousand people at Reading," Dave said. "I'm not sure, but it was a lot bigger than any show I had ever played. I think this picture was taken before the gig, and the reason I can tell the difference between pre- and post-gig is that Kurt was seriously injured by jumping into my drum set. That bottle he's holding out toward the camera was some kind of incredibly potent cough syrup, and he was carrying that thing around like a flask. So, this is preshow, and he was drinking that cough syrup, which led him to dive into my drum set, which put him in a sling for the rest of the night. That gig was definitely a triumph."[49]

Nirvana's former manager, Danny Goldberg, pointed to Kurt's keen insight and preternatural awareness of his devotees. Kurt capitalized on that even if it meant sustaining injuries for the sake of his art. When speaking with interviewers Rachel Martin and Vince Pearson, Goldberg explained that "[h]e also had this comprehensive, crystalline understanding of all the other aspects of connecting with a mass audience."[50] There appeared to be a telepathic resonance with each fan, every lyric unsheathed from the trenches of his war-torn brain, his performance at Reading a prime example.

Arguments regarding the depths of his lyrics were discussed during an interview with writer Erica Ehm in April 1993. Kurt referenced *Perfume* by Patrick Süskind, a book that he read "about ten times in my life . . . cause I'm a hypochondriac and it just affects me—makes me wanna cut my nose off." *Perfume* formed the basis of cult favorite "Scentless Apprentice," a lyrical prose he initially shied away from but resorted to as he was "running out of ideas more and more."[51]

In the same interview, Ehm questioned if Kurt had a hard time coming up with ideas for his songs. "I don't know, I just—I just noticed that people expect *[pause]* expect more of a thematic angle with—with our music, you know?" Kurt explained. "They always want to read into it, and before I was just using pieces of poetry and just . . . just garble. Just garbage, you know? Just stuff that just would spew out of me at the time, and a lot of times when I write lyrics it's just at the last second 'cause I'm really lazy. So . . . And then I'm—I find myself having to come up with explanations for it, you know, so I thought I'd—you know—prevent that this time and, and actually have an explanation for some of the songs at least."

People often point to the themes in Kurt's lyrics, most alluding to his anti-establishment persona. The corporations and establishment entities he railed against often served as the vehicles to deliver those opinions. It gave him a platform, but it also kept him inside the system he was pushing against.

But Reading '92 would not be Kurt's undoing. No matter how embittered he had become toward the entertainment industry (and rightfully so), his music remained just that—his. There were no hints of Muzak, no nods to corporate rock.

As the lights dimmed, Dave's drums were the only sound. Without warning, Kurt tore into "Aneurysm." Kurt's high-octane lyrics stretched for what seemed like miles over the Thames floodplain.

As he slipped into "School," he dropped to his knees, completely absorbed in the music. Watching this nearly thirty years later, you could feel the pressure of each note, each breath, hands gripping the neck of the guitar. As you watch, it's impossible not to root for him to get his shit together, to persevere, to be able to return to Reading for years to come.

A future never to be.

Blue light strobed across the stage as Kurt rose to his feet. Lyrics became secondary, serving the audience more than their creator. His guitar may as well have had veins, hemorrhaging if it were ever cut away from him. Was his playing technically correct? Who cares?

He screamed about being back in high school—unhoused nights couch surfing, being forced to fend for himself before he was ready. The song cut, and once again, he was bathed in complete darkness—a brief, desolate silence fraught with anxiety before the audience erupted in cheers.

There was a moment of idle banter on stage between Kurt and Krist as they discussed Reading being their last show, a deceptive conversation rife with playfulness but also possessing real undertones of a person who had simply had enough.

Next, the band dove headfirst into the instrumentals of "Sliver" while Kurt struggled to suppress a laugh, a carefree expression flitting across his quickly steeling face. If you blinked, you missed it. Although parts of "Sliver" possess a mirthful innocence and playful sarcasm, Kurt was a master of lyrical deception. Singing about waking up in his mother's arms tugs at the heartstrings to this day.

Although "Sliver" hinted at concealed childhood trauma, he resented the media's attempt to psychoanalyze his words and actions. We're invited to theorize about Kurt's relationship with his mother because he mentioned it first. But his drug use was to remain ignored. Artists often lack control over how their work is interpreted, and once substance abuse rumors enter the conversation, their explanations—and actions—fall prey to public scrutiny. The lighthearted nature of "Sliver" may serve as lyrical camouflage for a deeper, more traumatic experience.

Even if all of Kurt's lyrics—like his antics—were calculated, their intent wasn't nefarious. Each song invariably offered up a vantage point, albeit a limited one, into his life. The interpretations were often an amalgam of the listener's personal baggage and presumptions surrounding Kurt—whose life fans felt they deserved unrestricted access to, even when they were intentionally being kept out. But the more he pulled away from fame, the more it clung to him.

In a September 1992 interview with Robert Hilburn, Kurt explained that the rumors and speculation around his drug use were the biggest thing affecting him.

"I felt totally violated," he said. "I never realized that my private life would be such an issue."[52]

But Kurt spit in the face of adversity, refusing to cater to the slanderous comments that plagued his existence. Whatever he was dealing with, it was there onstage, and Reading '92 was a reminder of what he could do when he stepped out in front of a crowd.

★★★

"This song is called 'In Bloom'" echoed across the stage as Kurt's fingers navigated the neck of the guitar effortlessly, his penchant for power chords on full display. In contrast, his jaw roughly slid back and forth, perhaps marking his intense focus.

Kurt struggled with the low notes, a pained expression on his face. He quickly jumped octaves, trying to hit each note with a degree of accuracy. The fans couldn't have cared less. It was triumph. It was Nirvana. As the song came to a close, the audience screamed, as if aching to know what song the band would play next.

The lights dimmed, casting the stage in a warm, ethereal glow as "Come as You Are" tore through the air, its distinctive sound courtesy of Kurt's coveted EHX Small Clone Chorus pedal. Thick and familiar, it hung in the air.

The sound gave way to "Lithium," Kurt connecting with a sea of strangers. As he sang, "I can't wait to meet you there / And I don't care," the crowd answered in unison: "Yeah, yeah, yeah." They shared the moment with him; connected, together.

Kurt rose like a phoenix from the ashes of a media-induced firestorm. "Light my candles in a daze / 'Cause I've found God," echoed back, taking on additional meaning in the years following his death. He communicated most clearly through music, but the problem was not many people spoke his language. And perhaps he began to feel disconnected from himself.

An effervescent and final "I'm not gonna crack" is a portent we all missed—or refused to acknowledge. The stage faded to black. The anticipation buzzed in the floodplain. Krist tried his hand at comedy, adding a bit of levity to an otherwise stoic performance, while Kurt readied himself for another number, swapping out his Jaguar for his sunburst Strat.[53]

"About a Girl" fit Kurt like an old pair of Converse—intrinsically his, each word rife with smoker's grit, his arm awkwardly bent as his Strat growled along with his grainy vocals.

There was a break from all the crude distortion Kurt heaped onto the song, concluding "About a Girl." The band intentionally messed with music bootleggers, introducing "Tourette's" as "The Eagle Has Landed."[54] Kurt's screams were primal.

"Tourette's" ended as dramatically as it began and, immediately after, the chilling notes of "Polly" permeated the air. Only Kurt could straddle two forms of savagery so flawlessly, one song brutalizing his vocal cords and the other punishing humanity with its truths. Kurt wasn't one to shy away from disturbing subjects, "Polly" a testament to music born in pain. The soulful ballad depicted the true story of a teenage girl who, in 1987, was abducted, tortured, and raped but somehow managed to escape. What makes "Polly" that much more dour is how Kurt wrote it from her abductor's point of view.[55]

"Lounge Act" offered a welcome reprieve. But even these lyrics touched on pain points—fear, jealousy, undertones of neglect. Kurt infrequently shed light on the inspiration behind his lyrics, excruciatingly aware that fans often looked for meaning when there may have been none. But anyone listening to his words can tell there was more depth, nuance, and imagination than he cared to acknowledge. Regardless, Kurt wore his lyrics on his secondhand sleeve, a clear insight into his ethos, what he stood for, and what he demanded, albeit unassumingly.

Critics and skeptics had insinuated "Smells Like Teen Spirit" was the byproduct of stolen riffs from Boston's "More Than a Feeling." While the song, in many ways, defined *Nevermind* and catapulted Nirvana into the mainstream of American culture, Kurt never hid his distaste for *Nevermind*'s opening track, claiming it was nothing more than a Pixies rip-off.

"Lounge Act" was over, and Kurt was eager to confront the Boston plagiarism accusations. In that spirit, the band decided to once again flip off their critics, the unwavering lead singer playing what fans assumed was "Smells Like Teen Spirit." With an impish grin reaching across his face, he strummed the opening chords to "More Than a Feeling."

"I appreciate Cobain's willingness to act out in public," Nick Soulsby, author of *I Found My Friends: The Oral History of Nirvana* and *Cobain on Cobain: Interviews and Encounters*, told me. "I like that he would perform and refuse to please an audience if he felt they didn't deserve it, or he'd cut 'Smells Like Teen Spirit' if he felt pressured to perform it or was in an awful mood. He wasn't fake. He wasn't making 'happy.' He was real."[56]

Kurt reveled in taking the piss out of tabloids, and reminding them that he was still in control of his narrative. Meanwhile, Krist sang what few lyrics he knew, mumbling while Tony continued to dance about erratically on stage. But Kurt's point had been made, and with a series of sharp, discordant notes, he abruptly transitioned into the real "Smells Like Teen Spirit."

The chaos of the faux opening swirled into a wonderful, dissonant frenzy—Krist doing his best not to laugh, Kurt deliberately missing guitar notes in the verse and solo, and Tony bouncing around the stage while the lights strobed to the beat. The final frame of the concert video briefly panned to Kurt's unearthly shadow haloed in light against the amps. The end came as flawlessly as it began, and the trio was once again thrown into complete darkness. Perhaps an omen.

The audience roared, a deafening thunderclap of excitement. Krist and Dave played their hearts out. Kurt had delivered the performance of a lifetime. Reading showed him pushing back, reclaiming his narrative—but as with anything, it came with a price. A price those closest to him were forced to watch, because being caught in his orbit was unavoidable.

And despite the people around him, he was still painfully alone.

Gary Lee Conner, guitarist for Screaming Trees, and I talked about Kurt's meteoric rise to fame and the toll this undoubtedly took on him.

"Once they got big, he was fighting to still be in [the music scene]," he said. "Once you get famous, you have to do all the stuff other people say, and he just wanted to do his music the way he wanted to. He didn't want to worry about selling as many records as they did, but you have to do this. Plus, you throw in a drug problem, too . . ."[57]

We may never understand the full scope of what Kurt experienced internally as he belted out the lyrics to "Smells Like Teen Spirit." But we can guess. Although he never uttered these words, to me, his lyrics have undertones of "Never mind. Never mind it all. I wanted this. I got it. I'm unhappy. But never mind." But we'll never know the true meaning behind his lyrics simply because they often evade comprehension. That was by design.

"One thing I know from reading his journals and talking to people like Danny Goldberg is that Kurt said he did not want fame but also really seemed to desire it quite a bit," journalist Mark Yarm told me. "So it was a mix, like the rest of us. I'm sure many of us would love to be famous but don't actually want to deal with the pressures and the inconvenience of fame . . . there was part of him that wanted Nirvana to be the biggest rock band in the world. And there was part of him that wanted to be left alone. There were just so many facets to him, and I think he was brooding but also funny—there was kind of so much to him, and of all those singers from that era, he just seems to stand out. I didn't come from this background, but obviously, he came from a very broken home. I think people could relate to that. I think he was as famous as he was because there was a relatability factor. And, obviously, people just reflecting their own wants and desires onto him as well."[58]

Once Kurt got what he asked for, he was eternally tethered to the money he rebuffed and the fame he grew to hate—but also the nuclear family he desperately longed for. His addiction slowly caused it all to unravel, one secondhand string at a time. Doing what he loved—playing music—should have helped. Instead, it came with a level of fame you can't undo, a bell you can't unring. And in the end, living the dream damn near killed him.

The media only intensified that pressure, reducing a complicated person to something far easier to simplify. When I spoke with Nick Soulsby, we discussed sensationalism in the media.

"It seems as if a lot of websites, bloggers, and so forth tend to focus on Kurt's depression over his happiness," I said. "But the stories people have shared with me—yes, some are upsetting—have an overwhelming theme of a charismatic man who affected those around him and who had so much love and light inside of him. I try to find commonalities that humanize Kurt, reminding people that he was a person who deserved privacy and respect, regardless of his celebrity status."

"There's most definitely a desire to reduce humans to simple one-dimensional portrayals of far more complex beings who can be many things each day, can hold competing ideas in their heads without bursting, and can surprise constantly," Nick explained. "Maybe it's a lack of time, or a desire for what's easy over what's true, but Kurt Cobain managed to carry whatever burdens were on his shoulders while showing kindness, patience, impish humor, and empathy. An aging uncle once asked me, 'Why would you be a fan of this man?' because he'd only ever caught the drug addict/suicide headlines. It was nice to be able to say that this was someone who came from as close to nothing as society can produce and was able to touch millions, then to revolt against the idea that wealth and fame and professional life was all that a human might wish for or need. So many people are trapped by the lives they have built around them, by expectations, by the fear of losing face or disappointing others; it unites people at all levels of society—it's the reason alcohol and drug abuse impact the poorest to the wealthiest, why princes and paupers all wind up in psychiatric care—and it most certainly affected Cobain."[59]

Nick's reflections underscore how often Kurt's life was misrepresented, making it all the more striking when you watch him play, knowing full well what he had going on behind the scenes.

Nirvana was roughly halfway through their set, yet their onstage energy was unabated. Dave and Krist assaulted their instruments with razor-sharp precision, but it was Kurt who understood how to connect with fans without even trying, the antihero who represented a generation.

Several notes echoed across the stage as he tuned his guitar. A visceral groan pierced the night sky as the band readied themselves for "On a Plain." Eyes closed, face somber, Kurt drew the crowd in.

They left no room for hesitation, ripping into "Negative Creep" as Kurt growled into the microphone. The instrumentals were gravelly, filthy, and effortlessly distorted. As the music petered out, Kurt haphazardly strummed his guitar—sloppy but intentional. It was just him and a rosewood fretboard.

"Been a Son" played as Tony danced, lyrics tackling systemic issues like sexism. The song ended, and Kurt took a quick detour upstage before returning to his post, taking a drink and approaching Krist. Back at the microphone, a sweet sentiment followed.

"This song is dedicated to my twelve-day-old daughter."

The lights cut in and out. Even though his words were brief, he was a father who was endlessly devoted to the tiny human who changed his life for the better. The crowd answered immediately, a surge of cheers cutting through the dark, while Kurt stood still, focusing on what mattered most to him: his family.

"And my wife."

He didn't owe the media a thing, even as they demanded their pound of flesh, but he wanted the record set straight. He was concerned with his image, the same image his daughter would grow to know and understand: one of humility, resilience, and unwavering dedication.

He stared out at a sea of acolytes, many following him because of what he represented: hope. Kurt bled in front of the whole world, showing them how an ordinary boy from a small timber town could grow to do extraordinary things, changing the landscape of music forever. He even offered them a glimpse into his private life.

His next words were raw, but he spoke them just the same.

"And, um . . . there's been some pretty extreme things written about us. Especially my wife."

He might not have had control over media narratives, but on stage, he had the last word.

Kurt continued, "And she thinks everybody hates her now."

The crowd screamed.

"So, um . . . this is being recorded, so . . . why don't you give her a message and say, 'Courtney, we love you.'" He smiled. "Okay, ready? On the count of three. One, two, three. Court—"

The audience finished his sentence. "Courtney, we love you!" they screamed, and a genuine smile ran across his face, as though eternally grateful. His expression was serious at first, almost heavy. He wasn't flipping off cameras or playing to the crowd the way people might have expected. Instead, he seemed earnest, speaking directly to the audience. His face shifted and he smiled as the crowd answered him, like he wasn't expecting it.

"Thanks," he said, humbly.

Kurt's opinion of his audience softened over time, as evidenced in an interview for *Fender Frontline* in February 1994. Chuck Crisafulli asked, "It must be a very odd feeling for Nirvana to be performing in sports arenas these days. How do you get along with the crowds you're attracting now?"

"Much better than I used to," Kurt responded. "When we first started to get successful, I was extremely judgmental of the people in the audience. I held each of them to a sort of punk rock ethos. It upset me that we were attracting and entertaining the very people that a lot of my music was a reaction against. I've since become much better at accepting people for who they are. Regardless of who they were before they came to the show, I get a few hours to try and subvert the way they view the world. It's not that I'm trying to dictate, it's just that I am afforded a certain platform on which I can express my views. At the very least, I always get the last word."[60]

And Reading '92 hinted at that shift.

The audience may have been with him, but the rumors that followed him there hadn't gone anywhere. He still had to remind his harshest critics who he was and what he stood for, even as he shared his art with the world.

Kurt returned his attention to his guitar, the stage lights casting an eerie yellow-green glow across his slight frame, his vulnerability a fleeting interlude.

"All Apologies" melted from his fingertips as his hospital gown billowed in the breeze.

"What else could I be? / All apologies / What else could I say? / All my words are gray / What else could I write? / I don't have the right / What else could I be? / All apologies."

The distortion ripped through the night air, and he was a vision that lacked all vanity, blond hair scattered about his face as he sang.

"Married. Buried."

The words hung uncomfortably close, as if they were meant to echo one other.

"What else could I write?" poured from his lips, his eyes squeezed closed. He opened them and stared across the ebbing tides of fans once more. His eyes bore a hole into the audience, taking everything in, but lost in another universe. One we didn't have access to.

"I don't have the right."

His voice broke, and something changed. This felt less like a war cry and more like a moment of surrender.

"What else could I say? / All my words are gray."

Yes, these lyrics differed from the versions on *In Utero* when the album dropped in 1993. Swapping lyrics wasn't new to Kurt, but it speaks volumes that these were the words he initially chose.

As Kurt leaned back and tapped the distortion pedal with his foot, his fingers were all muscle memory, the song deeply ingrained in him, once again screaming his heart out.

"All in all is all we all are."

Kurt tore into another fan favorite, "Blew." His guitar solos never disappointed, and it was less about the notes and more about the feeling that emanated from his fretboard. The song ended, but fans were insatiable, hands raised, voices crashing back toward the stage. The band took a quick break, but before concertgoers knew it, Kurt was back. He took a couple of drags from a cigarette as the stage lights transitioned to blue.

Kurt had swapped his guitar out again, this time for a black Fender Stratocaster with a black Seymour Duncan Hot Rails humbucker in the bridge position and a Kramer neck.[61] "I'm not like them / But I can pretend," he sang, the lyrics to "Dumb" deliberate and powerful. "Wish away / The soul is cheap" offers up mesmerizing, perplexing, and haunting feelings, even thirty years later, holding new meaning for how Kurt may have seen himself.

"Stay Away" battered the air, and Kurt looked mired down by his thoughts, a trait those closest to him recalled in several interviews. He was Seattle's unofficial grunge sovereign, even as his life spun frantically about him. Having people stay far away was what he wanted, but fame ensured he would be hounded for the rest of his days. As "Stay Away" concluded, Kurt dove headfirst into "Spank Thru." The audience barely had time to catch up before the band attacked another tried and true favorite, "Love Buzz." Kurt's playing style was often haphazard, but that's what made him great.

After the song concluded, Kurt briefly disappeared. When he returned, he was once again donning his sunburst Stratocaster, chatting with Krist before blasting into the opening riff of "The Money Will Roll Right In." Kurt sang about Hollywood and all the subsequent money, his voice emblematic of his contempt. His choice of cover songs was always fun, but it was also oddly specific and calculated. The song ended, and there was no time to process, no time to reflect.

A Wipers cover sliced through the air; Kurt's rendition of "D-7" was delicate in its own right. The lyrics were haunting, exploring themes of rejection and isolation. This song had plenty of undertones, from the way certain marginalized groups were oppressed to the way Kurt may have felt about himself. As he sang about leaving, even through the words of a cover song, we were reminded that he lives on in those he affected. There was a pause, and the song immediately abandoned ballad territory and transitioned into something guttural; the audience was alive and demanding more while Krist sang the opening to "Territorial

Pissings." Kurt tore into the song, the trio reverberating flawlessly off one another. They were a powerhouse that performed the same way for an audience of one as they did for sixty thousand.

Krist threw his bass in the air, catching it as Kurt slowly began to trample over the amps. A distorted sound emanated from his guitar as Tony did cartwheels, exiting the stage. Kurt sat on the rubble he'd created, an endless stream of sound pouring from his guitar and visible blood splattering on its pickguard. His movements were slow, deliberate. Dave dismantled his drum kit while Krist proceeded to beat on what the drummer left behind. Kurt continued to create an endless outflow of noise as he worked to destroy the amp cabinets, pushing his guitar's headstock into the grill cloth. Dave kept destroying his drum kit while Krist beat on everything in sight. Kurt eventually made his way downstage, staring intently as Dave picked up a cymbal and hurled it at his drum kit, Krist still banging away on the remaining percussion while the audience cheered. Nirvana was a three-man wrecking crew, ripping the stage to shreds.

Kurt graced the audience with a sloppy rendition of "The Star-Spangled Banner" that bled into more aimless distortion. Kurt's off-key pitch somehow managed to represent the subjugated voice of a generation.

Kurt's generation.

Nirvana's generation.

Dave swung Kurt's mutilated black Strat around like a rag doll. Kurt left the stage and entered the audience, giving away his sunburst Strat before climbing back on stage. (A bouncer supposedly took it back and returned it to Kurt or his guitar tech after the show, but the sentiment was there.)

The enigmatic frontman looked back at the audience one last time. The show was over, and he had somewhere else to be.

"Thank you very much. Good night!"

That was also the last time Tony saw Kurt in person.

Several hours earlier, the media had questioned if he would even show that night. Hadn't the band broken up? Wasn't Kurt in rehab?

Depending on what tabloids you read, it was both. But despite the media-induced maelstrom, the trio persevered and secured what they rightfully deserved—legendary status. And no tabloid could ever strip them of that, no matter how hard they tried.[62]

"Skin the sun, fall asleep
Wish away, the soul is cheap
Lesson learned, wish me luck
Soothe the burn, wake me up"
—Kurt Cobain, "Dumb"

Chapter 10

"SLIVER"

Carlos "Cake" Nunez

WHEN THE SPECTACLE OF READING '92 FADES, WHAT REMAINS ARE THE people who were there when the stage lights went dark. A mutual friend connected me with Carlos "Cake" Nunez, a friend of the Cobains. I shared Walter's story and explained how I hoped to help others by showing the real Kurt—as told by his friends, fellow musicians, those who knew him, and the artists he inspired—and Carlos readily agreed to an interview. He's etched in Nirvana history, but he doesn't do many interviews. We set aside a few hours to talk—conversations about Kurt never take less time. It's a theme I've noticed while writing this book, and a worthwhile one, at that. Those who knew Kurt loved him with an unparalleled intensity.[63]

They're also fiercely protective of him and his memory, something I find admirable—though occasionally that vigilance feels exclusive. These are the gatekeepers of Cobain lore, a circle outsiders can't easily access. When their mission is purely to safeguard Kurt's memory, I have nothing but respect. When it leans toward exclusion at the expense of untangling the real Kurt from the media circus, my admiration wanes.

Carlos exemplifies the former—he protects Kurt's memory without exploitation.

He understands the craft of writing about someone as notable as his friend Kurt. A writer and journalist himself, Carlos knows all too well about the fragility of Kurt, his memory, and the best way to share these stories with the world. And it's through honesty. Carlos has written for respected publications such as *fLiPSiDE Fanzine*, *LA Weekly*, *Fiz Magazine*, and *Music Connection*. But one of his articles, "An Interview With . . . Kurt Cobain," sparked the beginning of Carlos's friendship with the Nirvana frontman and changed his life forever. This article was featured in issue #78 of *fLiPSiDE* in May/June 1992 and is often referred to in esteemed Nirvana and Kurt Cobain literature alike.[64]

Carlos and I became fast friends, and he shared an honest portrait of Kurt. When we talk, our conversation conjures up rare, up-close images of Kurt that are hard to come by. While he recalled the toll fame took on him, he mostly remembered Kurt for his kind, compassionate nature, especially how he made time for everyone—something I had heard before—and shared stories about Kurt's prankster side, the part of him that's often eclipsed by his depression.

Honest and genial, it's not hard to see why Kurt bonded with Carlos. How they connected is equally interesting.

★★★

"I had a friend who had a subscription to the Sub Pop Singles Club, and he got the Nirvana 'Love Buzz' single," Carlos begins. "Around that time, I got a job working at Caroline Records Distribution in Sun Valley, California. They also had a location in New York, and they needed distributors for Epitaph and all these other indie labels. I worked there between 1989 and 1991 and actually left the week *Nevermind* came out. I was a picker then, and I was just really into music; I really enjoyed Mudhoney. That was my favorite band at the time. I remember I would read about these bands in *fLiPSiDE* before I started writing for the fanzine, and I would read about Mudhoney in *Melody Maker* in the UK when Everett True would write. He was flown out to Seattle to talk about the Sub Pop scene and one of the first interviews Nirvana did was with him, actually.

"So I was working at Caroline, and I got moved up to a buyer position, and I started selling the *Bleach* album. I remember getting a fax from Sub Pop saying that there was going to be a TAD/Nirvana tour, and I got really excited. My friend Peter and I—he wound up being the drummer in my first band, DickTit—we were super into Sub Pop bands. I remember that it was a stormy night when Nirvana played Raji's in Hollywood. It was February 15, 1990, I believe. It's actually where the cover of 'Sliver' was taken from. I remember seeing that they were playing, and I took a couple of work friends with me to the show. My friends weren't too fond of Nirvana, but I thought they were great that night.

"But Nirvana was first mentioned to me in '88 before I worked at Caroline. I would go to this club called the Club With No Name, and my friend told me about Soundgarden, so I went and saw them in '88. And it was funny because Kim Thayil [Soundgarden] saw me—I didn't even know about the flannel thing at the time—and he was like, 'You look just like the people in Seattle, man.'" Carlos laughs. "Then I mentioned Nirvana, and he said, 'Yeah, they're better than us. They're kind of like The Beatles in a lot of ways.' It was awesome, talking to Kim about how great Nirvana was.

"Another time I interviewed the Smashing Pumpkins at the Peanuts club. They ended up playing a special event show where only a few hundred kids got to see them for the *Gish* debut album. It was amazing. I got to interview them; I took the soundcheck, and I remember during that interview, Billy Corgan says, 'Butch Vig is working on this great album by this band Nirvana. They're gonna be really big.' So Billy already knew how excellent they were, you know? This was back in 1990. This was when I got a job writing for *fLiPSiDE*. Earlier in the day, I had walked around the Caroline offices. Courtney was his girlfriend at the time.

"At *fLiPSiDE*, you don't get paid. You just get free records and get to go to free shows. So during the night, I saw shows, and during the day, I worked the records. It was amazing. I was writing and had my band going on, on top of everything else. And I saw Nirvana open for Sonic Youth at the Palladium [August 17, 1990]. That was the night where they really got a lot of buzz going for this band called STP. STP was actually formed by a member of the band Pussy Galore, Julia Cafritz. She was in STP playing guitar, and their seven-inch EP was produced by Thurston Moore. So STP was opening for them, and I remember Kurt went on stage in a Vincebus Eruptum Blue Cheer shirt. I actually have the whole show on soundcheck. I believe Dale Crover played that night—I have the soundboard and soundcheck. I got lucky. I have a board tape of that whole thing.

"And it's really funny because I remember Kurt went on stage, and people were already cheering; they loved that there was a huge buzz going on, you know? I remember this guy said, 'Oh, I heard they suck.' I'm like, 'Oh, I think you're wrong. You're gonna see how wrong you are.' This was in between STP and Nirvana. Kurt went on stage and up to the mic wearing a Blue Cheer shirt, and he said, 'Hi, we're Nirvana, and we don't particularly like heavy metal.' Just like in that voice." Carlos laughs. "Like, 'Let me just go into the music.' I forget what song it was; it might have been 'Aneurysm.' One of their best songs ever, I think. So I was in the pit, and I lost one of my jackets, if I recall correctly. I don't even know because I had such a great time. It was just great. I don't even remember Sonic Youth, that's how great Nirvana was that night. And I love Sonic Youth. I mean, they're one of my favorites. But with Nirvana—I just remember the buzz on them was huge.

"After that . . . I was about to leave the job because of some personal issues I had with the people there—I wasn't really very happy, and I wasn't getting a lot of respect—so I decided to move on. But we got this fax, and it said that *Nevermind* was coming out the next week, so we had to order some more copies of *Bleach*. I went up to my boss to say, 'We usually order about a hundred copies on CD of *Bleach* and hardly any vinyl.' And cassette, of course, because cassette was still popular then. I said, 'We need to order three to four hundred copies of *Bleach.*' Now, my boss was from the UK, and he said, 'Are you fucking kidding me? No.' Then he immediately got a fax from Caroline's New York office saying we need to order five thousand copies of the *Bleach* CD, and he just looked at me with his mouth wide open." Carlos laughs again.

Bleach was certified gold and platinum in 1995, and for good reason.[65] Kurt's harrowing vocals and gritty, distorted guitar playing added to the album's uninhibited sound. Carlos predicted its popularity from the outset.

He reflects on the times he saw Nirvana live and the gravity of those shows. It's one thing to have seen them in concert, enjoying the band as a fan. It's an entirely different experience to watch them as a friend, having knowledge of Kurt's private and public struggles, and the way the concerts affected him.

"I saw Nirvana nine times," Carlos tells me. "I was a very lucky young man, you know, back in the day. But when I first met Kurt, I realized how much we had in common. Plus we were both in bands. We both loved music. But when he first met me, he realized I was the one who conducted the phone interview with him for *fLiPSiDE*. I was at the Hollywood Palace, and I saw Kurt and Courtney; Courtney and I were already friends, but this was pretty much the first time I officially met Kurt. I went up to Courtney, gave her a kiss, and said, 'Hi, Courtney.' Kurt looked at me like, 'Oh, who's this guy?' So I said, 'Kurt! Kurt, I'm Cake. I'm the guy who interviewed you for *fLiPSiDE*.' He took his hoodie off and grabbed my hands in his hands, and he said, 'That was the best interview I ever did. You never misquoted me once. And, by the way, you're my favorite writer at *fLiPSiDE*. I just want you to know that.' I was like, 'Oh, wow,' and I remember Courtney grabbed him by the hand and dragged him into the Hollywood Palace, and he turned his back to look at me before the door closed. I'll never forget that. That was the first time I officially met him—when they were married.

"One day, I got a call from Courtney. She said, 'Hey, my band's gonna be staying in this hotel in Hollywood, and I told them to call you. So they're gonna be calling you in a few days,' and, sure enough, Patty [Schemel, Hole] calls me from a hotel in Hollywood. So I went and I hung out with them [Hole], and then I went and picked up Pat Smear [Nirvana's touring guitarist]. When I picked up Pat and took him to the hotel to hang with Hole, it was prior to him joining Nirvana, amazingly enough.

"So we went to the hotel and were hanging out and having a good time. Pat—I love the guy. Then everyone was like, 'Hey, does anybody know Kurt and Courtney's number?'" Carlos laughs. "And it's like two in the morning, mind you. I said, 'Yeah, I do,' so I called them. Everyone I was with wanted to prank them, basically. So they got on the phone, and all you hear is, 'Hey, who the fuck is this?'" Carlos laughs again. "They handed me the phone, and I said, 'Courtney, this is Carlos.' And she says, 'Carlos! Why are you calling me at two in the morning?' and I told her we were all over at the hotel and wanted to see how she and Kurt were doing. She told me how much she and Kurt loved me and that they wanted me in the family. At first, she was telling me she wanted me to be the nanny. And then it got to the point where she says, '[Gold Mountain Entertainment's John] Silva's gonna call you.' Eventually, I spoke to Ron Stone from Gold Mountain Entertainment, all so I could be the nanny. It was really interesting. But one day I called Silva after I hadn't heard from anybody, and he said that the Cobains went with a friend of theirs. They went with Cali [DeWitt] to be their nanny.

"Another time I was across the street after seeing The Jesus Lizard, and Kurt and Courtney got there late. Courtney saw me across the street where The Central was, which became The Viper Room. So she said, 'Carlos!'—she's talking to a member of Celebrity Skin—and tells me to come over there. Kurt was in the car—that's when he had his Volvo. So I went into the car, and I remember this so distinctly. He was smoking a cigarette, and he was playing the single 'Happiness Is a Warm Gun' by The Breeders again and again. Every time the song ended, he would play the cassette again. Well, we were talking, and he was looking at me, and I can remember his blue eyes, and he asked, 'How old are you, Carlos?' I said, 'I'm twenty-six,' and he said, 'Oh, you're older than me, but you have such a baby face.' We were talking some more, and I said, 'So is Steve Albini going to record your next record?' Mind you, this was in '92, so way before all this happened. Kurt looked at me, and he said, 'Is it that obvious?'—that's all he said to me. I got out of the car, and I went home, and I wrote in my column that Albini was going to record the next Nirvana record. I mean, this is what I heard from Kurt. And eventually, Albini said there were rumblings in the underground press about him recording and doing the next Nirvana record."

As Carlos recalls more experiences with Kurt, I asked what made his friend so special. Carlos is thoughtful in his response.

"Kurt didn't expect the success. I mean, he wanted Nirvana to be popular. If you see the early footage of when they were with [Jason] Everman, everybody was really getting into jammin'. He wanted everybody to be energetic on stage, and I know he always wanted to have a band that got signed. However, he didn't know that the record [*Nevermind*] was going to sell that many copies. I remember seeing a video of Mark Kates, who I'm friends with and who is an old publicist of Nirvana's, and he was saying if anybody said that that record was going to sell millions, they were full of shit.

"But Kurt always knew how to make people feel warm, you know? I remember this one day—I think this was a '92 call-up party. I was looking for a job. I couldn't find anything but had been working at Rhino Records on the weekends. I was going through estate sales that people bring in, and I would go through the records and sort the best ones and give them to the store to sell. That was my job. I remember I talked to Kurt. He called me up, and I was surprised he actually called me up about this, but he said, 'I heard you're looking for work.' . . . He asked if I was doing anything at all right then, and I said that I was working at Rhino Records on the weekends. And he said, 'Carlos, I'd rather be doing what you're doing than what I'm doing right now.'

His dream had been to be in a band, but he wanted to be in the background playing guitar. He didn't want to be the front guy anymore.

"I think that the next thing he was going to do . . . I think this would have been the fourth Nirvana record . . . but from what I felt, his idea was it was going to be more of an extreme kind of Butthole Surfers sound. He was a really big fan of the Butthole Surfers. That's also why he had all his friends' bands play with them [Nirvana]. All these bands. I mean, he brought Calamity Jane to play with them in Brazil. I mean this little band that played little clubs. Kurt was just a thoughtful human being. There's this great story that Kurt told me in my interview with him where he says that . . . I think it was the guitarist of Metallica who called him up, and he said, 'Hey, man, we got this great idea to do this concert. First us, then Guns N' Roses, and then you guys. What do you think?' But, you know, there was just one problem. Kurt said that he didn't really like Guns N' Roses and their misogynist attitude towards women. He once told me that he'd rather do something called Lots of Pale Losers and have them [Nirvana], the Cows, The Jesus Lizard, Melvins, and all those 'loser' bands play instead."

"Kurt could be very outspoken, and he wasn't afraid to champion the marginalized; he didn't care what people thought," I say. "He had a strong moral compass where society was concerned, and people just loved him for it."

And with that love came unwanted attention and focus from audiences all over.

"Do you think he had stage fright? He would go from standing at the microphone, not moving, to suddenly all over the stage."

"I don't think he could really see the crowd," Carlos explains. "I think the lights made it hard for him to see the audience. I think it would have been a lot harder for him otherwise. But I also think he just loved the energy, and I think that's what made him keep going on stage. It was the energy, you know? His music brought a lot of love. The Phoenix show in 1993 at Veterans Memorial Coliseum—that's the first show Pat Smear played with them. Not including SNL. But at that show everybody was singing along to 'Lithium,' and Kurt just jumped off the stage, and he went into the crowd, and he was being lifted around. And then after this show, backstage, he was in pieces. He was standing there, like, 'Cake, look at me. Look what the crowd did to me, man. They were grabbing at my cock. They were grabbing at my shoes. I'm missing a tennis shoe. They were trying to take my wallet. They were pulling my hair. I can't jump into the crowd anymore, Cake. Look at this. Look what they did to me.' He was showing me what they did, literally showing me. He's showing me, and it's like Jesus showing his wounds to you; literally what he's showing me, you know? It was only me, Bill Bartell, Nirvana, and John Silva backstage at that moment. It was very intimate. Nobody knows about that moment. But I'm okay if you want to include it [in your book]."

"Okay. Thank you," I say. Yes, it's a privilege to hear these stories, but it's also incredibly humbling—and at times, depressing—knowing that immense fame stripped Kurt of the ability to connect comfortably with his audience, something he once loved and did so effortlessly. He seemed energized by the rush of playing live, yet unprecedented levels of fame made even simple acts like crowd surfing impossible.

On October 18, 1993, Michael Alex interviewed Nirvana for MTV News where Kurt is referencing the concert Carlos describes. Kurt was asked if he could see the audience and if he felt their energy.

> "Oh yeah, I can feel it, I can sense it. At certain times when the house lights come on during certain parts of the songs, I can see everyone. I think 'Lithium' is a good example because when we break into the distortion part, the lights all come on and I can see everyone jump up and down and I realize it's not only just the front part that I can see, it's the whole audience. And it's great. There's nothing better than that much of a capacity of people in tune with the band and giving off that much energy. It's just like a little club but one hundred times more. Yeah . . . they always sing during 'Lithium,' which is kind of neat."[66]

As our conversation about concerts continues, Carlos recalls a night at Jabberjaw, where his band DickTit had played a few times. On May 29, 1991, Nirvana played a benefit show there for Mikey Dees of Fitz of Depression after his van broke down.

"Gary from Jabberjaw called me up after that news and said, 'Nirvana's playing tonight. Don't tell anybody, but it's two bucks to get in.' Of course, he tells the guy from *fLiPSiDE* not to tell anybody," Carlos says, laughing.

"But he tells everybody and everybody's there, of course. That's why he said that to me. I remember everybody was at that show. It was so packed. I saw Kurt, and he was outside in the back area of Jabberjaw. He wasn't talking to anybody. I went up to him—this was before I really knew him—and I said, 'Hey, Kurt. My band's playing [a different show]. Do you know DickTit? Would you like a flyer?' And he was like, 'Hey, man. This is a nice flyer. But I have holes in my pockets,' and he showed me the holes in his pockets. Then he said, 'Maybe you should give your flyer to somebody who can go to your show because I'm not gonna be in town for it.' That's just the way he was; he was thoughtful. He took his time and said, 'No, I can't take your flyer,' and he actually explained to me why he couldn't take it. And you know what's ironic? Somebody told me that the same flyer was on Krist Novoselic's fridge."

I've heard similar stories about Kurt. As one person put it, he was always gracious but, after he became extremely famous, harried.

"So, what happened with the whole *fLiPSiDE* interview?" I ask, referring to the night Carlos was supposed to go to Kurt and Courtney's house. "Did you end up missing it?"

"Yeah, I guess there was some miscommunication going on," explains Carlos. "Kurt wanted to have me over, but Courtney didn't. He was trying to be nice and bought all this food." Carlos laughs. "Al Flipside and I did a phone interview, and he [Al] apparently recorded over the tape or lost it. I don't know what happened, but that would be one of the most valuable interviews of all time if it could be found, you know? And Kurt was upset because we didn't come over and he bought all this food, so I apologized because Kurt said he didn't eat the sort of food that he bought for us. Also, Al didn't eat meat. Kurt got all these chips and fried chicken and was like, 'Oh my God, I'm sorry, I didn't know Al was a vegetarian.' It was so funny."

From fried chicken faux pas to benefit shows for broken-down vans, these are the kinds of moments that stand out to me. I ask Carlos if there were any other memories of note with Kurt.

"You know, there is another moment at that Phoenix show," he recalls. "Another band was playing, and I remember Kurt went to the area where the security guards were throwing the kids out for jumping off stage. Kurt went up to the security guard and said, 'I don't want any of these people kicked out. I want them back at the show.' Then Nirvana had a meeting with the head of the whole security team, and Kurt was yelling at them. He came up to me after and said, 'Cake, make sure they don't kick any of the kids out again.' I was watching the security guards, and they were watching me, and I kept watching them, and they didn't kick the kids out." Carlos laughs. "There you go. That's another moment I remember of his behavior."

"Kurt seemed like one of these people who wanted to connect with his audience, and then he got incredibly famous, and people stopped respecting him and his personal space," I say. "It seems like fans also stopped respecting that he was just a person and started taking liberties with him, like the story you told me about when he crowd-surfed. But he always seemed so humble and an eternal music fan."

Carlos takes a beat. I can tell he's thinking about what his friend was dealing with behind the scenes—and how that kind of fame changes things. But despite all of that, there was still another side of Kurt—the one his friends knew.

"You didn't know how big the band was at that point. It was '93 when they performed in that benefit show for Mia Zapata from The Gits. (I got to meet her by the way, too. She was wonderful.) But Kurt was very comfortable in his own skin. There's a photograph I just posted on Facebook again that Thurston Moore [Sonic Youth] actually had on Instagram a year ago. I forget who took the photo [it was

Lindsay Brice], but it's Sonic Youth at Castaic Lake. So in the picture, next to me was Tara Tavi, my friend and awesome vocalist and musician. Next to her is Mike Kelley [a friend of Sonic Youth's], and next to him is Kurt, on the ground, in his pajamas, just watching Sonic Youth."

I picture Kurt sprawled on the floor in his jammies, listening to one of his favorite bands.

"He always seemed very easygoing and just like an empathetic person," I say. "It didn't seem like fame changed his core values or anything. He seemed pretty much the same."

Carlos agrees without hesitation.

"Yeah, you could tell that he never acted like a rock star. I remember when he went to Phoenix. When I got there, we walked into the room, and he was surrounded by MTV. (This was before and after—MTV was not around him the whole day because it was the big tour.) Kurt was eating some food, and after the interview, he looked at me and he said, 'Cake. Are you hungry?' and he hands me his plate. I looked at the plate and said, 'No, it's okay. I just had something to eat.' But he was just always so kind. I've met so many other rock stars, but nobody was like him. Nobody else had that vibe. When you sat down next to him, there was an energy that would actually emit from him that I would sense. You know? He liked sitting next to me. He would always ask, 'You want to sit down?' and then he would sit down like we were little kids at the playground. I remember one day he was sitting down next to me, and I thought what a kind person he was."

"He seemed like a friend first and a rock star second," I say.

"You know, he wasn't going to be changed by everything around him," Carlos explains.

"He was always trying to help everybody. He also knew what he wanted. He would be like, 'I'm not going to have this fucking band open for us. No, I don't want them; I want *this* band to open for us.' And he also paid attention. I remember when I did the Boredoms' cover story. That issue had just come out, and Kurt said, 'Boredoms are playing,' like he knew that I did the cover story. Then he said, 'So you can come and see us when the Boredoms are opening for us.' I was like, 'What? Boredoms are playing with you guys? Wow.' So he said, 'Well, I saw your cover story, and I thought, *Let's get the Boredoms.*' I thought, *Oh my God. What a nice guy Kurt is.*"

The love that Carlos had for Kurt radiates through our conversation, along with the pain of losing his friend. As enthusiastic as Carlos was to tell me about all the good times they had together, he recalls one profound memory: his last in-person interaction with Kurt.

"This is the last thing Kurt ever said to me to my face: 'Cake, am I ever going to see you again?' Then he took a cigarette puff, and I shook his hand, and that was it. But I take comfort in knowing that consciousness lives on, and Kurt's still here with us."

I know this story is difficult for Carlos to tell me. But he still wants to share it, because talking about Kurt brings him joy.

In typical Carlos fashion, he quickly scrounges up a humorous little anecdote about one day when he was meeting up with Kurt. He knows that even though Kurt left this world and all his loved ones behind, his impression is permanent—and positive. And this is the Kurt that Carlos (and many others) hold near and dear to their hearts.

"I was sitting in my car waiting for Kurt to show up [where we were supposed to meet], and I saw somebody below the car, and I said, 'Who's there?' Kurt jumped up and said, 'Hi, Cakey!' in the funniest cartoon voice you could ever imagine. Then he got in his car, and we both drove off. We were going down the same dirt road, and he slowly started bumping my Celica with his car. I remember looking in my rearview mirror when he was doing that and just seeing him laughing."

Chapter 11

"RAPE ME"

Cow Palace, 1993

PLENTY OF NIRVANA'S CONCERTS SPOKE VOLUMES. MOST WERE ENGINEERED to entertain, but many served a greater purpose—Reading '92 included. Still, there was one show that struck a different chord altogether. Not because of spectacle. Because of what it stood for.

That show was the Tresnjevka Women's Group Benefit at Cow Palace and the date was April 9, 1993. Some attendees arrived in solidarity with the Bosnian rape victims Nirvana sought to raise funds for, spearheaded by Krist. Others were there simply to watch their favorite band. It didn't matter why people showed up—the trio used their platform to shine a light on an atrocity, and that says everything about who they were.

Krist explained the purpose behind the concert: "There's probably a lot of people who don't care. But that's okay. If they come, we'll still get their money. And if people do care, there are information booths directing them on what they can do."[67]

By the time the band played the show, fame had had plenty of time to wreak havoc on Kurt. The media's fixation on his personal struggles over his humanitarian work was well documented—and it was slowly eroding his psyche and spirit.

I spoke with Stephen Tow, the esteemed author of *The Strangest Tribe: How a Group of Seattle Rock Bands Invented Grunge*, who has deep insight into the Seattle music community and the media's fascination with portraying a certain angle.

"Kurt was a special artist," Stephen began. "He was like the John Lennon of the nineties. He wasn't the most musically talented person, but he had the 'it' factor, which made him and his music special. As a music fan back then, I first got into Pearl Jam, because they reminded me of sort of angry seventies music—and I tuned out the eighties mainstream. But after Kurt died, I switched allegiances and became much more of a Nirvana fan, because of that artistry. Nirvana's songs were simple yet so profound and heartfelt. As an aside, the parade of preteens wearing Nirvana shirts from Target is getting on my nerves. I'm tempted to ask them about their favorite song from *Bleach*, but I know I'll get blank stares. I'd respect them much more if they wore *Badmotorfinger* shirts."

Stephen touched on Kurt's staying power and how it tied into the media narratives surrounding Seattle's music scene.

"In terms of the larger Seattle music scene and grunge in particular, the media was intent on focusing on the darkness and pain of the music," he told me. "And heroin use, of course. An example is the 'All the Rage' *Time* magazine cover featuring a screaming Eddie Vedder. They missed out on the fun and especially the playful side of that music scene, notably that Seattle put on humor like the notorious 'Lexicon of Grunge' piece printed in the *New York Times*."[68]

The bruising appeared from beneath the surface—in full view. Kurt's interviews began to hit differently than they had just a few years before, in 1989. Something sharper had taken the place of his typical humorous and humble demeanor—and it would remain.

When Chuck Crisafulli interviewed Kurt, he asked him about *In Utero* and how he played "some of the most powerful 'anti-solos' ever hacked out of a guitar."

"What comes to mind for you when it's time for the guitar to cut loose?"

Kurt simply replied: "Less than you could ever imagine."[69]

While Kurt's enthusiasm may have waned as interview fatigue crept in, at Cow Palace, he still took to the stage that day to use his voice and intensity for change. Despite being constantly barraged by the media and—like Atlas—pulled apart fiber by fiber from the weight of the world, Kurt knew this show was bigger than him. He wanted to be more than an entertainer—and through his music, lyrics, and platform, he was able to enact tangible societal change.

★★★

Without warning, "Rape Me" assaulted the speakers. The song moved through the crowd, appeasing those who came to show their support, and permeating those who came to watch the decade's most infectious band do what they did best. Fans likely noticed Kurt's voice carried something deeper that day as he screamed the lyrics—a reminder of how vehemently he felt about protecting women.

Kurt's slight frame was covered by an inside-out Captain America shirt beneath one of his iconic secondhand sweaters and the same battered jeans that he seemingly wore at the 1992 VMAs, where producers begged the band not to play "Rape Me." (They still played a few opening licks, a reminder that the trio would not be stifled.) The song is often confused with Kurt's volatile relationship with the media, but the reality is that it was direct confrontation and rejection of the pervasive rape culture in society. Nirvana's decision to open with this poignant number spoke volumes, a stark reminder of what some fifty thousand women endured during a horrific period of systemic rape and torture during the Bosnian War.[70] In that room, on that night, the song wasn't just music—it was the whole point.

At the end of the show, Kurt climbed onto the amp cabinets, guitar still in hand. He savagely catapulted himself onto Dave and his drum kit, a physical manifestation of his disgust towards rape culture and the other monstrosities he railed against. But maybe that was the point. Nothing about Cow Palace was neat or tidy—the cause wasn't, the music wasn't, and his exit sure as hell shouldn't be. Krist threw his bass into the air, catching it without batting an eye amidst the chaos, then waved to the audience.

"Supporting a good cause," he called out.

He walked off stage as Kurt emerged seemingly unscathed from the rubble of Dave's drum kit, pushing his way past the cymbals and exiting the stage the same way Krist did.[71]

The choice to open with "Rape Me" at a benefit for rape victims wasn't subtle. That was exactly the point. The song was the statement, and the information booths did the rest. No speech needed.

Kurt had no patience for intolerance of any kind and stood up for anyone on the margins—anyone subjected to senseless, baseless intolerance. This was 1993. Nirvana could have played anywhere. Instead, they showed up at Cow Palace, chaotic and unfiltered as ever, and used every bit of that chaos in service of something real. The audience thought they were getting just another Nirvana show. They were—but they were also getting a front row seat to what it looked like when a band put their platform where their values were.

The show was over, but echoes of empathy rippled throughout the arena, especially for the recipients of the Tresnjevka Women's Group Benefit. Nirvana's contribution at Cow Palace helped raise tens of thousands of dollars for Bosnian rape victims, a gesture forever time-stamped in the trio's altruistic—and humanitarian—history.[72]

In an interview with Ivano Leoncavallo, Kurt commented on what he offered the audience that night.

> "Usually, when you attempt to make some kind of statement in a big place like this, people don't really understand what you're saying. That's why most bands—most rock bands

> will resort to saying, 'How you people doin' out there?! Alright! Party!' I don't think it's gonna be very effective to have a long-winded speech. I think the fact that we're doing this and the literature that people are going to be able to read will be effective enough."[73]

While being interviewed by Erica Ehm in 1993, Kurt demonstrated a vulnerability that captured his true spirit. He was the riveting nucleus of the conversation, fascinating not for his fame, but for his humanity. He wielded his influence for good, though tragically, he didn't live long enough to understand the gravity of his effect.

During this interview with Ehm, Kurt reflected on Cow Palace and the band's impact that day. He also reflected on other ways Nirvana had helped out in the community.

> "I mean, we really have been effective in certain ways, like being associated with this organization called FAIR . . . and I can't remember right now 'cause I have a mental block exactly what it stands for, but it's something like . . . ah, shit! I can't remember!" [Kurt laughed.] "But they're an organization who looks at the injustices that are . . . they look at the details that surround certain issues and certain stories that have been reported in magazines and newspapers, like *USA Today*, who tend to look over a lot of the facts."[74]

FAIR stands for Fairness & Accuracy in Reporting, Inc.[75]

The last concert Nirvana would play in Los Angeles would be on December 30, 1993, at the Forum. According to FAIR.org, this was a benefit concert to represent the organization, with Butthole Surfers and Chokebore part of the impressive roster of musicians lending their talent for another worthwhile cause.[76] Naturally, Kurt was happy to take part.

In the same interview with Ehm, Kurt reflected on other benefit shows.

> "So we've done benefits like that . . . No on 9 benefits to try to stop Portland's anti-gay laws that they were trying to pass . . . and we've done a Bosnian benefit and stuff like that . . . and it doesn't seem like much, but we raised like $50,000 for the Bosnian rape victims, y'know? And that's a lot more than we could have done griping about it and talking about it in interviews, and maybe putting out a fanzine, y'know?"[77]

★★★

Throughout all of these interviews included in this book, I learned from Kurt's friends about his strong social conscience. Considering the layers of Kurt's performances and public persona, Nick Soulsby—author and researcher who has dedicated years to meticulously documenting Kurt's life—offered his perspective on Kurt's misrepresentation in the media:

"Cobain's presence—rather than his intention—seems to have been what resonated most with people, it certainly did with me, and the equivocation of his words allowed people to read what they wished into him. He clearly despised the conservative machismo and aggressive vision of manhood that he felt he'd been force-fed as a young man and overtly mocked it when he had the public forum in which to make statements whether that was wearing dresses, supporting anti-war and anti-rape charities, the initial intentions behind the song 'Rape Me,' the various images on which he fixated in his lyrics. This was a guy whose idea of promoting *In Utero* was a video of the band pretending to give birth, a concept for the video for 'All Apologies' that would have involved male-on-male prison rape and male seahorses carrying babies to term."[78]

Nick's observations highlight that Kurt's values and intentions were often grossly misunderstood, a tension that played out at performances like Cow Palace, where his artistry and altruism stood in stark contrast to what the media obsessed over. Even posthumously, more attention should have been given to shows like these, rather than the "Rome incident," when he was hospitalized in a brief coma following a Rohypnol-alcohol overdose. Sensationalizing Kurt's mental health as it deteriorated had become the norm; his decency and compassion were degraded to an afterthought.

But no headline could undo the intent behind Cow Palace. The money was real. The message was real. And for the Tresnjevka Women's Group, so was the impact.

Chapter 12

"SOMETHING IN THE WAY"

Kirk Canning

KURT'S MUSIC OFTEN FORCED PEOPLE TO CONFRONT UNCOMFORTABLE truths, and "Something in the Way" is a blunt reminder of the relatable compounding obstacles he faced. As the song flows, we hear Kurt sing with the quiet voice of his younger self—unhoused and abandoned. Even in the song's imagery, the animals he catches for food become pets, companionship outweighing hunger.

The searing quality of "Something in the Way" could, in part, be tied to the hardships Kurt faced. Its title captured the weight of his experiences and internal contradictions because something always stood in the way of Kurt's happiness. Childhood demons that plagued him into adulthood, homelessness, struggles with substance abuse—whatever he was experiencing, it stood between him and something better.

His compassion was a blessing and a curse. Although it fueled his music and his advocacy, it also left him exposed. That duality lives in "Something in the Way," a song made from Kurt's humanity and struggles, even if he never slept beneath the bridge it's said to be written about. It's not just the lyrics that embed themselves; it's the instrumentals and their ethereal, if not foreboding, quality. That same aching vulnerability is amplified by Kirk Canning's cello as it moves through the track.

Just as its words offered a universality for anyone struggling, the completed version of "Something in the Way" formed organically through the people around Kurt. If someone was going to contribute to a song like this, it had to be a friend—and that friend was Kirk Canning. His cello's resonant sound elevated the already powerful song, each note adding a richness that matched Kurt's haunting vocals as he sang about an experience deeply personal to him.

Kurt talked about "Something in the Way" during an interview with Kurt St. Thomas:

> "That song really wasn't even written until a week before we went into the studio. And uh, I knew I wanted cello on it, but after all the music was recorded for it, we'd kinda forgotten about putting a cello on it, and we had one more day in the studio, and we decided, 'Oh, geez, we should try to hire a cellist,' y'know, and put something in, and we were at a party, and we were asking some of our friends if they had any friends who play cello, and it just so happened that one of our best friends in LA plays cello, so we took him into the studio on the last day and said, 'Here, play something,' and he came up with something right away . . . it just fell like dominoes . . . it was really easy."[79]

Fragmented, unexpected moments like these often led to Nirvana's most seminal work. Although Kurt never offered a definitive explanation of the song's origins, it's frequently been associated with the loneliness and uncertainty he experienced growing up in Aberdeen. Those feelings of isolation and instability made their way into Kurt's art, and "Something in the Way" was no different. Speaking with Jonathan Poneman, he reflected on its emotional roots:

> "I always wanted to experience the street life because my teenage life in Aberdeen was so boring. But I was never really independent enough to do it. I applied for food stamps, lived under the bridge, and built a fort at the cedar mill."[80]

Kurt's reflection offered insight into the song's origins, but how it came together in the studio tells a different story. Kirk Canning recounts his time recording one of *Nevermind*'s most poignant tracks.

★★★

"How did you become a cellist?" I ask.

"That was in grade school," Kirk explains. "The school that I was attending was giving hearing tests to all the children, and then based on your hearing tests, they were directing or suggesting to the parents where that child might be best suited instrumentally. So I had pretty amazing hearing, and they told my parents to push your kid into the cello. I studied cello all through grade school, junior high . . . high school. I was getting a little bored with it, plus punk rock just started happening here in LA. This is mid to-late seventies, and I gave up the cello and got a bass guitar and started playing punk rock. Played in a bunch of bands. It's [the cello] a very beautiful instrument and, most of the time, very sad sounding."

I ask Kirk how he came to record "Something in the Way," referencing my conversation with Carlos.

"Was it an L7 . . . I think it was a signing party? Could you just tell me how Kurt or the band came to ask you to play on that track?"

"I know the party Carlos is talking about," Kirk begins. "I don't think that's when it was actually brought up, but they [Nirvana] were out here just starting up with *Nevermind*, and Kurt and Krist had come over to our place to hang out and party in Venice. And me and Krist were in our front room, and we were talking about basses and stuff. I actually turned Krist onto that bass that he is so well-known for now, the Gibson RD Artist. He likes Gibson basses, and he was playing, I can't remember, an Olympic or something like that. But he always said, 'I'm always looking for a nice, heavy bass.' And I pulled out my bass and showed it to him, and it's a pretty massive bass, and he fell in love with it. . . . From that point on, [he] bought every single one he could ever find. I believe at this point now, Gibson has actually created a signature model for Krist.

"Anyway, my wife and Kurt were in the other room, and I think they were listening to The Beatles and such. Then, later in the evening, we were all hanging out and talking about how it's going in the studio, and they [Kurt and Krist] said they're thinking about hiring a cellist to put down a track on this song they're working on. I said, 'Huh, I used to play cello in high school.' And they were like, 'Oh, well, you know what? You've got to be the one who plays, then.' They're like, 'We don't want to hire a studio musician. We'd rather have a friend play.' And I said, 'Well, I haven't touched a cello since high school. This is going to be interesting.' And my brother's wife at the time played cello. She's a very good cellist. And so I gave her a call and asked if I could borrow her cello because she has an amazing cello. And I started messing around, getting my chops back. They [Kurt and Krist] didn't even have a tape of the song. So it wasn't like I could even work on it at home or come up with a part. We went down to Sound City and they put the song on. I just started plucking around, trying to find some nice parts for it. Came up with three different parts: a high part, a medium part, and a low part, and we ditched the low part—it was conflicting with the bass—and kept the other two parts. And I guess I got ahead of myself with the story here."

"No, no, that's awesome," I say. "I was going to ask all this because one of the people I interviewed was Steve Albini, and we had talked about some studio sessions. I wanted to know if you went and played with Nirvana live [in the studio] or if it was like you played over their recording."

"It was just a studio recording, which was unbelievably comfortable. I knew Butch before that day because he had worked with L7. So it was pretty much me, Butch, Kurt, and Krist. I don't think Dave was there that day. And they didn't really have that much on the song yet.

It was like a scratch guitar track, Kurt's vocals, probably scratch bass and scratch drums, too. And the guitar track was horribly out of tune. I play by ear mostly, and as much as I tried to force myself to not listen to Kurt's guitar, my ear kept directing my fingers to play along with what I was hearing. And then Butch . . . I believe that Pro Tools had just come out . . . which was very new at that time, and an amazing app for music and recording and manipulation. And he was actually able to bend the one note that I kept sliding to—I was sliding to what I heard on the guitar."

Recording a song like this wasn't just about the technical details, though. There was something else beneath it—something tied to Kurt himself.

"Having known Kurt, what stood out about him?" I ask. "I love the answers I get."

"I'll give it a shot," says Kirk. "I mean, Kurt was kind of an introvert, but there were times where he was just the opposite. I mean, get the guy into a party mode and he could be the craziest guy there. But then, again, he could also be the quiet guy sitting in the corner talking with my wife or something. He just oozed creativity. You put a guitar in his hand, and he could just make something up on the spot. He was very talented, very prolific. I mean, as you see from his music, an unbelievable writer. I mean, it's hard for me to say whether a guy is good-looking or not, but he did have something that drew you to him. I don't know if it's charisma. Just a very loving soul, I guess."

"I think that's beautiful," I say.

"And he had these eyes that just could melt you," Kirk adds. "I just kind of went in that day, got a few listens, came up with the parts, played them, and was very nervous about my playing. And yeah, actually after every take, Krist would come in with a bottle of Jack Daniels. 'Take a swig of this, that'll help you relax.'"

"I was a big fan of Nirvana's the second I heard *Bleach*, and it was shortly thereafter because of my wife and them being label mates, so I'm so pumped that I met them," Kirk explains. "But I just went in blindly, as I told you. And hearing it for the first time, I was amazed because, well, I hadn't heard them [Nirvana] play too many slow, ballad-type songs like that and wasn't really expecting that. So I was kind of taken aback. But at the same time, it made it a little easier for me to come up with some cello for [it]. I mean, if it was a fast rocker, granted there are certain ways you can play the cello that would work for that as well. But it was much easier for me to come up with something that enhanced and fit with the feeling going on in there.

"It is a great song. And it's just so different for Nirvana. I mean, you listen to *Bleach* and they're all pretty hardcore. I mean, they're very dynamic. They go up, they go down, but there was never really anything real slow or ballad-like like 'Something in the Way,' so it definitely stands out."

"It does," I say. "And listening to Kurt, his lyrics, and I know it's kind of hard to decode what he was saying . . . or not what he was saying, but what he meant. But the whole song, everything is just beautiful. And then when I knew I was going to be able to talk to you about it, I was just sitting there, listening to it, just really focusing on the cello, and it's just incredible. That must've been such a wonderful experience. Really such a beautiful song. So thank you for giving us wonderful music."

Kirk and I talk briefly about the book, about Walter, and what I'm hoping to achieve with this project. I ask him if he wants to weigh in on mental health awareness and the stigma surrounding suicide.

"I think the premise for your book is amazing," says Kirk. "I think that more needs to be done for people in those situations. Depression is just so hard to read. For other people to even think that they need help or for you to help them—I mean, like comedians, for instance. Most comedians, they make you laugh. You wouldn't even think, 'Oh, they're depressed.' But just to generalize, most comedians are depressed people or have issues that they've dealt with in their life that cause them grief in any way. Yeah, I'm glad you're doing this. And I think that it's much needed . . . for people in these circumstances."

"Thank you; I appreciate that," I say. "Although suicide is a theme in the book, I don't get into Kurt's passing. I'm hoping this book can do some good, that's it."

"That sounds amazing to me."

"Thank you."

"And it sounds like you did it in the best way possible without getting involved with what everyone else gets involved with," Kirk says.

"The sensationalism?" I ask.

"Yes."

From this book's inception, I refused to sensationalize Kurt. He wasn't a myth or a martyr—he was a person, with friends and family who still see what the media spins. Each interview I conducted reflected a real connection to him, regardless of the relationship. Some were simply friends hanging out, listening to vinyl; others were people who worked with him, played beside him, or admired him from afar. What mattered wasn't what might sell copies; it was sharing these stories truthfully, exactly as they deserved to be told—with honesty.

Kirk shared his experience recording "Something in the Way," offering a glimpse into how the track came together. Nirvana often brought in other musicians—especially friends—and this session was no different. Kirk's addition drew out the song's quiet intensity, note by note.

Chapter 13

"SERVE THE SERVANTS"

Danny Goldberg

AMID NIRVANA'S METEORIC RISE TO INTERNATIONAL STARDOM IN THE nineties, Danny Goldberg, of Gold Mountain Entertainment, was managing the trio, helping them navigate their unprecedented level of success. While speaking with Kurt's friends and fellow Seattle musicians helped me understand him better, I wanted to learn about him from another vantage point—the business side of artistry. Managers assume a different type of responsibility than friends, balancing empathy with logistics while offering another perspective and relationship dynamic.

I reached out to see if he would be up for an interview, to which he humbly agreed. Speaking to the man who once steered the most famous band in the world was surreal. He's had a brilliant career to date, so I knew he could help me untangle the man from the media-constructed myth. In addition to his illustrious position in the music industry, Danny's also a distinguished journalist and author, most notably penning *Serving the Servant: Remembering Kurt Cobain.*

Danny shed a brighter light on the life and career of the principled Nirvana frontman and how he persevered through the media's negative coverage and impacts of fame.[81]

★★★

"I think the biggest challenge was the media's interest in his private life," Danny begins. "That was something that he had not anticipated. Try to realize, because it was so many years ago, but at that moment, in '91, '92, Nirvana had the sort of fame that Taylor Swift or Beyoncé has. So there was a level of scrutiny in his personal life that was very unexpected, and very unpleasant for him."

This comment tracks with everything we know about Kurt. Fame had decimated the boundary between art and privacy, and nearly every aspect of Kurt's private life—every obstacle, every challenge, every setback, everything—became public for the world to speculate on.

"Just from reading things about him—that he overcame a lot of adversity, he had a tough childhood—he really still persevered," I say. "He had this incredible career. I know it was brief, but can you speak to his tenacity as a person and how he just pushed through this to do this, to be a professional musician?"

"Well, he was—like a lot of people—he had different sides to his personality and addressed different aspects of his life differently, but the area where he was the most disciplined and focused was to do with his art," Danny tells me. "He had an incredible work ethic as an artist. He insisted on extensive rehearsals before the band recorded anything. He'd work for hours on a song. So that was the one area in his life which he was able to really focus, and he had a very strong work ethic when it came to his art."

That discipline was his anchor—the one constant in a world spinning on a chaotic axis.

"When you watch Nirvana's concerts now, they kind of look . . . I don't want to say haphazard, but everybody's out there having a good time," I say. "There's a look that will come over Kurt's face, and you get the impression that it really is not choreographed, per se, but that there was a lot more thought that went into the overall appearance of the shows than maybe you'd expect. I don't know if that's accurate or not."

Danny clarifies this for me.

"He [Kurt] gave an honest thought to every aspect of being an artist, rock musician, rock personality. It was something that he thought about from a young age before he had any kind of a career, and anything to do with his career, he thought through extensively. Music would be very tight for the live shows, but how casual or anarchic some of the staging was . . . he looked at the performances as part of his art, and he took his art very, very seriously. That having been said, a live performance involves interaction with the audience and being in the moment. So, the Nirvana shows were not exactly the same, night to night, like a theater production. Part of the art form is to be in the moment. So, there were certainly very many spontaneous moments that were not in the context of the concerts, but they were in the context of the music having been rigorously rehearsed."

The combination of careful preparation and complete spontaneity was one of Kurt's greatest contradictions, especially as fame increased artistic pressure. It also forced fans to question why he didn't just quit if music proved to be too cumbersome.

"I'll go on to different Nirvana forums and something that people will ask is if Kurt did have some troubles with fame, why didn't he just quit? . . . I'm assuming there were all kinds of contracts and people that the band employed. I don't think it's that easy to just pull the plug on a band like Nirvana, if you could speak to that at all."

"They canceled shows and parts of tours when he [Kurt] physically wasn't up to it," Danny explains. "As for completely quitting Nirvana, I think he thought about that and talked about it sometimes, but he was ambivalent. His biggest problem, in my opinion, was not his fame—or what he was doing as an artist; his biggest problem was the psychological demons that had haunted him long before he was famous. It's not like he had the perfect life and then suddenly got famous. He came with depression and drug addiction. He was doing heroin long before he was famous. He had depression long before he was famous. There's no reason to have thought that just completely abandoning the one thing that meant the most to him—one of the things that meant the most to him that he was so proud of with himself—with his spiritual and psychological issues . . . Nirvana did not tour very much compared to other big bands, because he wanted to limit that. When he wasn't feeling well, they canceled shows. But the idea that his self-destructiveness and drug addiction was the result of being famous is just something that doesn't ring true to me because as I say, he had those problems before he was famous."

I could tell Danny's time with Kurt gave him an intimate understanding. I'd assumed Kurt stayed in Nirvana because of the people they employed, but leaving Nirvana wouldn't have quieted his demons. Music was, in many ways, what defined him. By quitting, Kurt would have lost the creative outlet that carried him through some of the hardest times of his life. Playing in Nirvana was a physical manifestation of his inner turmoil—an outlet that, if left to fester, might have consumed him entirely. Music became the way he released a lifetime of pain, his words and actions continuing to resonate long after. The tragedy is that he never saw just how powerful that impact truly was.

I ask Danny if there's a way that, as a society, we can assist those experiencing a mental health crisis. "I know we have websites if you need to talk to somebody—text or call—but is there any other awareness that we could do to help people?"

"I don't pretend to be an expert on mental health, but generally speaking, I think that the United States, with regards to health in general, is a backward country compared to other countries," Danny begins. "The sheer financial cost of healthcare in the United States is greater than it is anywhere else. The cost of prescriptions in the United States is greater than it is anywhere else. I think that in general, the US healthcare system needs to be modernized and compared with what other countries do. But mental health is a subset of that. In terms of research, it doesn't mean that there's any treatment that's a magic bullet, and for drug addiction, and alcoholism in particular, as far as I understand, the most effective treatment for the largest number of people actually has not cost money, it's been the twelve-step program. And I have many friends who believe their lives have been saved by the twelve-step program. Unfortunately for Kurt, he just didn't really connect with the twelve-step program. He experimented with it, and it just didn't speak to him. It doesn't for everybody. While criticizing the way that the economics of the US healthcare system are organized, they've also recognized the tremendous value to people of the twelve-step program."

The truth behind those words hides a quiet heartbreak; something that has saved others didn't resonate with Kurt. Danny's words are also an uncomfortable truth, especially when considering how many people face barriers to basic care even today, and that's just counting those fortunate enough to have health insurance.

Kurt's story lives inside this uncomfortable truth, and he's not the only one. When you consider that the United States remains the only developed nation without universal health coverage, the picture becomes even more stark.[82] Countless Americans live with chronic conditions that go largely untreated in a morally bankrupt healthcare system. Like millions of others, Kurt lived in a country where seeking medical care wasn't just an unfair labyrinth—it was one marked by exorbitant cost and unfounded shame. In the case of Kurt, his depression was misunderstood while his addiction was stigmatized. Could this have perpetuated his initial descent into addiction? Perhaps. Kurt himself admitted that drugs became a form of self-medication. But the takeaway is the same: Kurt's struggles weren't isolated—they were part of a much larger, broken system.

In an interview with Laurence Romance on August 10, 1993, in Seattle, Kurt elaborated on the impacts and extent of his drug use, and his initial romanticization of it:

> "I really don't care what anyone thinks about my past drug use. . . . I could put the blame on that kind of influence, but

> it's a mixture of rock 'n' roll in general, the Keith Richards thing, Iggy Pop and all those other people that did drugs. I just thought it was just one of those things that you do, you know, to relieve the pain. But, as I expected, before I started doing heroin, I realized that . . . I knew at the beginning that it would become just as boring as marijuana does. Like all drugs, after a few months, it's just as boring as breathing air, so . . . I just don't wanna turn . . . I've always lied about it, because I never wanted—I didn't want to influence anybody, you know? I didn't want anyone to even consider the thought of doing drugs, because it's really stupid."[83]

Pain played a significant role in his addiction. And I don't just mean emotional pain. Kurt suffered from chronic, debilitating stomach issues that plagued him for most of his adult life, so I asked Danny if that could have been part of the equation.

"Is it possible that the reason Kurt started using drugs was that when he was young, he had stomach issues and he didn't have access to free healthcare?"

Danny answers honestly.

"I don't know that. Millions of people have drug problems, including lots of people with plenty of money, so I think these are psychological and spiritual issues, and I think it's important for society to try to create mechanisms to be as helpful as possible to people. But I don't think, in Kurt's case, that there's any way of knowing. But there are quite a few . . . There are people of all economic standings who become alcoholics and drug addicts, people with all kinds of jobs. It's got a dynamic of its own. It has to be recognized."

"I agree. It's prevalent; it doesn't matter where you look."

Danny's perspective didn't just explain what Kurt experienced—it painted a broader picture of the challenges people face every day.

But despite Kurt's struggles, there was still a man worth celebrating—a man not defined by his hardships, but instead an artist who was more than a statistic. So I turned the focus back to the music. "Out of all of the shows, what concert would you say is Kurt's greatest one, or the one that you think represented him the best?"

Danny thinks about this. "Oh, goodness. I don't know that I could single out one show. There are a lot of films of some of the shows."

"I focus on Reading ['92] a lot; that one's great to watch," I say.

"I think Reading is—to me—it was an extraordinary show because it also came at a time when he [Kurt] was under a lot of enormous pressure with magazine articles that criticized him and Courtney," Danny explains. "There were rumors that the band was going to break up, that they wouldn't even do the show. And then it's definitely an extraordinary show. So that's certainly one of them. I wrote about it, and many others have as well.

"Generally speaking, they were a consistently good live band. There are some official recordings and some unofficial recordings. I think that the quality level . . . There are a few bad shows, but most of them were very high-quality level. . . . They didn't play that many shows, but the ones they did, a high percentage of them were very good."

But what stood out just as much as the music was who Kurt was offstage.

"He naturally empathized with anybody who was being ostracized, marginalized, or disrespected," Danny says. "He vocally was very supportive of feminists and the gay rights movement. This was 1991; it was a little edgier than it would be now. He was unapologetic and unambiguous about it from day one. It dated back to bigotry in high school, when he had some gay friends that were bullied and it really pulled him . . . He had very strong feelings about what it was to be a moral man, and the contrast with immoral behavior. All three members of Nirvana had been very much inspired and formed by the punk rock, the American aspect of the punk rock ethos. They were determined that when they got famous, to be supportive of artists that they admired and to help share the spotlight with them. Whenever Kurt did interviews, he shared a lesser-known band to try to bring attention to them . . . Every show, if you look at his appearances on British television, every single one of them, there was something like that. I think the group Captain America got a record deal because of Kurt wearing one of their T-shirts on the cover of *New Musical Express*, and then he toured with them. There's no question that he's part of the ethos and culture that inspired them, and they really took it to the next level."

It all came from the same place—Kurt did things his way, whether that meant highlighting a band he loved or pushing back against how he was told to perform, even on *Top of the Pops*.

"I was at that broadcast," Danny tells me. "Sometimes, when they would switch the songs, the TV producers would always get rattled, because they liked to know what the song is in terms of the length of it and the camera positions, and there was at least one show when there were complaints about it. But generally speaking, Kurt's feeling was that he wanted every performance to have something special about it, not to just go and robotically re-create. I think that even if it caused him stress from the producers at the time, it was that much more historical in that one thing; they were producing art, not just the repetition of something. But there was some grumbling sometimes from the TV producers, but no one ever decided not to air Nirvana clips."

Danny and I continue to speak for a few more moments, and before the interview ends, he adds one final sentiment about Kurt, expressing his gratitude.

"I'm so glad that Kurt's music still touches people," he says. "I live outside of New York City, but my office is in Manhattan. There's literally not a day that I don't see somebody wearing a Nirvana T-shirt, even though Kurt's been physically gone for thirty years or so. It's amazing that, in a short length of time, the music that he created still inspires people who weren't even alive when they [Nirvana] were putting out their records. So I'm glad that people are still moved by it and inspired by the good that he did."

Between Danny and Ryan Aigner, I felt as if I'd covered the band's various stages of management (both from the beginning and near the end), but my research was far from over. I had to speak with someone who understood the inner workings of the studio—the pressure, the creative demands, and the unmistakable desire to produce something raw and unfiltered. So I reached out to the legendary Steve Albini, who produced *In Utero* and captured Nirvana's unapologetic sound with unflinching honesty. What I didn't know at the time was that this would become one of Steve's final interviews.

Chapter 14

"IN UTERO"

A Tribute to Steve Albini

WHILE WRITING THIS BOOK, I FOUND MYSELF STEPPING INTO A WORLD I hadn't originally been part of, not knowing how people would respond. With so much written about Kurt Cobain already in circulation, people were understandably hesitant to give yet another interview. Once I explained my reason for reaching out, however, and noted the charitable aspect of this book, people were put at ease.

I wanted to learn more about Nirvana's *In Utero* recording sessions, so I contacted Steve Albini. He's also known for his work on albums such as the Pixies' *Surfer Rosa*, PJ Harvey's *Rid of Me,* and The Stooges' *The Weirdness*, and was a musician himself, playing in influential bands like Shellac, Big Black, and Rapeman. Beyond his impressive track record, I'd also heard a lot of good things about him as a person. He lived up to that reputation, responding to me right away and being happy to help. We eventually settled on April 5, 2024—the thirtieth anniversary of Kurt's passing. This was merely a coincidence, and it wasn't mentioned when we spoke.[84]

Steve's interview stands out in my mind for several reasons. For starters, I'd read he was "the crankiest man in rock." Naturally, I was nervous to speak with him—but in every exchange, he dispelled those rumors. He was nothing but kind.[85]

When I called Electrical Audio, Steve answered. My nerves were instantly calmed as his laid-back demeanor put me at ease. What resulted was a conversation with an astute man, a master in his craft, and an all-around nice guy. He graciously answered all my questions, even ones he had probably heard a thousand times. What I didn't know then was that this would be one of his final interviews.

Before we connected, I covered *In Utero*'s thirtieth anniversary release and thought about each track and what went into the album's original production work. When we spoke, I wanted to compliment him for an album that harnessed Nirvana's talent without the need for tracks polished to perfection. Steve's unparalleled production work allowed the band's artistry to stand on its own merit. And the music is as candid and captivating as a live album but with the technical proficiency that could only be achieved by Steve Albini.

Although each song evokes strong emotions, some are more unabating, relentless. Namely "Scentless Apprentice," one of my favorites. Based on the novel *Perfume*, this song is arguably one of *In Utero*'s most compelling tracks. Something about Grenouille—the disturbing protagonist of *Perfume*—and his tale of terror resonated with Kurt. Steve Albini flawlessly captured Kurt's primal screams as he howled for people to just go the fuck away. In many ways, he captured the real Kurt on *In Utero*, each track equal parts poignant, powerful, and unapologetically honest.

On the evening of May 6, I started working on Steve's chapter. I was on his Wikipedia page, just poking around. But the following day, the news hit—Steve had tragically passed away at the age of sixty-one. The stark change on his Wikipedia page—"is an American musician and audio engineer" to "was an American musician and audio engineer"—was a gut punch. I listened to *In Utero* throughout the day, reflecting on Steve and his impact on those who knew him and the world around him.[86]

My heart goes out to his family, friends, and everyone he affected, myself included, ever so briefly.

I wasn't sure how I could accurately express my admiration for and gratitude to Steve for his willing participation in this process. He made time to talk to me despite his many obligations, which isn't surprising since he was incredibly generous and selfless. Steve knew this book was intended to raise funds for those in need, and he didn't hesitate to participate, because that's just the kind of person he was. If you haven't heard of Letters Charity, founded and run by Steve's wife, Heather Whinna, and championed by the man himself, I highly recommend checking out this incredible and worthwhile organization—in honor of Steve. Their website is letterscharity.org, and it's an example of Steve's tremendous impact in this world. As a tribute to Steve, a portion of my profits from *Forever in Bloom* will be donated to Letters Charity.

This chapter is for Steve, recording engineer extraordinaire and one hell of a good guy.

★★★

It was April 5, 2024. I called Steve Albini.

"Hello, Electrical."

It sounded like Steve, but I asked to be sure.

"This is he to whom you speak," Steve said.

When he said that, I knew right away there was something about him. He was answering the phone at his own studio—it showed how many hats he wore. And the way he said it—it was overly formal, but somehow disarming in a way that was hard to explain. He was incredibly sharp—very aware, very present. I just knew I liked him, and he immediately put me at ease. Maybe it was his cadence, or how unassuming he sounded despite having worked with some of the biggest names in music history. He caught me off guard.

After I set up to record and later transcribe the interview, I begin by telling Steve more about this book, about Walter and how he inspired me to write it, and some of the organizations I'm donating funds to.

"[This book is] basically just a collection of sentiments and statements where people kind of come together to remember Kurt, his tenacity, and maybe share some stories. Just to kind of remove a little bit of this stigma around suicide and mental health, too, and just kind of have something that's a positive reflection of his life and his work. There's nothing sensationalized in it. There's nothing salacious or anything. It's all just a nice kind of quiet reflection. So that's it. . . . I wanted to open with that," I tell him.

As a quiet, honest reflection of who Kurt was, it makes sense to start with the environment that shaped him—the scene.

"Well, Kurt and I came up in music at roughly the same time," Steve tells me. "He was fractionally younger than me, but we both came up in the same sort of milieu, that being the underground punk music scene. And in the early days of the underground punk music scene, that being the late seventies and the eighties, there was a very close affinity between all the different subcultures in any scene. Meaning the queer underground in Chicago was absolutely instrumental in allowing participation in the music underground. Meaning that a lot of the, not just for a lot of the people involved queer or gay, but all of the clubs and all of the support systems that had been put together sort of surreptitiously for the gay and queer subcultures were available to the music scene.

"So, a lot of the shows were at gay bars, and a lot of the record stores, and hangouts, and other places were very queer-friendly. And so that persisted and became part of the identity of the music scene. And then as that music started to percolate out into a wider audience, and Kurt made explicit mention of this, it started to attract people who were not friendly in that way and who were not part of that subculture, not indigenous to that subculture, and weren't as open-minded and were, in some cases, hostile or abusive to people with different gender identities and people with different sexual orientations.

"And that feeling of being an outsider when you're young and forming your identity is similar and shared among all the different kinds of outsiders. If you're an immigrant, or if you're a minority, or if you're queer, or if you have neurological problems, or if you're disabled, all of those things make you feel like you're apart from the straight society. And in the punk scene, there was a kind of natural sympathy for all of those people and a natural shared identity with all of those people.

"And Kurt was uncomfortable with Nirvana moving from that subculture rich with those kinds of people and that kind of thinking into a mainstream where all of those people and all of those identities were marginalized. He was uncomfortable with that. And he made explicit mention of it. If you talk to a lot of veterans of the music scene of that era, of the people whose identities and musical tastes and participation was formed in the late seventies, early eighties, that will be a common thread. It's that we felt like we were outsiders and all outsiders felt like we banded together and created a safe harbor for each other. And then when that music started to filter into the mainstream society, it was uncomfortable."

I tell Steve about other people I interviewed and how they had similar comments, then ask about Kurt's drive and tenacity—his perseverance to push through and really see his dream through to fruition.

"I only worked with Nirvana very briefly," Steve says. "And I wasn't an intimate of theirs. I wasn't part of their circle of friends prior to working with him. And after we parted ways in the studio, we didn't really reconnect until many years later, so I don't really have any firsthand knowledge of his behavior in private moments or in times of stress. While I was working with him, he was intensely focused and extremely productive, and that was apparently not something that you could rely on with him. He had periods where he was somewhat unreliable and periods where there was a lot of drug activity, and a lot of domestic problems, and stuff like that. But I didn't witness any of that . . . I was insulated from all of that. And I also didn't observe anything like that during the relatively short period that I was working with him."

"What was Kurt like in the studio?" I ask. "He was very hands-on with everything when possible, and he was just very, very focused."

"They had made a few records by this time," Steve says. "And I think they realized that advanced preparation makes for an easier time in the studio, and so they didn't leave a lot of things undecided. When they came to the studio, they were well-rehearsed; all the songs were written in detail. Kurt had ideas for second guitar parts and production ideas that he wanted to bring to bear on the songs. He had a mental image of how he wanted each of the songs to sound. And they were articulate in conversation about how they wanted things to sound and how they wanted things to go.

"So they were extremely well prepared . . . and they had been touring, so they were in good physical shape, and they're just organically very good musicians. So, it was a very smooth session. We were done and dusted in twelve days. There's a kind of a detail there that is sometimes overlooked. In the seventies and the eighties, you were expected to put out an album that would have eight or ten songs on it, thirty to forty minutes, and everybody was happy. In the nineties, the record labels were really pushing the shift to compact disc away from vinyl records, and so they were insisting on having longer records delivered. That is, records that were fifteen, sixteen songs on an album plus additional tracks for the Japanese market or for various territories, or for uses, promotional unreleased B-sides, and that sort of stuff.

"And so, a band in the seventies could go into the studio for a week and make an eight-, or nine-, or ten-song record, minimal production, relatively straightforward process. But in the nineties, when they were expected to deliver fifteen or sixteen songs, then that kind of extends the workload. And so the fact that they were able to get it done that quickly meant that not only were they well-prepared, but all of the sort of secondary decisions, which songs are the priority songs, which songs are we tossing in as the bonus tracks or whatever, all of those secondary decisions had also been made."

"Wow. . . . They were really ready to go," I say in awe. "I saw online that there was a letter that you had given them basically kind of laying out the details of the way the production recording session would go. Did they have any kind of pushback with that, or were they okay with everything you laid out?"

"So that letter as circulated is slightly misleading . . . in that Kurt and I had a long phone conversation when he initially approached me about working on the record. We had a preliminary conversation, and then I said, 'Let's talk about some more details, talk it over with the band, and come back and call me back.'"

A few days later, Steve and the band had a longer phone conversation about how they wanted to make the record and why they wanted him involved. He suggested writing everything down so the band could review it together and avoid any confusion. "It'll all be written down and there won't be any hearsay or there won't be any misunderstanding about anything," Steve says about the letter.

"So I basically wrote up the content of that conversation that Kurt and I had had," he continues. "We talked through all of those points on the phone, and I just wrote it all up in kind of a document, which [was] sort of meeting notes, I guess, you would call it. And then I sent it through. I faxed it to them back when there were fax machines. I faxed it to their office. And then they got together and shared it within the band, and they all talked about it and they agreed, 'Yeah, that's the way we want to make the record.' So it sounds like it was me writing a proposal for doing the record, but what it was, was it was me sort of documenting the talking points of the conversation that Kurt and I had had in detail already."

"That's another theme I've noticed while writing this," "I'll talk to people and more times than not I get, 'That's not accurate. That's been misconstrued as X, Y, Z.' So basically the way I laid the book out was instead of doing a book where I . . . I had never met Kurt, I'm not involved with the Seattle music scene, who am I to rattle on for three hundred pages? It's basically just a very interview-heavy book, because otherwise I think that's how things turn into a game of telephone and get misconstrued and whatnot."

"I mean, I don't harbor any hard feelings about people taking things one way or another," Steve says. "I understand that all of this stuff is an oral tradition and nothing is going to be as anyone remembers it. It's just that that's one very specific thing that I was involved in that I can sort of clarify."

"I appreciate that," I say, thanking him for his honesty. "So let me ask you another question, and I don't know if it's silly or not. I mean, I really love *In Utero*. Obviously, I've listened to all the albums over and over and over while writing this just to kind of try to put myself in a certain headspace and analyzing lyrics to the best of my limited ability. But you listen to *Nevermind* and it's a great album, but sounds to me—with very limited knowledge about being a recording engineer—it seems like a sound that would've been harder to reproduce on stage. Versus *In Utero* which really, I think, captured the essence of the band and you really understood what they sounded like.

"Was there a song on that album that was particularly fun for you to record or that you really, really liked? . . . I mean, obviously, the whole album is great."

"I haven't categorized it in that way," Steve explains. "There are specific moments from that session that stand out in my mind as being really great moments. . . . The first song that we recorded was 'Serve the Servants,' which is the first song on the record. And they had done a brief sound check of all the instruments before we started recording, but in the interim between when we did the sound check and when we did the first take, Kurt had added a boost pedal or distortion pedal into his guitar chain.

"So when the first loud part happens, the guitar was suddenly like eight or ten decibels louder than it had been during the sound check, and it was overloading the channels on the desk and overloading the tape machine. And I had to very quickly rock the faders back to get it back into the normal range. And in a conventional session that would be . . . It was the first take. It didn't occur to me. I didn't presume that that would be the take that would end up on the record. The first takes are often fraught with mistakes and they need to redo things, or somebody's headphones weren't set correctly or whatever.

"So it wasn't a big deal, but when they came in to listen to the playback, they were very happy with it. And they said, 'Yeah, let's use this. That one's done, we can move on to the next one.' After one take, which was great progress and sort of set the tone for the whole session. And I mentioned to Kurt that 'Okay, when you hit your distortion pedal there, the guitar overloads, and there's a brief moment of distortion there before it comes back into the normal range. Do you want to punch that in and clean that up so that it's the same as the other choruses or whatever?'

"And he listened to it and he's like, 'Nah, that's fine.' And that just sort of being willing . . . It was an engineering mistake on my part, but it was handled in flow, and I thought it spoke toward their willingness to go with the flow or their willingness to leave in some of the imperfections that in a more controlled setting would've been ironed out pro forma. And my thinking about it was, *If you're cool with it, I'm cool with it.* Rather than it being, *Oh, no, we can't let a record go out like that. That has a technical mistake on it. That'll wreck my career or whatever.* [Laughs.] And I was very pleased that they were more concerned about what it felt like on playback than they were concerned about adhering to any kind of academic perfection."

In the middle of our conversation, everything started shaking. At first I thought something was wrong with the furnace, but then the walls began to rattle, and it didn't stop.

Steve had no idea what was happening on my end and kept talking. He was in the middle of a story and let out a small laugh—the kind where you'd normally laugh along—but I didn't. For a second, I just sat there trying to figure out what was happening before I apologized, saying I wasn't trying to ignore him; I was pretty sure we were in the middle of an earthquake.

Steve didn't waver. He asked if everything was okay and offered to reschedule. No judgment, no urgency—just calm. My son slept through the whole thing and our house was fine, so we kept talking.

It ended up being oddly comforting. I wondered if he had that effect with Kurt.

Any residual nerves I had were gone, and the rest of our conversation flowed with ease.

"I have another question, and this is just again, my limited knowledge with how bands record. Do they all go into one room and they play a song, everybody's playing at the same time, or is it like different—"

"I mean, it can be done in a lot of different ways," Steve says. "But the way Nirvana made that record—they were all playing at the same time the same way they did on stage. There was isolation. The drums were in a different room from the guitar amplifiers. But there was a glass wall between them, so there was a line of sight and everybody could see everybody. It is often done in different ways, but in this case, they made the whole record basically playing live together the way they would on stage or in rehearsal. The final vocals were overdubbed and there were some other guitar overdubs added and things like that. There was cello overdubs on a couple of songs. But it wasn't assembled with a microscope and tweezers the way a lot of records are."

"That's what I was going to ask," I say. "Some things like the chorus was that . . . Because I know sometimes certain studios will take the chorus and they'll put it . . . I don't know how to say it because again I don't do this professionally. They almost put it on a loop. I'll listen to certain things on—"

"I mean, that's a production technique where when you get one perfect chorus, then you just copy it and splice it in for all the choruses so that all the choruses are identical. That's a pop music production technique. That wasn't really germane to the way they thought about their music or the way that they wanted to make the record."

I told him this was exactly what I was hoping for—the kind of studio insight I wanted in the book—and asked if there was anything else he wanted to add.

"Like I said, my relationship with them was very limited," Steve says. "I was only in their company for a couple of weeks. I didn't know them beforehand. We got to know each other during the making of that record, and I came to admire them and respect them. And since then, I've maintained a friendship with Dave and Krist, and I value their friendship. And I think they're good people and good souls. And Nirvana were a remarkable band, and I'm obviously flattered to be associated with a band that significant."

After we got off the phone, I sent Steve a short email.

"Thank you again! It was a 4.8 magnitude earthquake that interrupted us. I really appreciate you taking the time for this interview!"

That was the last time we talked. My time with Steve was brief, but it left an impression. He didn't have to take that time with me, and I didn't take that for granted.

That was the innovator, the genius.
In Memory of Steven Frank Albini
July 22, 1962–May 7, 2024

Chapter 15

"MONTAGE OF HECK"

Jeff Danna

NATURALLY, I FOUND MYSELF DRAWN TO THE SOUNDTRACK FOR BRETT Morgen's rock-doc *Kurt Cobain: Montage of Heck*. The movie itself is stunning and evocative—laced with visuals and emotion that aimed to reflect Kurt's inner world. From the home footage of Kurt to the forlorn illustrations, the movie captured my attention. But what resonated most was the music. A stirring version of "Smells Like Teen Spirit" demanded a spot on my playlist, the song's string ensemble challenging my preconceived notions about Nirvana: that their music was purely raw, when it had hidden layers I hadn't fully heard before.

I reached out to Jeff Danna, an incomparable film composer and the person who arranged and produced the movie's score, hoping he'd help me understand more about Kurt's unmistakable talent.[87]

Jeff has won prestigious awards and carries a résumé that would make any director beg for his collaborative talents. He composed the music for *Resident Evil: Apocalypse*, *The Boondock Saints*, Pixar's *Onward,* Terry Gilliam's *The Imaginarium of Dr. Parnassus, Silent Hill*, and much more. I was eager to learn how he reimagined Nirvana's music and what he thought of Kurt's creative process, so we set aside time to speak.

★★★

Before Jeff shares his careful and thought-provoking analysis of Kurt's musical abilities, he first tells me a little bit about how he prepared for *Montage of Heck*.

"I read Kurt's biography, *Heavier Than Heaven*, before composing the score for the movie," Jeff says. "Reading the book was incredibly eye-opening. Every time I read it, it felt like a little cloud formed over my head because of the unhappiness of Kurt's childhood. It really blew me away. I thought, *This poor kid*. I think his childhood struggles clearly show up in his art. That book was tough to read, but its vibe helped me prepare for the movie. Honestly, I did a very humble job; I just rearranged some things Kurt did.

"To me, Kurt's work embodies a type of spirit that burns white hot. It's so undeniable that it leaves behind any concern about simplicity, dictation, or whether Kurt knew how to write music on paper, etc. It's rock and roll! It isn't supposed to be Strauss or Bach. It's supposed to be visceral. No one has ever had a more harrowing vocal delivery than Kurt, and that music reaches off the record and grabs you around the throat. His melodies were unusual and unpredictable; there's no mistaking them for other artists. He was in his own world doing his own artistic thing. I think that his work—and all the best 'art' if I can use that word—applies this architecture where the whole is greater than the sum of the parts. As everything comes together, it's absolutely transformative. The result transcends all the individual pieces. He was a supreme singer/songwriter, and we're all better for it."

"I agree one hundred percent," I say. I mention how Nirvana's shows, while rough-hewn and chaotic, weren't without intention. "I learned that Kurt had this whole big vision and plan for concerts that I think people wouldn't have realized watching their shows."

"That's really interesting," says Jeff. "I didn't know that. But there is an obvious parallel to the music at those concerts. There's that whole off-the-cuff 'sloppy rock and roll' sound that some performers deliver, such as Kurt and Mick Jagger, but within the rough-hewn sound, there's also this enormous amount of artistic intelligence and structure. Otherwise, we wouldn't care about the work; it would just sound unpolished and substandard. To my ears, Nirvana sat in that balance point perfectly."

That same balance of rawness and intention comes through in Jeff's renditions in *Montage of Heck*.

"There's a video we cut together from the movie, using the string octet arrangement I created for 'Smells Like Teen Spirit.' Honestly, I was a little afraid to touch that song because, in rock and roll, it is hallowed ground. But the film needed it, so I dove in. I wondered how Kurt would hear that song now, all these years later, and what kind of new view could be had of it. We tried our best to honor the legend, and the orchestra played it with boundless energy."

"You listen to the music in the film, and it's kind of hard to listen to, but not in a bad way," I say. "When you're listening to it and looking at the footage of Kurt as a little boy, like a toddler, it's tough. To see those pictures of Kurt when he was little . . . As a mother, that movie gets to me."

Watching *Montage of Heck* allowed me to quietly look at the life of a little boy who grew up to change the landscape of music. But his talent and success weren't enough to save him from himself. Seeing a young Kurt—thriving and full of promise—makes the ending that much harder, because you already know where his story goes.

"My approach to these childhood songs was informed by *Heavier Than Heaven*; what I learned about Kurt's childhood and saw through the prism of raising three boys myself," Jeff says. "Knowing what boys are like and raising them helped with reimagining these songs. It made sense to make some of them childlike. And a little bit eclectic. I worked with this one musician who plays a stone marimba for example, and we played that alongside an antique toy piano that I found—a Schoenhut, which was one of the original toy piano makers in the States. There are multiple elements that I used to make the music a little bit quirky and left of center, as we were still thinking about some of the score being childlike and dreamlike."

Jeff plays a clip from the *Montage of Heck* score.

"Temple bells were also used often," he says. "And accordion. Hammond organ. Empty suitcases were pounded on. I combined those disparate elements with the string section, and we went down and recorded at The Village in Santa Monica. It's a classic rock-and-roll space and seemed fitting for this project—we used the room where Fleetwood Mac recorded *Tusk*. There was a real vintage rock vibe in that room, which we fed off.

"As far as fitting these pieces into the film, there's a lot of intentional repetition in the movie's music because Brett wanted to keep it simple and cycling as the images changed on screen. Often when I'm working with Brett, I'm given the job of holding things in one place emotionally—or in a very slowly developing place emotionally—while the pictures tell an after-developing story. It's about the film first."

"You're watching *Montage of Heck* and the baby pictures of Kurt with the music, and it's like, 'Oh, here's this beautiful home video.' And you have a hard time not focusing on how the movie ends. Know what I mean?" I ask.

"Brett had access to everything," Jeff explains. "This is why we see those clips—the home movies when Kurt was a kid and some of those really intense moments with Courtney when they were both under the influence. That footage had never seen the light of day. It's tough to watch sometimes."

"It *is* tough to watch," I agree.

"I sat in front of Courtney at the premiere, and it was just a heavy kind of night," Jeff says.

"I saw *Montage of Heck* before I started writing this," I add. "And it was one of the things that propelled me to want to do this. It sat with me because it's a very haunting movie, and so is the soundtrack. And I knew I wanted to write something celebratory."

"That's great."

"You can read a lot of sad, depressing stuff about Kurt," I continue. "But I thought something positive would be a nice tribute."

"All of the film's music is reworked Nirvana songs. 'I Want to Die' is the name of the film cue on my YouTube channel," says Jeff. "But it's actually Nirvana's 'Something in the Way.' It's the track that uses the toy piano but also features an accordion, which was a neat sound in the context of Kurt and his life, for that moment in the film.

"When you're talking about rock and roll, simplicity is the recipe. If your knowledge of music is simple in a theoretical sense, you are in no way impeded. The music becomes about feelings, attitude, and the visceral energy that fuels it. Nirvana's songs aren't complicated or complex. They're like Beatles songs. They are Kurt's version of Beatles or Stones songs. But because he had his own original view of the world, an original guitar sound, and a *very* original voice, Nirvana's music became a new thing.

"I hear film music all the time," Jeff continues. "With many scores, they are 'technically proficient' but not very 'emotionally resonant.' Personally, I'll take a simpler orchestral arrangement with a tune that breaks my heart over a piece of music that just has a lot of elements flying around. And that's what the best rock and roll does; it's basically all of rock and roll because it stays down on that simple, visceral level. But when you put all these different ingredients together, it's extremely effective. Simple and stunningly powerful."

Emotionally resonant. That was Kurt for so many. When you listen to his voice, or try to recreate his strumming pattern, what comes through isn't whether he knew the pentatonic scale or had some polished technique. It's the feeling behind it—the thing you can't fake or recreate. It was his emotional intelligence, and that's what made him a genius and able to connect with his audience.

"When I was nineteen, I experienced something that changed me," Jeff tells me in his final story. "I was just beginning to figure out how to write orchestra music; I'd been playing punk rock and new wave rock and roll since I was about eight years old. But here I was, thinking about other ways that music can be expressed or more refined. I remember one Sunday night I went to see Handel's *Messiah* in Hamilton, Ontario, and it was this glorious, uplifting, and incredibly impressive experience with an orchestra and a choir. I could feel everyone around me—they were all in their forties and fifties—reveling in the spirit of the music, and it was almost a form of church. Then the very next night I saw Paul McCartney at the SkyDome with my friend, up close in the sixth row, and at some point, Paul sat down and played 'Let it Be.' The feeling in the room right then was exactly the same as the feeling during Handel's *Messiah.* It was eight chords and a man at a piano, and I realized it was the same feeling at both concerts. One a complex and rigorous orchestral masterpiece, and the other this very simple but stunningly beautiful piece of music. I thought, *There's this human channel that all music can tune into when it hits that level of truth and beauty in its own way, whatever the era and genre.* In that way, I think that Kurt's music cries out just as strongly and truly as Tchaikovsky's, but it's just a different way into that same human channel. During both Handel's *Messiah* and 'Let it Be,' I remember thinking, *These are all legitimate ways of evoking that same feeling.* That's why Kurt's music works at any level—it has that truth in it, with a capital 'T.'"

After we spoke, I found myself listening again to the *Montage of Heck* score. Learning about the care Jeff put into reinterpreting Kurt's recordings—and the unconventional instruments he used to make the songs feel worthy of the originals—made me want to revisit the music with fresh ears. I realized it wasn't just me who heard something in Kurt's work worth preserving. Anyone moved enough to engage with it seriously was responding to the same thing. It was never about technicality—it was about telling the truth. The ugliness he saw in the world—whether it was violence, misogyny, or some other type of exploitation—and his need to purge it, loud and unfiltered.

Chapter 16

"HAIRSPRAY QUEEN"

Cathy Faulkner

As the path to understand Kurt unfolded before me, I found myself connecting with more people who truly knew Nirvana—and Kurt—up close. Their willingness to share made an honest tribute feel possible.

Some of the most crucial vantage points came from those who watched Nirvana's rise from a public platform, especially as the band began dominating the airwaves. That led me to Cathy Faulkner, the music programmer for radio station KISW in Seattle.[88]

Cathy's unique experience allowed me to better understand the cultural phenomenon that was—and still is—Kurt Cobain. She worked for KISW between 1981 and 2001 and served as music director from 1991 to 2001. As a Seattle native, she had a front-row seat as Nirvana shifted the entire musical landscape. I wanted to learn more about her experiences at KISW to see how Kurt—and Nirvana—turned the music world upside down.

But first, we talked about Seattle itself.

★★★

"I truly believe there's a context that is helpful to anybody about how Seattle was at the time because I haven't seen anything as community-oriented, incestuous, organic, and . . . analog," Cathy begins. "We now live in a digital age, and it's something that people can't really relate to. And there was a context both at the time that Nirvana was starting out and then at the time when Kurt passed . . . I always refer to this strange website. It's called SeattleBandMap.com, and you can trace a member of a band and it'll take you through all the different bands that they were in. And it just shows this really tight spider web of how we all worked together, worked with somebody."

By now, I understood what Cathy was saying—many of my interviews snowballed from one conversation to the next, an invisible tether connecting the music scene Kurt was suddenly thrust to the forefront of. My research reaffirmed just how tightly woven the community was, each band deeply connected to the next.

We chat for a moment, and our conversation shifts to the intention behind the project and why raising funds and heightening mental health awareness is vital. Too often, headlines fixate on Kurt's struggles instead of his talent, kind soul, and social conscience.

"There's so much more than the sound bite," Cathy says. "There's so much more than the clickbait. There's so much more. I was in the same area as him, but we just didn't run in the same circles. I ran more in the hard rock circle, and he was more in the punk circles. But you know, there is so much more to a human being than just a couple of elements.

"The first time that I met [Kurt] was at a small club in Seattle called The Vogue. He was not a performer. He was actually there as an audience member, but kind of off to the side or in the back, and I just remember him seeming so shy. I can't remember exactly when it was, but it was around the *Bleach* album. It was certainly before *Nevermind*, and I just was so struck by how much power comes out on the record.

"And he was just a quiet, shy person, and I think that's one spot in my world that I remember. I didn't have many interactions with him. I had more with Dave and more with Krist . . . I became music director at KISW when *Nevermind* came out, actually. I had worked at the station for ten years prior to that. They [Nirvana] would come by the station on a regular basis, and it was like, 'Oh, okay, they're here,' and it wouldn't be something that you would imagine thirty or forty years later, somebody's gonna ask you what it was like, you know? You didn't solidify it to memory. And then, for better or for worse, the other memories were in '94, the very dramatic times of not knowing where he [Kurt] was or people being concerned about his well-being. And then, obviously, the frenzy around the news breaking locally and being part of a media machine when that was happening. Those are the stamps that come to mind first, and then just as a music fan and a music programmer, how his lyrics and Nirvana's music and his music touched me as a person."

"And that's what I want to know, too," I say. "How did his music touch you? Because he seems like he's affected so many people in so many different ways."

"From a music programmer standpoint, when I listened to any record, I thought with my radio station's format, audience, and focus in mind," she tells me. "When I was working at the station, I would always listen to a record first. And with Nirvana having more of a punk background, a commercial formula . . . rock or mainstream rock radio station—we were harder than the average bear—we played a lot of hard rock and heavy metal. It isn't an exact fit. So, on first listen, it's like, 'Okay, I can see the local angle. I can see the hard-edge angle. The rawness creates that hard edge, whether it's punk-influenced or rock-influenced.' But it still would apply more like—in the early days—to a college radio station or a more alternative radio station or a smaller market radio station kind of a thing."

Cathy described those early years, roughly 1987 to 1990, when bands played wherever they could. Nights, weekends—wherever there was an opportunity to get in front of people. What mattered was being part of a scene that didn't quite fit anywhere yet, and what came through wasn't just about Nirvana, but about the Northwest as a whole. Being removed from the constant scrutiny of cities like New York or Los

Angeles let musicians exist free from the pressures of conformity. That creative freedom let artists be unapologetically themselves, paving the way for a sound that was distinctively their own.

"Personally, when I listened to Nirvana, there was no denying that there—as with many bands that succeeded out of Seattle, regardless of their musical origins—there was a passion," Cathy says.

"There was an authenticity. There was, for lack of a better term, just not giving two shits and saying it like they saw it. From the first moment that I heard Nirvana, there was a rawness there. Absolutely no filters were the other kind of adjective that I would put to it, that you couldn't put it in a box with anything else."

Cathy's description of Nirvana's impact—their raw, unflinching attitude—made my next question unavoidable.

"What was it about Kurt that stood out? I feel like, even writing this, I've had a hard time putting my finger on it."

The repetition of this question throughout the book isn't accidental or lost on me; hearing the answer to the same fundamental question from different voices is the only way to understand who Kurt really was, if only through the eyes of others.

"The words that I would choose—and part of this has a little bit of 'hindsight is 20/20'—I mean, if you were to ask me this thirty years ago, my answer would probably be different," Cathy begins. "But whether it was intentional or not, there was an authenticity, and just being where he was at, if he was in a shitty mood, it went on stage with him. If he was in a good mood, it went on stage with him. If he felt like the audience was connected with him, you got a different performance than when he was performing in a crowd that expected him to perform like a corporate puppet. And with not giving two shits, he was willing to go in areas where most people are uncomfortable and would do this instead [*she lifts her hand as if to say 'go away'*]. And you have to admire that in a world where everything we say is analyzed in a right or wrong mentality, and everybody is allowed their truth. And he was one hundred percent true, flaws and all."

"I've noticed that in watching a lot of Nirvana videos," I add. "One of my favorite interviews with him is with Erica Ehm at the Edgewater

Hotel. He's just so unapologetically himself. He seems very comfortable in the interview."

"Yes," Cathy says. "And he was calm. And you know, he also had a little irreverence, like, 'Whatever we're gonna talk about absolutely means nothing in the grand scheme of things.' But he still was respectful and just kind of matter-of-factly answering the questions, like, 'Your question is redundant, but okay, we're just gonna answer it anyway.'"

I laugh.

"That's what I was thinking. He must have answered these questions a million times, and some of them were dissecting the lyrics. But I love that interview because he just gave her his time, his undivided attention. The questions, asking what a song was about or what he meant by something. And he's just so gracious, and he doesn't cut her off, and he answers the questions. But what I thought was really interesting about him was that he talked about not knowing how to be a musician, saying he didn't know the chord names. But then you listen to the music, and it's so—it just works. It's so good."

"And Dave Grohl did that, too," Cathy says.

"They toured incessantly early on," she continues. "They played incessantly . . . Kurt undeniably had a direct line speaking to a generation."

And that responsibility and power was more than he could handle at times, especially with all the negativity that came with it. He dealt with scrutiny constantly, and I got a very small taste of that while writing this book. I share a few stories with Cathy about some of the "negative creeps" I ran into along the way.

"Some people questioned why an 'outsider' was writing about Kurt," I say.

Cathy reflects on how Kurt would have handled that kind of adversity.

"Just from seeing interviews and seeing things over the years, if Kurt was marginalized, he would push back on that person. You know, labels were very common in the eighties and nineties, so I think he would be critical of somebody he felt was ignorant. And just would push back.

"Not Kurt-related, but the Seattle music scene is very protective, and that's for justifiable reasons. In addition, there's an element to the punk culture that is almost like its own curse. It's like, you can't be successful if you're punk. But if you become successful, then you've done it, you know? Then you've either sold out or you've proved the corporate guys wrong. It's a weird kind of culture of judgment. And when you were telling me these stories about facing adversity, it's almost like, 'I'm part of the Kurt Club, so I would know better. Nobody else gets that club card but me.'"

"I'm not speaking from a 1994 lens," I say. "I'm speaking from a 2023 lens. And at a certain point, we can't keep pushing the narrative that people are destined to do things." When young people look up to Kurt, there's a responsibility to tell the whole story, not the sensational one, especially when so much of the long-standing narrative centers on the idea that his death was inevitable.

"There are substances and there are addictions of a variety that can take hold of a person," Cathy says. "In certain instances, you can't say whether you're seeing the person or the substance—or the trauma—and I think with many interviews and many performances, that can be very true for Kurt. That said, it's what we do as a society. What are the avenues? I mean, when he was missing, everybody in Seattle was looking for him. We were on the air in the mid-nineties, and it was at a time when there were three stations that were highly competitive. It was KISW, KXRX, and KNDD. So being the first to play new Nirvana, or being the first to play new Pearl Jam, or being the first to have any insight or info on these bands, was our charge. Right or wrong, that was our charge, and so I believe the station that went first [and announced Kurt's death]—I don't know if they had confirmed sources. Did they announce it to be *first* based on one phone call or take time for official confirmation after his family was notified? We waited till we did [have confirmation] from the Seattle Police Department because we wanted to make sure Kurt's family was notified. And I think that, on one hand, we're all waiting to hear—you know, everybody was looking for him—so we would hear these little pieces of information that he was seen here, he was seen there. And somebody said that he was seen with a shotgun, and then there were other people that said, 'No, he's disappeared, and he was over here.' Or somebody connected and talked with him but didn't get anywhere. It's just like all these different rumors and the helplessness, I think, that I can say I felt. It's like, how do you—even with a 2023 lens—how do you save this person?

"You know what? Everybody's gonna die. How can you predict that one person is gonna [die] and another one's not? The only thing you don't know is when and how. It's the only thing you don't know. And I think the narrative got to a point where there was no way to know [what would happen]. I mean, there was no way to think other than *It's going to be a tragedy, regardless of how it turns out*. It had all the markers. So yeah, to say you knew it was going to happen sounds insensitive. But my room has four walls, you know? It's something that's so obvious. And at that point, it was going to be tragic regardless of the end game."

As Cathy describes the panic and helplessness of 1994, the narrative comes into crystalline perspective. The real question isn't whether Kurt's death was inevitable—it's what could have been done to prevent a tragedy in the first place.

Cathy and I try to move on, circling back through Nirvana's history and the Seattle music scene.

"The thing that was also amazing about the Seattle music scene was when Nirvana came out," Cathy explains. "Cobain, specifically, and his love for the Melvins, and being a part of that. I think he was a guitar tech for Buzz, or roadie, at some point. But that was very much a part of Seattle . . . I think there was one benefit that Nirvana did in Seattle, and it was for Mia Zapata. It was for funding money to help find Mia's killer."

The Mia Zapata benefit concert took place on August 6, 1993, a month after her murder. Mia's friends started Home Alive, "a Seattle-based anti-violence organization, started in 1993, offering empowering self-defense classes on a sliding scale," and Nirvana was one of the bands who played at her benefit show.[89]

"And these details are things that the mainstream media doesn't usually focus on," I say, my thoughts trailing. Mia Zapata's benefit show was yet another example of Kurt's selflessness being overshadowed by his death. The two things aren't mutually exclusive. His death was tragic, and no one is arguing that his life wasn't difficult, but he also gave back. It's a side of Kurt that often comes through in photographs of him with his daughter.

"We see pictures of Kurt and his daughter, and he's so lovingly looking at her."

"I think of her growing up," Cathy says. "I mean, that's all the narrative she's been able to see on social media."

"And it's so exploited." A human being's life—Kurt's life—was publicly reduced to the most shocking parts, largely for profit and attention, while his family mourned the loss of *all* the parts.

"The magic question that you're trying to answer is, 'How did he connect with other people?'" Cathy says. "And even though our time with Kurt was so short, and even though the performances on a whole—it was only a few years of touring, and that's such a small amount of time—he still resonates with people on a massive scale. So there is something there. Why not explore it from that lens? Why does it have to be from somebody who's an expert? The only expert on Kurt is Kurt. And Kurt can't speak . . . Everything that I have heard thus far in this exchange and in your emails, you are not speaking for Kurt. You are exploring why people resonate so strongly with him and that there's more to him than his substance abuse and his suicide. It sounds like Kurt's your muse. You have a greater social question that you're exploring. And Kurt is your muse to do that."

I didn't realize it at the time, but learning about Kurt became its own kind of catharsis. Suicide leaves a hole, and it's only when you speak with others—hearing how they carry their grief and how they choose to honor the people they lost—that you begin to understand your own. Listening to Kurt's friends laugh about the good times and falter through the hard ones gave me something I didn't know I needed. It gave me permission to stop treating loss as something that must be mourned forever and instead let myself be human in the company of others who understood.

Through their stories, Kurt became a person again, not a sound bite—more human than myth. I watched this happen to Walter over the years, even if it was unintentional. His death became the focal point, a kind of hindsight no one had access to before. The funny, charismatic man who did the worm at my wedding was suddenly the Veteran who couldn't escape his PTSD. His work with traumatic brain injury patients didn't come up as often as his suicide did. It didn't come from a place of disrespect—if anything, it came from reverence, from not knowing how to talk about what happened. But for me, he was still Walter. Funny, charming Walter.

Cathy also understands how a person's final moments often pull focus.

"The other memory that comes up—I wasn't present for," Cathy tells me. "I was actually out of town when Kurt passed, but as assistant program director for the radio station, I was on the phone in my hotel room like, 'What do we do? What do we do? What do we do? What do we do?' And then the gentleman who helped coordinate the memorial at the Seattle Center . . . children and people around the area congregated around the fountain. There's a fountain in the Seattle Center that plays music, and the water shoots up according to what music's being played. It's a pretty cool fountain. People collected around that fountain, and then there was a stage. And to be fair, because of the competitive radio market, one disc jockey from each radio station was going to go up and speak. There was certainly a moment of silence. There was a lot of time for reflection, and the thing that struck me is, here we are reeling, you know? Our innocence is struck yet again by losing somebody in our music community. And the three people from the radio that were probably closest to him, as radio personalities, had to represent the entire power that was Kurt Cobain while also grieving his loss. I believe it was on the same day that he passed. But I could be mistaken. I was watching it from my hotel room, just watching the pain and how these people were put in front of a microphone to try and say some words of wisdom, or some words of comfort, you know? So that was, to me, the awful thing for people who were very close to him.

"But, in spite of it all, with the 2023 lens that you've referred to, the one thing that the three disc jockeys did to honor Kurt was they spoke from where they were. They were real, and they were raw, and they weren't trying to be a philosophical leader and give words of wisdom. It's like a current audience wouldn't really . . . It was just a, 'We're all here together,' sort of thing. And then, as I'm sure you're aware, they played the recorded message from Courtney at that event as well.

"The thing that I loved and celebrated the whole time . . . it's kind of like you're rooting for your hometown team, regardless of the success. Because there is no denying that success of music in the music business comes at a price. There is a price. It's a business, and it takes a passionate personal art form and makes it a monetary commodity. And it will clash. It will get so big it will either break, or it'll get so big and the person or the artist that is going along with that finds that balance to maintain their sanity in the process. And watching [Nirvana] go through a success that rarely happens to any artist . . . They came, I won't say out of nowhere, but their ascension to a mass phenomenon came so fast that they went on a rocket ship ride and still managed to do the majority of it on their own terms. So, many of us were cheering for them from home, because you can sell your soul so many times in the music business, and even if you go to the *Unplugged* performance, there was still that authenticity that made you fall in love with the band in the first place. And made that connection with Kurt Cobain in the first place. That connection was still there."

Nirvana became a cultural phenomenon almost overnight, and they managed to hold on to a sense of themselves in the middle of it. But when Cathy talks about selling your soul in the music business, I can't help thinking that Kurt never would have done it. He was true to himself in a way most people aren't, even under far less pressure. Perhaps it was sheer luck, or fate, that his authenticity ended up being something corporate machines found profitable. But I believe he would have made the same choices even if it weren't. He still would have followed his instincts and written what he felt, pushing back against the horrors of the world—even if it was harder to sell. Music was how he experienced the world, how he processed it. That kind of art isn't something you compromise. It's rare—almost unheard of—to see someone stay that raw and unfiltered when everything around them is pushing them to bend.

Cathy shares some final thoughts about the Seattle music scene and how today's musicians still honor the values carried by those in the eighties and nineties.

"There's a lot about Seattle that's changed," she begins. "And certainly, with the divisiveness of politics, Seattle gets a bad name, with a lot of the growth struggles that it's going through, that many other cities are going through. But it still has that special quality. I recently did a benefit show. We celebrated the thirtieth anniversary of the *Singles* soundtrack, and a lot of artists came together who were too young and never got a chance to work with the artists that, you know, blew up. And they wanted to celebrate it, and I was watching all of these musicians. It was like three bands and a bunch of guest musicians through the course of this evening, and we raised like $5,000 for MusiCares to help with musicians and their healthcare and their mental health. But through the whole evening—at the end of the evening—they were like, 'It probably wasn't anything like an Alice in Chains show or a Nirvana show that you saw.' And I said, 'This is actually like those shows. And I'm glad you asked me to do this because I got to see a music community that still exists. You guys are doing the exact same thing that musicians did thirty years ago. And if you think you're any less valuable than them, you still have the magic.' That is what made the Seattle community special, and all of them looked just like deer in the headlights, stunned. But they were a family, and they were talking about their kids, and they were talking about their shows, and they were talking about, 'Well, you know my amp is broken,' and then another member offered their amp. It was exactly the same that we saw in the eighties and nineties, where if the drummer of Alice in Chains couldn't play, somebody else was gonna play for him. And they brought a few other bands on the bill. And it is still very much true today.

"So that really warmed my heart . . . I worked really closely with Alice in Chains, and when they were doing the demo for their record deal, they—I think it was the weekend they signed with Columbia—they spent the night under the bridge with their gear, like they didn't have a place. I mean, the poverty or the sharing living spaces just to get by . . . how many weeks you lived on Top Ramen and SpaghettiOs, stuff like that, to Pearl Jam selling a million albums in a week; Nirvana going to number one on the charts from September to January . . . I think, for better or for worse, the Seattle music explosion happened at a time, and nothing—nothing has happened comparatively since—both geographically and to the time. And now we live in a digital age. I don't know if it can happen again because of the world that we live in. Not because of music or an explosion. But because you can put it in a digital format and analyze it and almost change its trajectory. So the only thing is that we came from an era of innocence where we kind of just spoke our minds, and now it's all part of this time capsule. You can take a little snippet of it—take it in or out of context."

After speaking with Cathy, I envisioned young artists, unsure of where they'd sleep that night but completely certain of their love for music. I felt their hunger and drive to pursue their dreams, helping one another instead of tearing each other down for sport. The community worked together; it wasn't a zero-sum game—and Nirvana proved it. As they climbed the musical ranks with an unparalleled swiftness, they did everything they could to bring the bands they loved along with them. That sense of camaraderie came alive for me through Cathy.

Those conversations—that tight-knit community—helped shape this book. Through them, I learned about the importance of perseverance. Kurt wasn't the only one who persevered. There was no denying he affected his community the same way it affected him. And when he passed, that loss was felt far and wide.

But I still had more questions about the Seattle music scene. To revisit its wider orbit, I wanted to learn more about the time pivotal musicians spent with Kurt and what they thought about his overall impact on music. So I reached out to Gary Lee Conner of Screaming Trees.

Chapter 17

"LITHIUM"

Gary Lee Conner

THE HUMOR LEAVES GARY LEE CONNER'S VOICE.

"It wasn't like, 'This is cool, I'm gonna kill myself.' It was like, 'I'm in horrible pain. I'm gonna end it.'"[90]

Up until that moment, our conversation had been lighthearted. Gary Lee from Screaming Trees—one of the founding fathers of the grunge movement—lauded Kurt for his musical brilliance, his unparalleled talent, and his quiet charm. His candor amplified what so many others had shared—that Kurt left a space in people's lives no one has ever fully filled.

Hearing Gary Lee speak so bluntly about Kurt made it clear that talent was only part of the equation. In a scene where nothing came easy, you either figured it out or you didn't. There was no in-between. That kind of environment created more than music; it formed the people who made it. It didn't take long for Kurt to learn that if he wanted something, it was up to him to create it.

"Back then it was a 'do-it-yourself' scene," Gary Lee explains. "There wasn't a lot of drinking and drugs—that came a little later. We were all in our early twenties. It was a cool thing and everyone was just friends and doing their thing. Kurt was from Aberdeen. With the Seattle music scene, a lot of the bands came from outside of Seattle. I think that outside of Seattle is just really conservative."

His point about conservatism—and the kids who rejected the belief that there was only one mindset to inherit—is exactly why the DIY culture thrived. Punk represented an anti-establishment, fuck-corporate-rock attitude, and Seattle was alive with revolutionary music that didn't just push back against the mainstream—it rivaled it in popularity, commanded attention, and proved that power could come from not just what sells, but from what bleeds.

What began as a raw, unfiltered rebellion born from garages and secondhand gear would eventually find its way behind museum glass, a testament to the irrefutable impact not just of Nirvana, but of a burgeoning Seattle music scene. Alive with pain, grit, and unrest, this discontent was seldom singular. Unstable home lives, isolated towns with antiquated ideologies, and an increasingly disconnected, commercialized music scene added to the frustration.

"We played our last show at the Experience Music Project—at MoPOP [Seattle's Museum of Pop Culture]. They have tons of old guitars and shoes and things like that, and it's just like, 'My guitar is in a museum.' Krist Novoselic was backstage with us and one of his basses was in the museum and we were like, 'This is so weird.' Krist was like, 'I should break in and take that.'"

Gary Lee laughs.

It's hard to remember a time before the Seattle grunge scene—before Nirvana and Kurt tore the music world apart—and Gary Lee agrees.

"I separate everything into the Paramount show in 1991, before that and after that," he says.

The impact of that night marked a defining moment in the scene—culturally, and for Nirvana—when their trajectory veered sharply upward, carrying them beyond the band fans had known just weeks earlier. But Kurt remained who he always was: humble and unassuming.

Everyone I spoke to had their own memories of Kurt, their own version of who he was, and their own moments that stood out. I wondered what version of Kurt Gary Lee remembered most, so I asked him my standard question next: What was Kurt like?

Even when talking about Kurt's humility, the topic of drugs is never far away. They were the catalyst for so much of his pain but also the temporary antidote to it. He was a product of his environment—of stomach pain that went untreated for years, of instability, and of limited or inconsistent access to healthcare when he needed it most. He took matters into his own hands—not because drugs were a solution, but because Kurt treated them as a necessity. And the tragedy is that he isn't the only one. There are other ways forward, but when you're in pain and you don't have access to the help you need, it doesn't always feel that way.

"People were pretty much just regular people who do it [play music] because they like to do it," Gary Lee tells me. "And then when we got signed to a major label it was, okay—the big time. The drug thing in the late seventies and early eighties—everyone was on cocaine, but by the time we got in there, it was really frowned upon. The label people, the workers, plenty of the musicians did [drugs], and that just goes along with bands more famous. There are more drugs and alcohol and people enabling you. And you're on a tour bus at shows and you can just get on the bus and you don't have to drive so you can just drink and do drugs. Then harder drugs get involved, and it sort of ruins everything. It destroys the whole creativity process, especially heroin and cocaine, too. I never did either, and I'm really glad I didn't."

Conversations about Kurt, although beautiful, are often laced with the painful consequences of addiction—the circle inescapable, no matter how positive they begin. And it wasn't just the pain he carried while he was alive; it was the pain so many felt that followed in the aftermath of his death. It's impossible to celebrate his life without acknowledging the weight his passing still carries forward.

The topic of copycat suicides comes up—a phenomenon where others take their own lives in the aftermath of high-profile deaths—and I ask Gary Lee what he thinks Kurt would have felt about the possibility.

"If Kurt could come back to life and knew that [copycat suicides exist] . . . it would just horrify him," Gary Lee tells me. "They're not seeing what Kurt really was. They're [kids] seeing his image that's been set up [by the media]. It wasn't like, 'This is cool, I'm gonna kill myself.' It was like, 'I'm in horrible pain, I'm gonna end it.'"

That's the cycle. Someone's pain becomes myth—the "27 Club," the tortured genius—and then it just feeds itself. The same stories, over and over. Kurt was flawed, no question. But if that's all we hold onto, we lose the beauty that was there too. The myth swallows the man.

"The music ended when Kurt died, and what he did when he was alive is what we should celebrate, because it was amazing," Gary Lee says. "I can see how people who got into Nirvana later might not understand why it's so big, but from my perspective, it was like, 'This is so refreshing.' We were part of actual rock history. It was like London in the sixties but instead was Seattle in the early nineties."

Gary Lee reflects on his own experience in the scene.

"Ever since '91, it's been my whole life and, in a lot of ways, has been surreal. We saw the whole major label feeding frenzy. Every band from the eighties and early nineties was getting signed to major labels. The bigger you get, the more money they put into you and the less money you get. It takes time for the money to come in, and I doubt Kurt saw most of the money while he was alive."

Gary Lee then shares a sentiment I know he looks back on fondly.

"Kurt was a fan of the Trees, and he wrote Mark [Lanegan] fan letters," Gary Lee says. It was the kind of thing you or I might have done. "It's weird to think in the context of what he [Kurt] is now."

He was unpretentious and unassuming, yet he went on to become one of the most influential musicians in rock history. But Gary Lee remembers Nirvana before any of that, when the songs were still being created.

"A lot of it [Nirvana's music] was really celebratory, like 'In Bloom' or 'Lithium.' We heard all these songs way before *Nevermind* came out because they'd [Nirvana] been playing them, especially 'Lithium.' The whole 'yeah yeah yeah' thing was just so uplifting. *Bleach* had all this dark stuff, but then it had all these really neat sounds and bright power pop. He [Kurt] definitely had an element of power pop in him. *Bleach* isn't that type of record, but it has a lot of those elements in it. They [Nirvana] didn't get rid of the heaviness, but he started writing more power poppy sort of songs. They didn't want to get popular—it's just what he was writing. I saw 'Sliver' live the first time and I was like, 'This is just really fucking good.'"

Gary Lee quotes a line from "Sliver," one of my favorite Nirvana songs, and I smile.

"They were my favorite band, and it really was so amazing to be around the same time and the same scene as them," he says. "*Screaming Life: A Chronicle of the Seattle Music Scene*—that was like looking at my high school yearbook. It was a warm and fuzzy feeling."

It's incredible to me that Gary Lee considered Nirvana his favorite band. Naturally, I want to know more about what it was like to watch them perform—especially the moments when they refused to play by the rules, like *Top of the Pops*.

"He probably got tons of shit for that, but I imagine, personally, it must have felt really fucking good," Gary Lee says. I couldn't agree more.

At that level of fame, Kurt had the power to do whatever he wanted—to say no, to blow it up, to make it weird. And he did. Which is what makes it so hard to reconcile. You can have the world and still be disappearing inside it.

But conversations about Kurt have a way of moving between the joyful and the heartbreaking. Gary Lee and I briefly discuss what may have led him to take his life.

"It was a combination of one, the drug problem, and two, I don't know if he wanted to do the heavy music. I know him and Lanegan did that Lead Belly stuff together, but you know he obviously had to do more big rock records."

Gary Lee's mind moves the way conversations about Kurt tend to—freely, between grief and admiration. Even the things Kurt couldn't bring himself to buy outlived him.

"He wanted to buy this Lead Belly guitar, and it was $500,000," Gary Lee continues. "He didn't know if he could spend $500,000 on a guitar back in '92 or '93 when he was just [starting out] making a lot of money, but now his guitars are worth that much or more."

Kurt's 1959 Martin D-18E—the acoustic he used to play *MTV Unplugged in New York*—fetched an astounding $6,010,000 in 2020. It's one of the most expensive guitars ever sold at auction, according to *Guitar World*.[91]

As we talk about what Kurt left behind—the guitars, the legacy, the price tags that would have made him cringe—I think back to where so much started: Olympia. The Washington city that defined so much of his story. It was where he found his footing, his sound, and the DIY scene there gave him permission to be exactly who he was.

"His association with the Olympia music scene was really important," Gary Lee says.

He then shares one final sentiment about Kurt, and I've heard it before but find it interesting that everyone says something similar:

"I see it in pictures but, at the time, I never noticed how blue Kurt's eyes were. But maybe he was always looking down." Laughing, he adds, "The whole introverted thing."

What struck me most about Gary Lee was how easy he was to talk to, and how human Kurt sounded from his perspective: not an icon—just a guy who wrote fan mail. Unassuming. A little quiet.

Kurt came up during a time when home lives were complicated and politics felt like something happening to them, not for them. Frustration had nowhere to go and the world wasn't rising to meet them, so they built their own space: a sound, a scene, a place for everyone to exist. And at the heart of it all, Kurt was just looking for somewhere to belong.

Gary Lee suggested I reach out to Kurt Danielson next—his labelmate on Sub Pop and another voice from the same Pacific Northwest scene that changed everything.

★★★

I want to take a moment to acknowledge the passing of bandmates Mark Lanegan and Van Conner (also Gary Lee's brother). Their musical contributions were prolific and revolutionary, and they won't ever be forgotten.

Chapter 18

"PAPER CUTS"

Kurt Danielson

KURT DANIELSON WAS THE NEXT NATURAL PERSON TO SPEAK WITH—not just because TAD helped shape the Seattle sound, but because he experienced Nirvana before fame flattened Kurt into a monolith instead of a human being. During their early European tour together, the bands were packed into cramped vans, surviving everything from puke buckets to the uncertainty of what came next in their careers. What no one could predict was the immortalized figure Kurt would later become. Looking back now, memories that once carried excitement for the future became enmeshed with something heavier.

Danielson is genuine, humble, and remarkably perceptive; he possesses the ability to analyze people with a clarity that makes his perspective different from anyone else's. Through his eyes, Cobain isn't an icon or a headline but a deeply complicated person whose struggles were more universal than people want to admit. What he shares isn't always easy to stomach, but it's necessary.[92]

***

"TAD got together in late '88, early '89, and we recorded our first record in the summer of '88," Kurt Danielson begins. "It came out in '89, and we toured the States, and then we got booked for a tour in Europe and Sub Pop decided that it would be best if they sent two bands over there, so they chose Nirvana and us. That was our first tour together, and after that, we toured in the States a bunch as well. This was before Nirvana was famous. They were promoting *Bleach* and *Blew*, an EP that came out after *Bleach*, and we were promoting *God's Balls*—our first record—and *Salt Lick*. So, neither band was very well known, and we got to know each other really well because we were thrown together a lot. We toured in a tiny van throughout Europe. Both bands, all of our gear, all of our luggage and merchandise, all crammed into one small van along with our sound man and our road manager and, in circumstances like that, you get to know someone fairly well.

"On the other hand, I'm not really sure how well I knew Kurt. At the time, I thought I knew him pretty well, but in retrospect, I'm not sure how well I knew him. He was the kind of person who could be many different people. He had a multifaceted personality. To one person, he could be everything that person was looking for; that's what they saw. And to the next person, he could be something completely different, depending on what that other person was projecting or needing to project. And that was one of his gifts. He was someone for everyone, almost, if that makes any sense."

"Yes, it does." Cobain had a way of becoming whatever the moment required, something Danielson had seen up close. He could read people, often showing them a side of himself that best fit each conversation.

"He had a great sense of humor," Danielson continues. "A dark sense of humor. And I don't know . . . when a person becomes as famous as Kurt became, he gets mythologized, and his humanity gets sheared away to some degree by the process of mythologizing."

Fame reduced him to something far less human than the person his friends actually knew. Before Danielson continues, I note that Cobain was a son, father, husband, friend—and reiterate that he was, in many ways, a chameleon.

"This happens to anybody that reaches that level of fame," Danielson explains. "They become this sort of legendary figure—one-dimensional, monolithic, without any nuance or dimension to him—whereas real people have a lot of different dimensions. Like you said, they are someone's brother, husband, friend, relative, whatever. They play many different roles. And this is true of anybody. But when a person reaches that level of fame, it's almost as if they lose the right to be a human being and become this one-dimensional figure. I ran into this problem before, when discussing Kurt and the complexities of his character. People oftentimes push back and say, 'No, that's not what he was like . . . he wasn't like that.' I'm not going to give you specific examples, because they upset too many people."

In the process of writing this book, I've experienced that pushback myself—people challenging the memories of those who actually lived beside him.

Danielson continues, "Like you said, he was a chameleon. He could be different things to different people. He was highly creative. Always in the process of working on his art. Everything that he saw, did, and experienced was fodder for that art. And he was like a magpie. He collected bright things—bright objects, bright images, phrases, ideas—and when it came time to write the lyrics for a song, which he did last, he had the melody and the guitar line, and then he would come up with the vocal line. But he had no words until he came up with some in order to record them. And that's when he would plug in all these different ideas that he'd been collecting.

"It was a fascinating process to watch him work on and to discuss with him on the road. We had a lot of downtime; it was unbelievably boring. There are ample opportunities to chat when you're thrown together like that, and we did talk a lot. But we used to joke around a lot, and I really enjoyed his sense of humor. And we would talk about . . . He was from a small town . . .and I'm from a small town as well, a town called Stanwood. So we had similar experiences and similar backgrounds. Both towns had characters living in them, and most small towns do have a lot of eccentric, freaky kinds of people. The kind of people who buy booze for minors. We shared a lot of those experiences . . . I mean, the main thing is that, despite his tragic passing and his addictions and whatnot, he was an extremely intelligent, very creative, empathetic kind of individual. Very rare in my experience. I think, when I met him, I had the feeling that I already knew him, because he had this ability to project onto you what he thought you wanted to see, and he was very skilled at that. It was one of his many gifts."

"Like he knew how to put people at ease?" I ask.

"Yeah," Danielson says. "He did, but I realized later that it wasn't that he was who I thought he was, or that there was a kinship between us, or anything like that. It was more like he read me and others very quickly and accurately. He knew what they were expecting. Knew what they wanted to . . . how they wanted to bounce off you. So it seemed one way, but it was actually another, and it's hard to explain. I don't have much experience with people like that, except for him. When we would be on the road together, you get to know pretty well about their circumstances, their goals, their interests, their tastes, things like that. But as far as the real Kurt underneath all of that, it was very hard to find, and well hidden, out of a desire to protect himself. That part of him took a longer time to find and to know, and you never really knew if you were at the bottom of it, if you ever found the real person. In fact, maybe there was more than one real person; maybe there were many. Hard to say."

Self-preservation was key for Cobain, and adapting to whoever stood in front of him may have been the only way he ever felt remotely comfortable. I knew going into this project that my role was to uncover the real Kurt Cobain—not to project who I *thought* he was.

It was the same with Walter. He was funny, charismatic, and happy on the surface, and then one day, he was gone. I don't think Walter was ever anything besides himself in different situations, but it still goes to show that people can outwardly project one version of themselves and inwardly feel completely different.

Danielson and I couldn't ignore the reason this book exists: suicide and its aftermath, the profound impact it leaves on the people who remain. I told him about Walter.

"You can't blame yourself," Danielson begins. "It's like when a person reaches that point where there's a chemical imbalance in the brain, they are no longer themselves, and there's nothing you could have done. If they want help, then they can go out and get it. You can't help them; they can only help themselves. And the other thing is, there's no way to second-guess them. There's no way you could have intervened and saved him. He was on his path. He was motivated by what he was motivated by. It was what it was. It's a mysterious thing, but I've been through this numerous times with friends who were going through depression or were addicts or, for whatever reason, it was time to go, and Kurt is one of those people. Chris Cornell is another. I just know that when it came to that point, they weren't themselves. They weren't a rational person. They weren't someone who was thinking straight. They were working through serious problems, emotionally unbalanced. And their brain chemistry was not healthy. And you can't imagine what it's like to be in that spot. And they couldn't have explained it to you anyway. And even if they did, what could you have done? You would have tried, and you might have felt better for trying, but you couldn't have done anything."

Danielson's words settled heavily, pulling Walter to the front of my mind. Everything he said was heavy but necessary. When I think of Walter, and his death threatens to eclipse his life, I find myself trying to reach the part of him defined by compassion, not by catastrophe, and that felt like that was the most sensible approach with Kurt Cobain, too. I understood what Danielson was trying to say about not blaming yourself. With Walter, I didn't see obvious signs. On the surface, he seemed okay. But that doesn't mean society couldn't have done more. Walter was a Veteran, and mental healthcare should have been effortless for him to access. Healthcare is a right, not a privilege. This is why we need to do better removing the stigma surrounding suicide and making mental health resources accessible to people who are struggling, even when their pain isn't immediately visible.

"Kurt [Cobain] seemed very . . . just from the videos I've seen, the interviews, he seemed like a very gentle, kind person, who really would have gone out of his way for others," I say. "I think it's . . . I was watching Cow Palace, and . . . Nirvana raised $60,000 for Bosnian rape victims. Kurt seemed like a very vocal person who stood for equal rights, and I think that's really amazing."

"That's all true," Danielson agrees. "He was all those things, and I always admired that about him as well. The other guys in the band, also . . . Krist and Dave . . . and Kurt had a social conscience and acted on it. At the same time, Kurt in particular was a complicated person, and although it's true that he felt for others and he championed the downtrodden and marginalized, he was also sort of a deeply wounded person and had been since childhood. . . . As he grew older, he went through puberty, and like a lot of people, he learned to hate himself and blamed himself for things. When things . . . I don't presume to know what happened, but I know that he was having problems in his relationship with his wife, and there are all kinds of stories circulating around about that. I don't want to get into that."

"No, no, no, that's fine," I say. I don't press him. Some topics aren't mine to excavate, and part of writing this book is knowing when to honor those boundaries. The point isn't to rehash tabloid debris—it's to celebrate a remarkable life, not reopen old wounds.

"I believe that he blamed himself for certain problems," Danielson says. "His addictions. And then if he was facing a big decision like divorce, or not divorce, that would have conjured up all of the betrayal and guilt that he had from his parents' breakup, and that would have made him feel like he was doing to his daughter what his parents did to him, and you can imagine the kind of conflict that would create. A fatal conflict, in fact. He just did not compute. He did not permit himself to go there, where he had been forced to go as a child.

"And also, addiction is a very difficult position to be in, especially when it's heroin, because the withdrawals are so profound and recovery takes such a long time—and a lot of effort—and you need a lot of support for that. He was in such a lonely place, having been put on a pedestal by his fans, plus he didn't know where to turn. And in public, you feel like you're judged all the time, and he just felt like he was so alone and without resources, and then there was all this hatred and guilt churning about him. And that's kind of where he was when the endgame finally came down. You can imagine how complicated that would be, how lonely he must have been. How driven by these violent and very negative emotions. There's no worse feeling than going through the withdrawal syndrome because you no longer have the ability to feel pleasure of any kind. You are completely outside that. Talk about depression. It's the most profound depression there is. Having been through it myself, I know. I can tell you that there are times when you are going through that where if you had access to a gun, you would gladly use it because it's too terrible to endure. That does happen from time to time. I believe that was where Kurt was at. If he would have held on, he would have gotten through it. His brain chemistry would eventually have shifted. But he was young; he was impulsive. He was looking for a solution. He couldn't find one. Nothing was simple. Nothing was easy. He's a very sensitive person, and maybe that kind of pressure and fame was not healthy for him."

His words were gutting—because of how human they were. The belief that "if he would have held on, he would have gotten through it" is something I've felt for years about Walter. No one is beyond repair.

"The paradox at the heart of Kurt Cobain is that there's nothing more human than a junkie," Danielson continues. "Because there's no one more frail and vulnerable—whereas a person at the high level of fame he achieved loses the right to be human due to the mythologizing process. This contradiction—and Kurt embodied many—trapped him in an impossible position."

Danielson's words affected me deeply. Kurt Cobain's passing was thirty years ago, yet the people who knew him still have to revisit that loss every time his name comes up. By that point, I felt we had said what needed to be said about Kurt's final days. It was hard on both of us. The conversation mattered, and I do believe this book can help people, but there comes a point where asking someone to walk back through painful memories stops feeling productive. So I knew when to stop asking questions. It's the same respect my family asked for Walter.

A person's life should not be reduced to their final moments, and I was determined to remind others of Cobain's light and the best parts of how he lived his life. I wasn't negating the bad—I was just finding the good, something that doesn't get enough space on the page, and I refuse to let that part disappear.

Cobain's pain was often witnessed by artists outside of Nirvana's "inner circle." To paint a full portrait and show his far-reaching impact, I felt it was important to speak with those who experienced him from different vantage points. This includes those who knew him best and those who witnessed his struggle—and those who were merely inspired from afar. Otherwise, you're missing the bigger picture of Kurt's influence on the greater music community and beyond. And because my goal has always been to understand Kurt Cobain by examining his place in music history, I knew where to go next.

Chapter 19

"DRAIN YOU"

Jimmy Drescher

KURT'S LOVE FOR PUNK WAS UNDENIABLE, BUT I KNEW I NEEDED TO connect with someone outside of the Seattle music scene. What did Kurt look like to someone observing peripherally?

Hailing from New York City, Murphy's Law is a pivotal part of the punk rock scene. The band is fronted by Jimmy Drescher, who has been entrenched in that world for decades and has seen it all—Nirvana included.[93] His candor and brutal honesty highlight what others might miss or simply shy away from saying themselves. It didn't matter if he briefly crossed paths with Nirvana or watched everything happen from across the country; Jimmy has his own insight. Kurt was undeniably punk rock himself, so I was curious to talk about him with someone still deeply embedded in that culture.

★★★

"I did know Dave Grohl from when he played in the band Scream, which is a Washington, DC, hardcore band," Jimmy begins. "And then, of course, he went on to Nirvana and now to the Foo Fighters. I saw Nirvana play—I believe it was San Diego with Pearl Jam and it might have been Stone Temple Pilots. One of my friends worked with Sony, and he took me out there to see one of the concerts, and that's when I actually met him [Kurt]. It was just a brief meeting. Another time I saw them [Nirvana] was here in New York City at Roseland. It was a big dance hall place; it should have been a landmark, but they tore it down. They were great, and the band was great. There was nothing weird that happened at the show—the band performed. It wasn't like one of the shows where they smash everything. They were a professional band and played, and the place was packed, and everyone had a great time.

"He was having fun with music, and then it became popular, and then it became super popular, and you have people who start taking over your career. I don't think he ever planned on it becoming a career, so he was overwhelmed. He was overwhelmed with life as it was, it seemed—from the things I've seen and read about him. So to become such a famous person where you can't even walk out your door without people waiting outside to take photos of you and interfere with your life . . . or you're trying to get your own head together . . . I'm sure it was affecting him greatly. Some people bask in fame—I think he was very uncomfortable with it."

"Why didn't Kurt just quit the industry?"

"Why didn't he just quit dope?" Jimmy is thoughtful, serious. "It's not that easy when you get caught up in something. You get entrapped into a situation, and you're uncomfortable in your own skin as it is, so it's hard to escape that. . . . And you can just help a person so much—you can't save a person from themselves. It's inside the head, and all the money in the world obviously can't save a person from what's going on in their head. That's why he got into the opiates, I believe to escape everything. If you've ever been under anesthesia, you're not thinking about problems when you're under anesthesia. And he was pretty much putting himself under to get away from everything."

Jimmy elaborates on his own experience in his band and contrasts his experience against Kurt's.

"I've been in my band for forty years," he says. "I started as a kid running away from home to go to the Lower East Side to get away from my parents, and here's this form of music which nobody knew about, which is punk rock. I mean, people knew about it, but it was a very underground culture at the time. There wasn't the rapid gratification of trying to find out stuff as we do on the internet and our phones—the way the media is instantaneous now and also manipulated. So I wound up in the [punk rock] culture with a group of kids that came from broken homes, and we started to make music, and it took off. And then the music took us to Europe and took us to Japan and continued to grow to the point where I finally got to go on tour with the Beastie Boys and did the Licensed to Ill tour with them. And then we toured with the Red Hot Chili Peppers, toured with the Ramones, you know—it took me to greater places than I ever could have expected. There are people that are completely destitute, and there are people that are insanely rich and have the same void in their life. No matter how broke or rich you are, if you have an emptiness inside of you, there's nothing that's gonna fill it. And that's what Kurt was."

Jimmy's point wasn't really about fame or money. To him, Kurt's struggle was internal and no amount of success would fix it. He couldn't—wouldn't—have quit. Music defined him. It was how he experienced and interpreted the world, even when that world tried to commoditize his pain. He cared about others, too. He had more than bandmates counting on him—Nirvana employed people. Fans depended on him. Walking away wasn't just stepping out of a band; it meant stepping out of a movement—an era he helped create.

Who was he without music, without Nirvana?

Maybe that's why music wasn't just a career to Kurt. It was his identity and an escape. It also offered a sense of community, all tangled together.

"Kurt loved punk music," I say, and Jimmy laughs.

"He *was* punk music," Jimmy says. "When we were on tour in California—in Los Angeles—that's when 'Smells Like Teen Spirit' came out. And I remember being with my guitar player, Todd Youth, watching TV in the hotel and the video came on. (Sadly, Todd is no longer with us and struggled with opiate addiction.) But as we watched 'Smells Like Teen Spirit,' it was the first time I saw kids dancing and moshing and jumping on each other. One of them had a Bad Brains shirt on. Bad Brains is one of the bands that came from Washington, DC, to New York and helped found a lot of what goes on here now with our hardcore punk culture."

For Jimmy, this wasn't just MTV playing a hit song. It was the moment punk culture—something raw, underground, and deeply personal—entered millions of homes. But for Kurt, that transition to the mainstream came at a cost. He valued honesty above all else, and the pressure to become a corporate product must have felt deeply alienating.

As we keep talking, the conversation shifts to how Kurt used humor to cut through the absurdity of the music industry onstage—still finding ways to have a good time despite everything he was battling behind the scenes.

"Yeah, he was definitely having fun with most of the music he wrote," Jimmy says. "It didn't come off as depressing, a lot of the songs. But I don't think becoming famous was helping him at all. The people around you also reflect on how you behave."

"The general population—with a famous person—wants to focus on the persona that's put before them by the industry, not by looking deep into the person themselves," Jimmy explains. "The smoke-and-mirrors effect, really. They throw you up there and they make you smile, they put makeup on you, and then you go home and you're alone and suicidal. Once that hotel room door closes, you're alone. And I'm sure he was alone a lot."

But Jimmy isn't just focused on who Kurt was when he was alone with himself. He also thinks about the people around him and the role he played in their lives.

"He was absolutely a nice person. Look at him with his daughter. Look at all the pictures. The whole deal is sad; the whole thing is sad with this guy. But there's so much left to celebrate. You think about the people who left nothing and felt useless and took their lives. At least he left something. He left a talented, beautiful daughter; he left a legacy of great music that influenced so many other musicians. Then you get the guy that's a janitor in a bar and he's got nothing. That's the person where it's really sad. Kurt lived a life already. Unfortunately, he took it and had so much more to live, but he lived more than many people live their entire lives in a small microcosm."

Jimmy keeps returning to the same idea: Kurt never felt manufactured to him.

"His nonchalant, carefree way of handling his popularity, the rawness of his music, the accessibility of his music and him and the band, 'cause the first show they played, they were just playing to their friends. And then they just kept making more friends, 'cause that's how it goes. He was just very approachable. He's me and you. He definitely wasn't phony. He was putting his emotions right there up on stage.

"I have people that saw my band play, and I was the first band they ever saw. Now they're bringing their kids to their first shows. So I drag the kid on stage and do a song with them, or if their kid learns to play one of our songs, I pull them up on stage. It's more of a family thing where I'm going to see old friends. I'm lucky enough to have so many friends as opposed to the impersonal view of a bigger band where you can't even step out from backstage. I at least can walk through the crowd and hug people and be at one with my friends and family."

But Kurt was part of the rare "can't even step out from backstage" menagerie Jimmy spoke of, and he amassed an extraordinary level of fame that was more than he could carry. All eyes were on him, his every move analyzed and dissected. To some, this was simply the byproduct of fame—something he signed up for. But that didn't mean he deserved to lose his privacy, and it certainly didn't mean he deserved to lose his humanity.

As Kurt involuntarily wove himself into the hearts and minds of millions, however, there was simply no way to disentangle himself from the mythos. Among those millions were legions of musicians

Kurt inspired—even posthumously—to pick up instruments and make a difference in the world.

Just as Kurt championed the bands he loved, I wanted to highlight emerging and independent artists—musicians carving out their own factions, people with something real to say and a deep respect for Kurt and the world around them. So I sought out the stories not covered in *Rolling Stone*, but the ones carrying the same DIY spirit and sincerity Kurt always admired in underground music, and aimed to amplify them.

Chapter 20

"POLLY"

Darrin Walters and Michelangelo Iansito

TODAY'S MOST ESTABLISHED MUSICIANS PERFORM NIRVANA SONGS WITH great aplomb, sometimes dressed in looks evocative of Kurt's signature floral-and-thrift-store aesthetic—proof that the band transcends time, space, and genre, their message still vital. Well-known musical acts from diverse genres have covered Nirvana, from The Polyphonic Spree to Post Malone and Tori Amos, each putting their own spin on the band's most iconic tracks.

But it's not just established musicians who feel his impact. Indie artists picked up instruments because of Kurt, hoping to enact the same kind of societal change he set out to accomplish more than three decades ago. Some of these artists have endured deep traumas; Nirvana—and specifically Kurt—became their unwavering beacon while they navigated their own tribulations.

Kurt colored outside the lines, embodying the authenticity of an underground, word-of-mouth, cult rebellion—a cultural independence he showed by supporting the bands he knew deserved attention, particularly bands that hadn't yet gained widespread recognition. In that spirit, I wanted to write outside the margins myself, honoring him in a way I think he would appreciate in a book celebrating his life and work. So I reached out to some indie musicians to hear their stories, and many shared how Kurt had inspired their love of music.

One of these musicians is Darrin Walters, also known as Walters Fall, a Canadian singer and songwriter. While checking out new music for various culture magazines I write for, I came across Darrin's work and was immediately drawn to his stance against domestic violence. He's been recognized by the International Singer-Songwriters Association, receiving award nominations for International Male Songwriter, International Male Rising Star, and International Male Emerging Artist. Staying true to his DIY roots, Darrin's candid approach to topics such as domestic abuse and misogyny is evident in his work, all while spearheading a music program for disadvantaged children.

"I want to keep Kurt's flame burning," Darrin tells me. "I feel like the media had their own agenda, and they were trying to push Kurt to a certain point—what they wanted him to be. They were almost trying to mold him into what they wanted their stories to be."[94]

"What do you think people wanted from him?" I ask.

"I think most people just wanted to profit from him. And I think that's the bottom line of it. People just wanted to profit from him. They thought they could push him around because they thought he was a mindless drug addict."

"Just another cog in the wheel," I say. "I don't think he cared what people thought about him, and if he saw some sort of injustice somewhere going on, he was going to say something."

"I think that was probably just who he was," Darrin says. "Once Kurt got famous, he thought, 'Wow, I can use this to make things better, maybe to just get some voices heard.'"

When breaking into the industry, the trials musicians often face are why organizations like MusiCares exist. These services offer mental health services, help with addiction and recovery, medical assistance, and support with basic living expenses. Many musicians know what it is to be unhoused or financially unstable, and they're not alone in these hardships. But still, they persevere, just like Kurt.

"I guess when it comes to persevering, musicians—I feel—are really well-adapted to that. I was homeless myself two years ago," Darrin tells me. "I was homeless for a good year. The only thing that I didn't sell—to get myself going again—was my guitar. And then I finally became housed and worked my way back up to where I am now. It's always been in the back of my mind that your choices . . . my choices really affect if I'm going to have a place to live tomorrow, or if I'm *not* going to have a place to live tomorrow. Or maybe you find a job you weren't planning on taking. You've got to fund the dream somehow."

Darrin's honesty—and the way he channels hardship into helping others—made me wonder how he believes Kurt would want to be remembered.

"I think that he would like people to remember the good things that he did, and how he helped the marginalized," Darrin says. "It kind of reminds me of what's going on now with opiates here [Canada]. My town has 2,500 people. I'm surrounded by towns that are maybe 20,000. There are ten to twenty people per week dying through the opiate crisis here. The healthcare system again—they've cut these people off from opiates after they had given them to them, and now there's no help for them. There's no weaning them off them."

Darrin's concerns reflect a much larger crisis. In Canada, there were 42,494 reported deaths between January 2016 and September 2023, just for poisonings connected to opioids.[95] In the US in 2022, there were almost 108,000 drug-involved overdose deaths, from both prescription and illegal drugs.[96]

"I just wrote a song two months ago," Darrin continues. "I wrote it with Kurt in my mind. It's called 'Addicted to the Dinosaur.' Dinosaur is another word for heroin. It's just a song about addiction, from the beginning to the end of somebody's battle."

Darrin's compassion extends beyond his songwriting. He and his family focus on charitable efforts—one of the things that initially caught my attention about his work.

"I run a charity with my wife: the Guitars for Kids program. We take kids that are in vulnerable situations, maybe abusive homes and stuff like that, and we create a list and we get instruments donated. Drums, guitars, whatever they need. And we give these instruments out to these kids that are in rough situations, and we try to provide them lessons afterward as well."

I think Kurt would have liked that.

"This all sounds wonderful, and it's amazing to think that Kurt influenced you and inspired you in so many ways," I say. "And how you write these songs that shine a light on people in abusive situations."

"You know, I feel like they don't have a voice as loud as mine is at this moment in time," Darrin explains. "So I'll use my voice for them. I'd just like to say that everybody should remember Kurt was a champion for people. Let's remember him as the champion he was. Keep his name going. Keep his music strong. Celebration instead of mourning. Keep him alive through music. I wouldn't have written music at all if it wasn't for him. I wouldn't be involved in music whatsoever. Everything I'm doing, it's all in his name. Do one thing in Kurt's image. Help somebody out. Do something. Donate some food to the food pantry. Bring a can of something, anything. Feed a homeless guy."

In that same spirit, it felt right to put this book's earnings toward the kinds of communities Kurt came from—the people who know hunger and instability the way he once did. I used my initial royalty check from the first edition to buy food for the Aberdeen Food Bank, and Aaron Burckhard delivered it with Curtis Van Roland Thorfinson from the Tangerine Tree. I also donated the profits from a virtual writing workshop to Camp Victory in Aberdeen, which offers free summer camp to children who are survivors of sexual abuse. It wasn't about grand gestures or to pat myself on the back; it was simply a way for the book to reach back toward the version of Kurt who had once gone without—the kid who needed help long before the world ever knew his name.

Inspired by Darrin's story, I thought about other ways Kurt's influence continues to ripple through the lives of musicians. While having some work done on my guitar—a replica of Kurt's "Vandalism" Strat—I met a musician who goes by the name "The Color Pink." His real name is Michelangelo Iansito. I asked him, on a whim, without mentioning my project, whether Kurt Cobain had influenced him at all. To my surprise, Michelangelo's answer was enthusiastic, describing the Nirvana frontman as pivotal to his budding music career.[97]

Like Kurt, Michelangelo has a strong social conscience. He told me his music, which he's been self-releasing since 2020, "subtly critiques the disillusionment inherent in American culture."

I asked him how he first came to music—and to Kurt.

"I became a musician out of exposure and mental necessity," Michelangelo tells me. "I grew up in a very old-school Italian household with my grandparents. Grandpa smoked, drank, and sang opera, while Grandma cooked and yelled from the other room. But it was happy and music was everywhere. As I got older, these get-togethers were happening less and less. I think this feeling of loss and not fitting in at all socially because of my upbringing made me feel like I was all alone for a long time and is something I still deal with. I write, play, and record everything myself in my basement, and I think my music attempts to speak to/about social issues that I'm passionate about, love, and just anything I'm feeling, really. I think loneliness is a theme that pervades through my work a bit.

"I felt and still feel like an outsider in school and just about everywhere else. Whatever morals my family had instilled in me didn't seem to match up with the world around me. I think this is something that Kurt must have felt at all times. The feeling of nobody around you understanding why you do what you do is an incredibly isolating experience. My loneliness eventually gave way to boredom, which began my true fascination with music. I started to learn how to play the drums as a teenager and found I could put all my rage, anger, fear, hate, and feelings into playing. I don't think I even understood that I had anxiety or depression or whatever when I was a teen; it just felt cathartic to play. Writing words and poetry was just a logical next step for me. I always drew and wrote stories; now I had a vessel for all that.

It took me a long time to be able to be 'comfortable' enough to put it out there, but here we are."

"What about Kurt or Nirvana speaks to you?" I ask, wanting to understand where that connection began.

Michelangelo offers up a thoughtful response. "I think I resonate with Nirvana—and Kurt specifically—because it feels like a stripped-back, raw, authentic expression of feelings. I especially love their live 1991 Paramount show because it's just three guys playing their guts out, and with barely any equipment. Kurt wasn't afraid to let himself explode on stage. It looks like he feels what he is playing. I think if most people had the chance to take the stage and let their anger and frustration and sadness out, it would look like Kurt flailing with his guitar.

"I think Kurt's words—or sometimes lack thereof—take center stage with his music. They have something to say not only as words but through his delivery. He's not afraid to sound gravelly or out of tune. He can be angry and sad in the same sentence. That's just a perfect mirror of life."

As we talk, the subject turns to mental health and suicide prevention—work that has now become central to my life since Walter's passing.

"I think Kurt was heavily tuned into life and the world around him," Michelangelo begins. "I think that's probably why he used drugs and struggled. America, for being the land of the free and so rich, has its fair share of problems. Mental health is a big one, and I can attest to this dealing with many things myself. I was in therapy for years dealing with depressive thoughts and episodes. You have to have a massive amount of empathy to be able to support and understand people who are going through something you're not. I'm sure he took on a lot of others' pain without realizing it himself. Panic attacks can feel like you're dying, and when the world around you feels indifferent, it can feel hard to go on. I have had close friends commit suicide, and it is one of the most confusing, painful tragedies for someone to deal with.

"Music has become one of the ways I deal with the world, the craziness of everyday life. The craziness of this country. Writing music and performing is how I connect with the people around me and show them how I truly feel. I think this is why I resonate with Kurt, because I think he was doing the same thing. Kurt said what he felt and put it in song. He wasn't afraid to critique social structures or poke fun at our terrible nature. We should all be allowed to say what we want to say and what we feel. Kurt and Nirvana as a whole gave the uninteresting, the uninterested, the vagabonds, and the outcasts a voice."

Kurt's music wasn't about spectacle—it was about inclusion, about giving people a place to feel seen when they couldn't find it anywhere else.

As Phil Barbetta, lead singer of the New Jersey band Corevalay, put it: "I think that music can sometimes be the only way to say something; and I think everyone deserves a chance to be seen and heard."

Kurt's legacy is still growing, shaping artists in ways I believe he would have welcomed. In Darrin and Michelangelo, I saw that connection still working in real time—personal and deeply lived.

But my research was far from over. I wanted to connect with more artists to see how Kurt continued to echo through their work and their lives.

I reached out to Stephanie Phillips from Big Joanie, a UK-based Black feminist punk band. The group has garnered widespread acclaim, praised in outlets like *Pitchfork*, *Rolling Stone*, *NPR*, *The Guardian*, and *The New Yorker.* Today's indie scene is shaped in part by Big Joanie's politically charged music and bold stage presence; although their sound is completely their own, they continue to embody the DIY mentality Kurt championed.

Chapter 21

"ABOUT A GIRL"

Stephanie Phillips

KURT HAD ZERO TOLERANCE FOR ANYONE BEING TREATED LIKE LESS than human—sexism, homophobia, racism, it didn't matter. He couldn't stand injustice in any form. As much as I needed to discuss the foundations of Nirvana with those who were there, I knew I also had to talk to women who've been on the front lines of the music scene. Big Joanie is known for their fierce, unapologetic music, carrying forward not only a legacy Kurt set in motion decades ago but also embodying the very reason he fought for inclusion.

Composed of Stephanie Phillips (guitar and vocals) and Estella Adeyeri (bass guitar and vocals), their work reminded me why he gravitated toward challenging the status quo—so much so, I think Kurt would have worn one of their shirts on stage. Stephanie and I find time to talk, and her perspective shows just how far-reaching Kurt's influence was—from the haunting backdrop of the Pacific Northwest to the vibrant music scene in the UK.[98]

"I think it's a really interesting fact about Kurt and about the band, that they came of age in this era where there was this little bubble and pocket of feminism and left-wing activism that was kind of making its mark in music," Stephanie begins. "You know, a lot of the music scene in the early nineties could be incredibly sexist and gendered, but he was very influenced by that kind of early Riot Grrrl scene that was going on. They kind of felt comfortable to say that, obviously, sexism is bad, but also that we should be working on doing something towards it. I think that it should be the basic line for most male musicians, that they could not only state that these things are wrong but maybe they try and do something about it and play with other women in bands and promote the women in bands, which I know Nirvana did as well."

Stephanie's response reinforced what I'd been circling throughout this experience. Nothing about Kurt or his allyships was performative. He amplified and stood beside those he believed in, especially when certain scenes excluded women by default. At a time when that was rare, his words—and actions—rang out.

Stephanie tells me, "It wasn't until I went to uni and started getting into different things that I listened more to Nirvana beyond 'Smells Like Teen Spirit.' And, yeah—I was just so taken aback with how pop-centric and different and unusual they were, that you could kind of meld a very glossy pop sensibility—in terms of the lyrics and the melody and the catchiness of it—with this almost harsh industrial gritty sound that was kind of the earth and the bed for it. And I just thought it was endlessly, you know, endlessly entertaining and [I] should delve into it. I think a lot of people compare Nirvana and those kinds of lyrics and song structures to The Beatles, which can seem far removed. But it does make a lot of sense; they get to the point very quickly, and their songs are usually quite short. And they are kind of pop songs, but they're just like *[laughs]*—"

"They are. They're catchy," I say. And that accessibility mattered. Nirvana didn't just reach kids who already lived inside underground music; they reached listeners from the far corners of the earth. Their melodic quality certainly didn't hurt, but it was the infectious pull of their sound that ensnared even those who missed the symbolism behind the songs. And it's still happening today, with Nirvana's albums continuing to gain additional accolades. According to the Recording Industry Association of America, *MTV Unplugged in New York*, released on November 1, 1994, was certified 8x Platinum on February 24, 2020, just four days after Kurt's fifty-third birthday.[99]

So I ask Stephanie why she thinks Kurt is such a cult phenomenon to this day.

"I think it's the same with a lot of cult figures where he reached the end of his story—and it was an interesting story, the same way with Jimi Hendrix and Amy Winehouse," Stephanie tells me. "They lived difficult lives, and there's kind of a lot for people to go back and look at morbidly, you know? You look at any interview with Dave Grohl or Krist, and in every single interview the interviewer asks about Kurt or his death. So the people around him are always kind of trapped in that moment when it first happened and are just perpetually suspended in that grief.

"This is very odd because it's all for someone else's entertainment and, I mean, I think the music is obviously amazing; it really defined the era. It was some of the best grunge music that came out. There were some amazing bands, and there were some not-so-amazing bands from the grunge era, but it was kind of perfect for the time. It really explains a kind of slacker [mentality] and how teenagers felt at that time and how teenagers still feel now. But in terms of Kurt specifically, there's so much in our obsession with it [his suicide]—it reflects the best and worst of our society, at all times."

There is a relentless romanticism surrounding Kurt's death. But when speaking to those who knew Kurt or felt his presence, his depression wasn't at the helm of our conversations. Yes, we discussed his struggles and demons—often through the lens of universality—but they didn't define him or shape how people remembered him. He was flawed but still a good person: deeply human, and someone people genuinely loved. Rather than dwelling on his suicide, we should focus on preventing similar tragedies in the future. His music touched countless lives—and still does.

"I always connected with music; it always helped me process things, and it was just something I wanted to understand fully, inside and out," Stephanie says. "That's why I've been involved in so many different aspects of it—music journalism and I've started bands as well. It's just always been a lifelong obsession of trying to understand music, really, but there are so many influences from X-Ray Spex—they became a big influence—along with Bikini Kill and PJ Harvey and definitely Nirvana, as well. Even though we didn't really mean to—I didn't really mean to—but people have said that a few of our songs sound like Nirvana. His impact is so wide and was so vast, it's kind of hard to imagine [it's been thirty years]."

Stephanie's story made everything we spoke about come full circle. Women in music never needed permission to create boldly, honestly, and unapologetically, but it still mattered that Kurt used his voice to stand beside them.

Chapter 22

"SMELLS LIKE TEEN SPIRIT"

Chris Enriquez

Spotlights is a post-metal band hailing from New York with a raw and imaginative sound, and their tether to Kurt is felt through drummer Chris Enriquez, who credits Kurt's overarching message with shaping his path as a musician. When I saw that Spotlights toured with the Melvins for Geek Show 2023 and learned that their drummer, Chris Enriquez, was tremendously affected by Kurt, I reached out to see if he'd be up for an interview. I wanted to keep exploring Kurt's impact beyond traditional oral histories—which rightly focus on those who were there, but may not focus on the legacy, the domino effect, and how his influence continues to move outward.

Chris and I connected to explore influence and legacy, our conversation opening with feminism as a natural continuation from where I left things with Stephanie.[100]

★★★

"[He was] a feminist as well," Chris says about Kurt without hesitation. "And he was also the first—you could call him a pop icon, probably like the first male, when there weren't too many males who were doing that aside from Freddie Mercury. But you couldn't even compare the two, because he was also coming up in a time where it was a little bit even more taboo than it was in the nineties, where people were starting to come out, and the New York drag scene was sort of becoming more prominent. So his timing and the fact that he was coming from punk rock but could also be heavy—like if you were into metal—was really special for someone like me, getting picked on every day and called, you know, the 'F' word. You know, that kind of stuff. So it was very refreshing and surprising.

". . . I was also at the Rock and Roll Hall of Fame when Nirvana was inducted," Chris continues. "We were also at the after party when they [the remaining members of Nirvana] played with different singers, and I watched Michael Stipe's speech that he gave. It was beautiful when he said something to the effect of this being for all the goths and all the fags and for all the rejects. But you get my point. He was really speaking to people like me and my friends who found salvation not only in his [Kurt's] music but in what he stood for in the way that he conducted himself in interviews.

"He spoke about more than music; just him showing up on stage as a man in a dress, you know, was incredible . . . And he and Krist Novoselic both identifying as heterosexual males but then making out with tongue on television, just to make a point . . . And while that was happening, my friends and I in grade school were kind of imitating this kind of practice in front of football players that were throwing shit at us or calling us names. We would be like, 'Oh, yeah, well, we *are* fags,' when we weren't. We just did it for the sheer shock value, and the kind of, 'Fuck you, maybe we are. Maybe I *do* want to hook up with you guys.' That was something that we took from the philosophy of how Kurt kind of—how Nirvana embodied punk rock.

"Nirvana was incredibly prolific in changing culture. And I feel like today's youth—and what we're seeing that's progressive—absolutely wouldn't be the way that it is without Cobain being one of the first people in the mainstream to portray these sorts of ideas. . . . Kurt knew how to say things and be sensitive to any side of the coin. When he was explaining 'Rape Me' on national television . . . he explained how it was an anti-rape song and that Nirvana was telling a story about that, and I believe that fans were taking it the opposite way. There was some sort of assault that I remember being discussed, and Kurt was saying that it's actually an anti-rape song. So that was super cool, and he didn't have to think about it [an explanation]. It was just like he was ready to go."

In her 1993 interview with Kurt, Erica Ehm mentioned the band's concern with sexism, asking, "How do you make people aware of that problem?"

Kurt answered:

> "By writing songs as blunt as 'Rape Me' *[laughs]*. Having to resort to doing something like that is almost embarrassing, because, um, people didn't understand when we wrote a song like 'About a Girl' or 'Polly,' and having to explain that and having misunderstandings about it, it just—I decided to write 'Rape Me' in a way that was just so blunt and obvious that it's like no one could deny it, you know? No one could read into it any other way, you know? Although some people have, actually, because some of the lyrics in it—some people have thought that maybe, um, it had something to do with my disgust with the media and the way they've treated us and stuff like that, but it's not true. That's not what the song is about at all. It's just my way of, in a sarcastic way, almost, of like just saying, 'How obvious do we have to be, you know?'"[101]

Kurt didn't falter when questioned about his convictions. Unfortunately, that clarity doesn't always translate to audiences.

"I have mixed feelings when I see how popular the Nirvana shirts are with the smiley faces because of what it's turned into," Chris tells me. "And then, you know—no disrespect to Post Malone or Travis Barker for doing their tribute—them wearing the dresses I thought was a cool gesture during their Nirvana tribute, but I just feel like it wasn't as political as it could have been. Like the way that they [Nirvana] would do that sort of thing. Like it was more deliberate and more obvious what they [the members of Nirvana] were trying to do when they would wear dresses, when they would do that sort of thing. Like, they all would have made out at different points, just to prove a point."

The liner notes to *Incesticide* declare: "If any of you in any way hate homosexuals, people of different color, or women, please do this one favor for us—leave us the fuck alone! Don't come to our shows and don't buy our records."[102]

That message of inclusion was often wrapped in music—loud, confrontational, and impossible to ignore—that continues to inspire.

"Music is a beautiful thing because it's a place where I can get my negative energy out," Chris says. "That's what it is for me. And my negative energy stemmed from being sort of a reject and carrying that through my life and sympathizing with people who feel rejected. And I love that the music that I make is something that people who need some kind of solace can go and listen to."

Consider the following: over 20 percent of students report being bullied.[103] Studies conducted internationally have reported that as many as 54 percent of children are bullied. If that's not shocking enough, it's reported that children who are victimized by bullies are upwards of nine times more likely to experience thoughts of suicide.[104]

We need to take this horrifying reality seriously. Bullying was a traumatizing part of Chris's youth—a disturbing experience shared by countless children—but Nirvana and their message of acceptance made it bearable.

"It's traumatizing," Chris says of bullying. "Growing up as a 'rocker' . . . in the eighties and nineties was extremely tough in certain places. For me, this would be suburban Long Island . . . in a particular area that was very Catholic, very conservative, very homophobic, and very sexist. And there were people that I knew who were just wearing a Metallica shirt or a Slayer shirt at the wrong place at the wrong time who are now permanently handicapped from their teenage years. Metal plates in their heads, partial blindness. People who were literally kids. I mean, we're talking about sophomores to seniors in high school . . . And the rest of their lives are now forever changed because of the shirt. And much like the stories that you would read about Kurt Cobain, like in the biographies, it was jocks. That's what we were dealing with.

"It's an ongoing battle that got worse somehow, and it's nice to know that at least today there are a lot more progressive ideas being promoted through social media and online and through mainstream media. But it also has brought more of the 'naysayers' out to the surface with more methods of communication that didn't exist when Kurt was doing his thing. Who knows what social media would have been like if those platforms existed in 1991? It's a tough world to navigate. Going to school today in the town where I grew up—apparently, there is a little bit more done to prevent bullying than when I went to school, at least from the signs I've seen hung up in the town when I drive through it. But it doesn't ensure the safety of your child, and it's a weird thing because on one end, I could have died a million times as well as the people around me; I could have been permanently handicapped like the people I referenced before, and it toughened me up and made me who I am. But if I had a child, I don't know that I'd be able to stomach knowing that they were going through that [bullying]. And the risk factor of it."

What Chris, Kurt, and countless others have gone through is traumatic—and that's putting it lightly. While no one should have to endure experiences like that, it shaped Chris's path, one that ultimately led him to tour with a band connected to the artist who influenced him most.

"We actually just toured with the Melvins up until a couple of weeks ago," Chris tells me. "It was our second time touring with them, so being around them feels like a weird extension to some level of what Kurt was maybe like. But then again, not necessarily, because the

Melvins couldn't be more anti—I don't want to speak for them—but they walked the non-mainstream path and somehow were the biggest influence on Kurt . . . in more ways than one. And it gave me a weird glimpse in trying to imagine that these were his high school friends.

"Dale talked about Kurt once around me, and I totally played it cool, and I couldn't tell you what the story was because it was so surreal. I looked at him, and I'm like, 'You were in Nirvana at one point,' and it's just bizarre because he's just a guy standing next to you. I think it's really interesting. Even if you talk to non-associates—anybody that's relevant in any way or who was around in one way or another or just has strong political views as a musician—is just worth getting their take on Kurt. It doesn't have to be his best friend or someone who went to high school with him."

I explain how I speak with people who knew Kurt personally and those who were just influenced by him, sharing stories and sentiments.

"I'm super pumped to be part of this because I grew up reading books about Kurt," Chris says. "And I also saw things that I didn't really like from documentaries and books [about him], so I have the ones I think are great, and most of them I thought were invasive and weird and fucked up or biased. But I also just have my memories, and I'm glad I was alive and paying attention when he was around. I talked about that recently with someone who opened up for us on this recent tour we just finished. They were in awe that I was alive to watch some of these things on television. Whenever I recall seeing Kurt, maybe something from television or *SNL* from 1993—it looks old to younger people, but I watched it on television when it first aired.

"I got into Nirvana coming out of glam metal . . . But it was very profound because, initially, getting into rock music felt rebellious. I was sort of rebelling against jocks and the clean-cut white kids that I would see at Sunday church, and they were the same people at church who were calling me all sorts of homophobic names and racist things.

"Listening to rock and roll music was my salvation, my escape . . . And when 'Smells Like Teen Spirit' was on MTV . . . It was unexplainable. . . . I just knew that I was watching something really different. It was angry. People were moshing. It was nuts. . . . There was the anarchy sign, and people—all these cheerleaders—and people just jumping on top of each other and crowd surfing. So I was on board immediately and I got the record on cassette tape and then the second that 'In Bloom' hit . . . I had already been playing drums at this point in my life . . . It was just—something about it. . . . I heard Kurt's riffs and I heard Dave's drumming and I knew that I could do it. So it was empowering as a musician, but I still didn't know what they stood for, necessarily. . . . And then I saw footage of him [Kurt] at some outdoor festival wearing a dress and a guy on stage [Tony the Interpretive Dancer] was dancing with smeared lipstick on his face without an explanation. I immediately knew that they were mocking homophobes. I don't even know if I knew the word homophobic, but I knew that they were mocking people that discriminated against others, and I identified with it very quickly . . . I just loved that they exposed me and my friends to Bikini Kill and Sonic Youth and other bands that also went out of their way to speak on our behalf. You didn't know these people, but they had your back, and they were on television or in a magazine that you would pick up and were speaking for you. So it opened up a whole new world that changed our lives forever. Because now I'm a forty-two-year-old tattooed punk rock guy playing in a band still, and it's because of that. I'm glad that I heard Nirvana and I ended up this way."

What Chris says is a testament to Kurt and like-minded artists creating safe spaces where young people could feel seen, supported, and part of something bigger, despite external hostility.

"At one point in my life, I definitely would fight back with violence when it came to these sort of situations where people are messing with you," he continues. "I think that because of somebody like Kurt Cobain—who would be my number one influence philosophically on so many different matters—as I've gotten older, I feel like the way that I'm able to make a difference in the world is by embodying the beliefs that I've learned from someone like him and his band, and the things that he stood for.

"And I educate people on why using your fists or resorting to violence or other ways of harm have unfortunately either taken lives or harmed people permanently. I explain that we could be preventing this with a more thoughtful, peaceful approach, and in this case an artistic approach that has elements of rock and roll and rebelliousness, but a message all at the same time.

"A guy like Kurt Cobain who played in a rock band—he did heroin and he committed suicide. But we don't talk about people that are, you know, successful dudes that work at offices that also do drugs and commit suicide, that do horrible things to their families. We look at them and say, 'God bless them!' and 'What a tragedy! What a great father he was!' Whatever, you know? 'He was so successful.' But then we look at Kurt and people go, 'Oh, he was a junkie,' and yada, yada, yada. And that's another problem because we're going back to the idea of what the American dream is and what you're supposed to look like and what your house is supposed to look like and all this bullshit."

Chris touches on something more insidious: the double standard between what's socially acceptable and what's condemned; how society celebrates conventional success while dismissing Kurt and others like him simply for being different.

"And honestly, Kurt Cobain was a very successful, compassionate, sensitive, and educational figure who didn't need to have the same accolades or degrees or whatever we celebrate in American society, like when we talk about people who are successful but might have committed suicide or died," Chris adds. "So we should be talking about the things that Kurt stood for that, honestly, no one has really done a better job of speaking out against. He was never accused or even questioned about doing anything strange with his fame. Aside from being depressed and doing drugs by himself which is, you know, what ultimately ended his life.

"When I went to the Rock and Roll Hall of Fame, they chose only women to sing on stage. That was the most perfect thing . . . Having Kim Gordon, Lorde, Joan Jett, and St. Vincent was the most Kurt Cobain tribute that they could have done on that platform, and that's still the greatest moment of any band that played at the Rock and Roll Hall of Fame. Because they chose to do it that way, even if they had just chosen one of those women [to perform]. But the fact that they did generations of women from top to bottom, past and present—was amazing.

". . . I was backstage at a Melvins show in Seattle just a few weeks ago. And Buzz was laughing because I was so excited to be in Seattle, especially playing with them, and because I was going to go to Sub Pop to buy some souvenirs. But he had nothing but negative things to say about Aberdeen. And I embraced that. I soaked it up because I realized that he was talking about the place that he's from in the same way that I was just talking to you about the place that I'm from—which I hated—but which caused me to be who I am. And Aberdeen was like that for them."

I ask Chris if he ever visited Aberdeen or Kurt's childhood home, as so many people have. He did.

"About twenty years ago, I did go to Kurt's house, and I looked at it, and I just remember crying," Chris says. "And I just was so curious, you know? There's the fun of their music that you get to enjoy, and the more open-minded nature of the band, you know? It's perfect."

Chris circles back to bullying and its long-lasting effects. Nirvana—Kurt in particular—worked to show him that he was so much better than any hatred thrown his way.

"I still walk around looking behind me and feeling like I have to be alert because of what happened to me in the suburbs, even though it's not happened to me here," Chris shares with me. "Because it's just in me; it's almost like PTSD, kind of like it's ingrained in me . . . It's just that I walk down the street at all times, assuming that anything—like the worst thing—could happen to me at all times, and I just have my own way of dealing with it and go from point A to point B. But that's what bullying does. And people just don't realize it."

Speaking with Chris about the way bullying left a lasting mark on him—shaping how he navigates the world—reminded me of countless young people who face the same kind of trauma every day, which can erode self-esteem or take lives through suicide or acts of violence. Hearing Chris's story made one thing painfully clear: society still isn't doing enough, and we need to do better to protect kids from this kind of harm. Connection to a support system, community, or movement is vital for survival. It wasn't just Nirvana's music that made people feel united; it was the band's message, the reminder that you could come exactly as you were, and as long as you weren't a raging asshole, you'd be accepted.

The positive, inclusive worlds Kurt helped create—spaces where outsiders and misfits could belong, a place where originality was celebrated and self-expression wasn't just allowed, it was a prerequisite—thrived in the underground. You'd see it in handmade zines, in house parties, in a DIY community that began as a punk subculture but expanded into something wholly its own. You had to be self-reliant. You had to not give a shit what other people thought of you. You had to be unapologetically yourself, and in doing so, you became part of something greater than yourself. It was a world Kurt not only inhabited, but one he inspired and expanded. And this world is still felt in the footsteps of those he influences as they navigate today's indie scene.

Chapter 23

"ON A PLAIN"

Alex Share

Countless publications rushed to sensationalize and subsequently profit from the trauma that Kurt endured, his substance abuse and personal demons often at the forefront of conversation. And these narratives had devastating consequences. At one point his wife, Courtney Love, was called into question, along with her alleged drug use during pregnancy.

The media wielded tremendous power, often controlling certain narratives. For example an article in, *Vanity Fair's* September 1992 issue, written by Lynn Hirschberg and titled "Strange Love: The Story of Kurt Cobain and Courtney Love," said, "There have been rampant reports about the couple's drug problems, and many believe she introduced Cobain to heroin. They are expecting a baby this month, and even the most tolerant industry insiders fear for the health of the child. 'It is appalling to think that she would be taking drugs when she knew she was pregnant,' says one close friend. 'We're all worried about that baby.'"[105]

This became a turning point that led to daughter Frances Bean's temporary displacement from her parents through child welfare officers at less than one month old. The investigation was ultimately dropped and the newborn was reunited with her parents a short while later, but the damage was done. The trauma of having his child taken from him seeped into Kurt's psyche.[106]

In his letter to David Geffen (which sold at Julien's Auctions for $28,125), Kurt had severe comments regarding Lynn Hirschberg and her article, saying that she "must have her karma broken." As the letter continued, so did Kurt's profession of love for his wife and unborn child.

> "I love my wife and soon to be new daughter too much to let everyone's low opinions of us ruin our lives together. I am now in rehab going on 18 days and I'm really looking forward to having a family at this point fuck NIRVANA. I've never admitted to using drugs in articles because I don't want my fans to do the same. We are capable of displaying a healthy attitude before our audience and the next record is easily as good as the last one, but I'm so extremely pissed off about this piece of trash journalism that I'll lay anything on the line for the love of my wife and daughter."[107]

I don't condone drug use, especially during pregnancy. What stands out to me about this story is how much power the media holds in shaping outcomes when facts are still incomplete.

But Kurt wasn't the only one affected by the media. I came to understand that its power doesn't stop at megastars; it reaches artists at every level of visibility. I reached out to Alex Share, guitarist for British band Phoxjaw. Kurt's influence remains central to why he became a musician, and to how he navigated some of the most difficult moments of his life. I knew that Alex was deeply inspired by Kurt. I also knew he had been profoundly affected by cancel culture.

In 2022, Phoxjaw's lead singer was the recipient of serious but unfounded criminal allegations. Even though Alex and his bandmates were not implicated in any way, Alex's career was suddenly placed in jeopardy. The experience took a severe toll on his mental health, derailing his sobriety and pushing him into a dark and dangerous place.

It isn't the same, but it forced me to think again about the *Vanity Fair* article and the media's immense power to shape narratives, careers, and lives, often without all the information.

Alex and I connect, and he begins with a clear point: Kurt is the reason he became a musician. He played a formative role in Alex's upbringing, acting as a kind of surrogate father—if only metaphorically.[108]

★★★

"Honestly, he's everything to me," Alex tells me, devoid of hubris. "I remember the first time I heard *Nevermind*. I didn't know any of the mythology or stories about Nirvana. I hadn't even heard of them at that time in my life. I was given a Nirvana record by a local kid on my council estate one day. He gave me *Nevermind*. I was about nine or ten, and I remembered saying to myself, 'I want to play guitar and write music forever.' In an instant, I thought, *Whatever this guy is singing about, I'm behind it*. Obviously, Nirvana was huge when Kurt was alive, but certainly, his death encapsulated them in time; it added that kind of mystery to them. But I heard Nirvana before I knew any of that stuff, and I instantly fell in love with Kurt. He was like a father to me, he really was. He set the moral standard of how I live my life.

"[He] was such a sensitive soul . . . He got bullied often as a young man, and I hate to say it, but I feel like a lot of the time—not always—people who have been through shit, people that have been through hard times, they are often some of the funnier, more grounded people. They look at other people and go, 'I don't know your story, so I'm not going to judge.' Some people just go through life manipulating and bullying. I think that really added to the beauty of Nirvana, that he was this incredibly good-looking guy, amazing person, but he didn't ever see that in himself. It's almost like he didn't have the ego that went with the rock star cliché. . . . And I think for a lot of people growing up, it was like, 'I can be that guy. I can be this nerd. I want to wear dresses. I want to be into weird art,' whatever it is, and still be considered 'cool' by the masses. Kurt changed the landscape of what 'cool' was, I think. Suddenly, the nerds were hip."

Kurt created a space for people who didn't fit, offering a kind of permission to exist as they were—that sense of safety is something Alex connects to deeply.

"I had a bit of a drug problem a few years ago. . . . On the outside, it looks like you're having fun. You're flaunting around, you're doing drugs, you're having a good time, but it is self-harming. . . . I think that drugs are like a mini-death, almost; you can escape your soul for that short amount of time. I know on the outside it looks dirty; it does look dirty. I can see that. And there's the whole rock-and-roll mythology of rock stars taking drugs. People have seen it a million times, but I think in some circumstances, someone's in pain. Someone's not partying. Kurt never wanted that . . . He did drugs very privately. He didn't want people to know about it, because he was worried about fans copying him. He felt so much shame when it all came out. I heard one story where there were some teenagers outside a gig smoking heroin off some tinfoil, and they went, 'Hey, Kurt,' and he sobbed for days, saying, 'I didn't want any of this.'"

Even when Kurt hid himself—and his family—from external sources, the media had a way of intruding, amplifying his pain and creating a false narrative for impressionable fans to emulate. I mention the *Vanity Fair* piece to Alex simply to acknowledge the power of media narratives to shape perception and produce real consequences.

"I understand completely," Alex says. "Being on a stage—being in the public eye—people can be quick to judge you without knowing the truth. In many ways, being on stage is a dangerous place to be. You can be loved as quickly as you're not; you can be dragged through the street, without the eyes and ears bothering to learn the truth. Being on stage, you're at the mercy of the people who run the businesses. Kurt and Courtney losing brief custody of Frances was horrendous. Without cheapening the love of a father and his daughter, I made the choice to make my band my family. I feel like what Phoxjaw went through caused me to lose my children—my community, my scene—for a short while. I don't want to diminish Kurt Cobain's experience with temporary custody loss, but the media tried to take what I love from me just like it temporarily broke Kurt's family.

"Even if the intentions were good with the pursuit of perceived justice, protecting Frances and the people who made the allegations against the Cobains, everybody went about it the wrong way. I feel like Kurt and I were both forced to an unjust sentence with the failings of the justice system. But people forget that musicians are human beings, too, and we don't want our lives exploited. We deserve privacy."

It was no secret that the Cobains were struggling with substance use, and a child's safety should always come first. Still, it feels unsettling that a magazine article carried enough weight to influence a custody decision—something that should rest on evidence, not headlines. And yet, so much of who Kurt was falls by the wayside when headlines take center stage.

"He was apparently a really funny guy," Alex says. "Kurt really was just a guy, and he just happened to nail it as a songwriter—he put so much time into his art, and he really resonated with so many people."

One of the things that resonates most with Alex is Kurt's unhoused years.

"The mad thing in the UK—I've had experiences of that—is sofa surfing," Alex tells me. "It's not fun. You're living under someone else's rule the whole time, and you have to be just politely moved on. But the mad thing is during COVID, during the lockdown, the UK government managed to house every unhoused person. . . . As soon as officials deemed things safe, the unhoused were put back out on the streets. The government proved that the unhoused crisis is solvable . . . It's definitely a societal problem. And the fact that Kurt was without a stable home as a teenager is so heartbreaking, as the solutions are there, but underfunded."

Talking about the unhoused crisis led us to a broader topic: the many public challenges musicians face and how society often overlooks that they're human, too.

"I think a lot of musicians and a lot of songwriters are generally quite sensitive people," Alex says. "They're looking at feelings; they're looking at the world. They're analyzing it, and then they're thrust into this meat factory of an industry. They're not prepared for it. I wasn't prepared for it. We're still waiting to get paychecks from our band. I'm very lucky that my mother and sister respect the power of music and the dedication it takes—they know I work hard. But the amount of jobs that I've had to leave. I've not been able to progress in my life because I need to take a month off to tour, which I'm not going to get paid for because it has to go back into the band or to the record label. It's tough, and I'm personally lucky that I have a few strong women around me who very much see that I'm working hard. It's like you've got this thing in you, and you're just like, 'I need to do this, I need to do this.' People who don't have that support—I can see how things can get pretty nasty pretty quick.

"There's no mental health support. My mother always said, 'Be whatever you want, but don't ever cause anyone any harm. As long as you're happy, whatever it is that you're doing, just work hard and do what you want with good intentions.' I did that. I'm not going to lie, I've definitely experienced some personal adversity. Just being more of an androgynous person, I can definitely walk into a room and I'm instantly a target. But artists like Brett Anderson, David Bowie, and Kurt Cobain always made me feel like I'm doing the right thing. They dressed however they wanted, and their spirit was true. To the right people, that will be reciprocated."

Alex's comments about authenticity and self-expression made me think of Kurt's childhood and the obstacles he encountered. Regardless, he followed his own moral compass even when he struggled to find direction. He was comfortable in his own skin.

"I just think Kurt was the coolest guy," Alex adds. "I grew up without a father. I needed male role models in my life. The first time I bought a magazine with Kurt in it, he was in a dress, and I thought, 'This guy's brilliant, he's doing what he wants.' He was a huge part of the alternative world. Kurt used to say, 'I wish I was homosexual just to annoy homophobes.' Subsequently, I like to dress in quite an androgynous way, wearing lacy shirts and things like that because I think it suits how I look. It suits my body. I just feel good in it. But the amount of hate I get for that—people think that I'm trying to show off or something. My good friend Aaron Fish nailed it. He said, 'You walk into a room dressed like that, you're going to get attention. Half the room might hate you, but half the room is going to love you.' And that was the impetus that propelled me forward; I was able to keep dressing how I wanted."

Alex receives pushback simply for dressing in a way that's organic and comfortable to him—a choice that harms no one but seems to invite criticism nonetheless. But this is what Alex took away from Kurt: it's not about what you wear, but the integrity you bring by refusing to compromise who you are.

"I've had fans of my band come up and say, 'You really inspire me to dress how I want to dress, be who I want to be.' And that's exactly what Kurt did for me," Alex tells me. "He used his public image in such a subtly political way. I was never out there to make a political statement. I really wasn't. But I realize that it kind of was, without realizing it. People say that everything is politics. If you're doing anything outside the norm, kind of left field, you're making a statement, whether you like it or not.

"Some people wear costumes and follow a script because that's an easier life. There have been times that I've thought if I just shave my hair and wear a tracksuit, I could be anonymous; I could exist without being attacked. I could be seen for who I am. But the number of times I've been chatting to people in a social situation, and they've said after a while, 'You're actually all right, mate,' I'm like, 'I am. I'm just a person. I live a life.' But some people only see the exterior. Maybe if you look deep in yourself, you might respect what I'm doing, but some people can only turn the unknown into hatred.

"I think you should dress how you want to dress in life. You really do project who you want to be, and there's nothing wrong with that. Eventually, you find the right people—you find your tribe. The people that you're going to get on with are going to say, 'Oh, you're my person, you're my people.' I've had many a night where I've had people just come up to me and say, 'I love your outfit,' or 'I love this,' or 'I love the band on your T-shirt,' and then you strike up a conversation, and you meet a lovely human being."

All too often society judges others on how they look—their clothes, hair, tattoos, piercings—forming baseless opinions. That's part of what made the grunge aesthetic so magnetic. It wasn't about expensive clothes; it was about freedom of expression, no matter one's means.

"How timeless is Kurt?" Alex asks, referring to his style. "How cool does he still look now, because he didn't follow any of the trends? He didn't have the big eighties hair or capitalist sportswear. He really was a very cool guy, I've got to say. Very effortlessly cool."

"How has he influenced you and your music?" I ask.

"Kurt massively affected me," says Alex. "I feel like the songs were quite simple, but when you look into them, they weren't. His chords moved in this . . . not wrong way, but—unexpected. The way the chords moved are definitely quite jarring. He was into his dissonance, and you could tell he wanted to do something weird, but he was also a big lover of pop. Also, his lyrics—some of the words he used—were incredibly abstract but also poignant. When you think about these pop songs that people sing, and how strange some of the lyrics are . . . It's kind of amusing how big these songs are that are heard by millions of people. I just felt like Nirvana was something different. I really do. I think Kurt had a really good ear for hooks. I think the guy could and did write great pop songs. But it was all a bit twisted. I feel like that set the tone for music that I love. I love good pop, but I love it to be just a bit twisted. I think some of the chord progressions Kurt uses, I've not ever heard since. Every song is so recognizable, even if there are four or five chords in a song."

The originality Alex focuses on isn't just heard in Nirvana—it's etched in *Montage of Heck: The Home Recordings*. Every word, every chord reflects a highly imaginative artist whose music was, in so many ways, as limitless as it was original. And Kurt never missed an opportunity to be his own person, especially on stage.

"I think, is it *Live! Tonight! Sold Out!!*, the tape?" Alex asks. "I don't know if you've seen the film . . . Kurt started to create and edit it. It's all just clips of their time as a band. Obviously, Kurt didn't finish it, but Dave and Krist did. But it's got all of the golden moments of their career. It's worth a watch."

We chat a bit more about other Nirvana videos, focusing on their creativity and impact, before the conversation shifts to some of the adversity I've faced throughout this experience.

"I think Kurt would be honored," Alex begins. "People writing about the specific things in his life and putting their spin on it is a bit more invasive, and that's the kind of journalism that he wasn't big on. Whereas I think his legacy being used as an artistic place for something to build would be way more down his way of thinking. Genuinely, I really do. I think it's a great idea, what you're doing. I think that Kurt has become beyond—he was a person, but he has become such a culturally relevant face but should be also respected as the artist and human he is."

"That's what I'm hoping for," I say.

Alex zeroes in on another phase of Kurt's career, exploring not just his personal legacy, but the directions he might have boldly taken later in life.

"With *Unplugged in New York*, I think Kurt wanted to lean more into that acoustic world. I think he felt like he didn't want to become this 'grunge' novelty. It seems as if that was the direction he wanted to move into for a little while. I think he would have come back to Nirvana, but I really do think that he was in a happy place at that moment, playing a show like *Unplugged*. He just needed a little break from Nirvana, but gigs like the Lollapalooza tour were getting booked when he needed some time off for self-care."

But Kurt seldom got more than a brief pause, and we'll never know what he might have pursued next.

Alex shifts to a subject that weighs heavily on him: the ease of accessing firearms in the US and how that can turn moments of crisis into tragedy.

"I've got to say that the gun laws in America are a big, sad solution of escapism when one is pressured by social and career-based pressures," Alex says. "I heard this sentence once and it's stuck with me always: 'People that take their own lives, they didn't want to die forever; they just wanted to die in that moment.' . . . Whether they used drugs or something more violent, they just wanted to escape for a moment. It's tragic."

The human cost he describes is reflected in national data: according to the CDC, in 2022 there were 50,000 reported suicides. An estimated 27,000 of these suicides were firearm suicides. In the last two decades, suicides in general—including firearm suicides—have increased by approximately one-third.[109]

Alex turns back to the permanence of the music and the struggles that often go unnoticed.

"Nirvana's songs go beyond novelty rock songs. They are almost like hymns. Like old folk music, old blues, where it just flows through people. But the idea of songs belonging to people—I get it when the artist is alive, and royalties for family if they do pass away—but songs and music belong to everyone. They really do; just because that artist wrote it . . . these songs still belong to everyone. And these songs have affected certain people in a way where they want to cover them. As long as it's done with respect, do what you will with them . . . Money, fame, drugs—that ain't gonna fix it. You'll still have that hole in you. That pang of something, just because on the outside it looks like somebody has everything, they still feel the same pain. They may have fewer struggles than you, but they still feel that same pain, that depression, and that voice in their head when they go to bed. All these things and people forget that fame does not bring happiness.

"It is wild, the way Nirvana's success happened. A guy from a little logging town moved to Seattle, all while learning more about what punk rock was. It's wild how big Nirvana got. It is absolutely wild . . . Kurt was just a music fan. He never saw himself as anything like we see him. But after he got famous, he knew how to work the media. He was an amazing artist. He was an amazing painter. He was an amazing father. He was a beautiful human being. As an artist, though, I've seen all the live shows. I've listened to all the audio recordings. I mean, who are you going to get to know better through music, though? Somebody who sings 'Welcome to the Jungle,' or someone that demands, 'What else should I be?' I feel that was part of the appeal with Kurt. You know him even though you never met him. You listen to his lyrics, you hear his music, you feel his energy. You think, *You're my mate. You'll never know me, but I know you.*"

Part of that unspoken connection, of course, comes from learning about Kurt from those who loved and admired him, a sort of bridge in a liminal space between memory and music. But some of it also comes from his relatability, his candor, and his quirks.

"Oh, Kurt was a strange little man." Alex laughs, circling back to *Montage of Heck* and Kurt's home recordings. "He was talking about his childhood and recorded it on tape. That's brilliant. I've got to say, as a lifelong fan, I really heard Nirvana and Kurt Cobain in a different way after watching that movie. It affected me so much as a lifelong love. It really did. I saw him as a human being for the first time, really truly as a human being. Kurt worked really hard, perfecting the craft of songwriting. He did it very well."

With this in mind, Alex shares one final sentiment about music and the way he'd like to be perceived—something that was true of Kurt: "Honestly, if I could have one lyric—maybe it's about the way I dress—that makes somebody think, *Maybe I can be unapologetically myself,* just one positive thing in the world that will cause a ripple effect, then that's great."

Speaking with Alex reaffirmed that Kurt didn't just influence people—he gave them permission to exist exactly as they were through his humor, defiance, and an unapologetic refusal to conform.

That idea of refusing to comply didn't end with his generation; it rippled forward, especially within punk circles that value honesty and autonomy.

Chapter 24

"PENNYROYAL TEA"

Nick Chiericozzi

MANY INDEPENDENT MUSICIANS INSTINCTIVELY CONNECT WITH KURT'S themes of defiance, longing, and isolation, even if the personal experiences shaping their creativity differ from his own. Passion doesn't necessarily have to stem from instability through divorce, constant change, or growing up without a steady sense of home, like Kurt experienced. Yes, his childhood may have shaped the way he wrote and informed the risks he took, or even the emotional weight behind his art. However, some believe it's simply what he stood for—a bold, exploratory, and honest career fueled by real life and completely devoid of meaningless corporate polish.

I reached out to Nick Chiericozzi of the Brooklyn-based punk band The Men because their approach to music reminded me of Kurt's unpretentious spirit. The band has played everywhere from theaters to boats, prioritizing music and honest expression over cultivating an inauthentic image. I wanted his perspective on how Kurt's experiences continue to influence musicians working outside the mainstream.[110]

***

"It's been well documented that there's an urge to create because of the past," Nick says. "You got to burn the past to make the present real."

This perspective helps him understand why artists create, their motivation ranging from instability to basic survival.

"It's possible that he [Kurt] never had to sleep under that bridge or sleep in that waiting room," Nick continues. "Any good songwriter is trying to find a way to tell a story, even before you know you're a songwriter. . . . If things are messed up at home, you go out and you look."

When you grow up without clear guidance or solid role models, you end up pushing boundaries simply because you're navigating the world alone. Stepping into a creative life takes a kind of social risk: putting yourself out there without a map, just an internal compass, hoping the art is worth the potential backlash or fallout, especially after achieving worldwide fame.

"I have no fame and most musicians are not famous," Nick tells me. "I would never want to be famous. Success is a wild ship. Something that no captain would sign up to captain. Nirvana's particular ride did blaze a trail, but it got smashed. What did survive is their music. The records do speak. *Incesticide* is really beautiful. Hearing that after the first two [albums] made the band that much deeper. When you got something good, like *Bleach* or *Nevermind*, and then there's another strange and intriguing thing on the horizon, it kind of seals the deal."

But the same chaos that feeds creativity can also open the door to complications.

"Heroin will kill you if you don't quit," Nick says. "It's really that simple."

"What if Kurt was part of a larger, systemic issue?" I ask. "His drug use may have been precipitated by a lack of affordable healthcare and self-medicating being the readily available option for stomach issues."

"There really isn't healthcare for rock-and-roll music," Nick explains. He isn't wrong. Kurt may have first grappled with stomach ailments during a time when the eighties saw an increase in how many people went uninsured. Additionally, there was a decline in the percentage of people with private insurance coverage.[111] Access to care wasn't guaranteed, and even when it existed, it wasn't always reachable.

When systems fail people in life, culture tends to mythologize their deaths instead of examining those failures.

"I romanticized his death," Nick tells me. "It was strange and unnatural when I heard the announcement on NPR on Highway 95 in the back seat while my parents were in the front. I was on a break from school, and we were in Washington, DC. I thought it [Kurt's death] was terrible, but curious. . . . That put my parents in a tough spot because he did that [died by suicide], and they were left with a kid who really liked Nirvana and having to explain that event. I don't know how I would explain that to a child. There's an emptiness to suicide. I can't tell you from the other side if there is one, but it doesn't seem to have a resolution other than the physical. I did hold vigil for him in my own way. . . . As an American, I'm supposed to love fame and the press and all that. . . . I burned a candle for him one night, and my mom ran in at like 2:00 a.m. and said, 'You're gonna burn the house down!' I kept the covers of *People*, *Rolling Stone*, and so forth in a folder under my bed for years. We [Kurt and I] also share the same birthday, and when I found that out, after he died of course, I really felt I was locked into destiny."

As he learned more about Kurt, Nick gravitated toward his more stripped back and honest performances, like *MTV Unplugged in New York*.

"The acoustic show in New York is something I've seen more than any live performance," Nick tells me. "I think my brother or sister taped it on VHS, and I watched it relentlessly. I can quote the commercials in between. It's really what made me interested in the guitar because it [the concert] was so naked. I never had cable or whatever, so seeing someone play without a cheesy music video and being able to translate the chords onto my mom's acoustic really was fun. I had no idea how to tune the thing, so I turned the tuners to match Kurt's. Probably sounded crazy. It's true, I'm a product of television. In that show, I learned about Lead Belly, Bowie, and the Meat Puppets all in one shot. It's not my favorite of theirs, however. To quote your subject, it's really about freedom. As many ideas and sets of eyes. They [Nirvana] had a lot of different sounds. The stuff that I like most now is their exploratory stuff . . . like *Incesticide* . . . That stuff is awesome."

Even for the time, Kurt's lyrical prose pushed into uncomfortable territory, especially when confronting themes of misogyny.

"This was a pretty new philosophy to me when I was eleven in 1993—not necessarily equality, but a recognition of the fact of inequality of male versus female participation and acceptance in music," Nick begins. "I think there are more groups now with all women than ever. That's great, and as is always the case, when the music is good, made by people, it's the best thing. Ending discrimination starts with music and things that are common in life among all people. I think people construct this kind of crap and act it out for a lifetime thinking they're doing some service to the past. When you really just hang out and talk to people, the albatross falls from your back . . . I remember feeling that way, wondering about sexuality, even before puberty, and whether I'd end up on this side of the fence or the other. Now that seems silly because I have human affections regardless of gender."

Even though Kurt's lyrics pushed back against sexism and discrimination, it was Nirvana's sound that initially drew Nick in.

"The music is really what brings me here," Nick explains. "The guitar tone and rhythm are what set the course for Nirvana songs. The vocals are great, but they are secondary, as he [Kurt] said. The idea of the wild solo without jackass technicality but with sensitive placement and presence makes me feel. I like the quieter songs, too, when the bass and drums are carrying the song, like 'Dumb.' Maybe my favorite songs are 'Pennyroyal Tea,' 'Dive,' 'Aneurysm,' or 'Been a Son.' That's kind of where I'm coming from. . . . Nirvana certainly had an impact on me becoming a musician. I don't think actually learning the guitar would've happened had I not heard them or at least not when I did. There is a simplicity within the music. . . . They also just sounded good. Music is sound. When that hits, it can change days and kill time."

It's easy to overlook the role a musician plays in a person's life. They're not just corporate cogs designed to fulfill quotas in a contract. They're magnetic, and their sound imprints.

"People think musicians and all stage performers are puppets who are acting out a role," Nick says. "That may be partially true, but music is not that; writing or designing is not that. It's feeling and sound in an organized manner, and you're going to get a version of reality when you see it in performance. It's just a band, but it can really lift you up if you don't lock into expectation. . . . I really think Krist Novoselic was the secret weapon of the band. Nirvana was a band, you know? His humor and groove made them unique. For Kurt to bounce songs off of someone like that, it must've been reassuring that another intelligent artist had his back. It's a collective universe."

Nick said the music made him "feel," and I knew he wasn't just talking about nostalgia. Kurt mattered. The whole band did. Nirvana's signature quiet-loud cadence, where melody slams into distortion, pulls people in and refuses to let go. For some artists, that influence doesn't stop at connection—it shapes their work and career trajectory. And it shows just how much Kurt affected musicians. That's why I reached out to Paul Wandtke of Smells Like Nirvana Tribute.

Chapter 25

"LOUNGE ACT"

Paul Wandtke

TRIBUTE BANDS EXIST FOR ALL KINDS OF REASONS. SOME HIT NERVES, others lean on nostalgia. But the ones centered around Nirvana run on something different—longing. Decades after Kurt's death, people still cram into bars and theaters hoping to feel even a fraction of that old electricity, even if someone else has to be the conduit. Smells Like Nirvana Tribute is one of those groups, fronted by Paul Wandtke (Dead Original, ex-Trivium, ex–*Rock of Ages*). The lineup also includes drummer Ty Del Rose (12 Stones, ex-Smile Empty Soul) and bassist Mike Petrasek (Dead Original, Bedlem). They're professional musicians, but at their core they're fans trying to manage their own grief and admiration the only way they know how—by playing the songs that built them. Their shows aren't just about recreating a sound; they're trying to tap into the same ache that lives in every other fan who still feels Kurt's absence.

When I watched some of their shows online, what stood out wasn't imitation or even nostalgia—it was the crowd. The room felt charged, like some emotional muscle memory firing back to life after decades of silence. Smells Like Nirvana Tribute wasn't resurrecting Kurt; they were giving people a way to gather, to feel something, to celebrate a band that somehow defined the undefinable. For some, tribute bands are sacrilege. For others, it's the closest they'll ever get to standing in the blast radius of Kurt Cobain.

★★★

"You know at the start of our tribute shows, we clearly state that we do this for Kurt—and only Kurt," Paul tells me. "If he was around, we wouldn't be doing Smells Like Nirvana Tribute because that would be really lame."[112]

For all the theatrics that come with a tribute act, Paul's explanation was honest and raw.

"If anyone besides Kurt had spearheaded Nirvana, do you think the level of success would have been as great?" I ask.

"Well, look at AC/DC," Paul says. "They were able to replace Bon Scott. But you can't do that with Nirvana."

"No, you can't," I say. "And something I've asked many people is, 'What was it about Kurt that stood out?' And people have a hard time putting their finger on it. He just seemed to be a very kind, empathetic person. No one has ever said anything bad about him. Everyone I've talked to has said similar things. Kurt had time for everybody. He was just that type of guy."

"He was just himself. He put everything he had into everything he did. I wish I could do that with my own music maybe one day. There's a YouTube video of some vocal analyzer, and he's comparing Dave Grohl to Kurt Cobain, and the difference is that Kurt Cobain was just fearless when playing live. The way he sang, he was just fearless. And honest. That's why, to me, even though he was a little pitchy live, it didn't even matter because the emotion is what matters, and that's why people love him.

"Songwriting-wise, his music, to me, is like a cat that's looking at you . . . but it really isn't looking at you as the cat is actually looking right through your soul. A lot like those blank-stare pictures of Kurt Cobain, ya know? But Kurt wasn't searching down anyone's soul in those pictures; he was simply spacing out and daydreaming amidst conversation . . . kinda like looking through a blurry glass entering another universe. His spaced-out look, I think, is represented in his music, creating a magical space where you can think and feel. I met a fellow Nirvana fan once that I shared my 'cat stare opinion' with, and he said, 'Yes, you know I've always thought his music was like a child throwing paint on a canvas—sloppy during the process but then it turns into this beautiful piece of art.'"

Paul is circling the same thing so many fans try to explain—the inexplicable way Kurt disarmed people.

"Is Kurt the reason you got into music in the first place?" I ask.

"Yes, totally," Paul says enthusiastically. "My older brother Brian on guitar and my cousin Martin on bass would jam all the time. We'd watch MTV, too, and always wait in anticipation of anything Nirvana-related. I'll never forget seeing Nirvana play *Live and Loud* on MTV—it was so different from anything else I'd ever seen. Brian and Martin were more experienced than me on their instruments, so when we jammed, they'd make me play drums on a makeshift cardboard box drum set. I was only about seven at the time, and it was really fun, so I continued to play the drums.

"We got into other bands like NOFX, Lagwagon, Screeching Weasel, Blink-182, and more. Later I got into the metal scene, then the nu-metal rock scene, and then the hardcore scene. But musically, I never felt anything as close as I do playing the tribute shows to Kurt and Nirvana. There's just something really cool about it all. Something really heartfelt that exists because he really connected with people through his music."

"What is that like for you?" I ask. "Playing on stage, as him—how do you feel people receive you? They can come to your shows to immerse themselves in all things Nirvana."

"Only on stage," Paul explains. "On stage, I feel like there's this aura and maybe—somehow—I'm tapping into it. We've had a lot of great responses, where people come up to merch and are like, 'Oh my God, I felt like I was watching Nirvana.' It is emotional for me, too, because some days I cry after a show and it's really, really weird and crazy. I just break down and start crying, and I think they are tears of joy, pain, happiness, and sadness, but I think it's just the emotion from the crowd and vibe of the show that gets me worked up and feeling sappy because at the end of the day as a fan of Nirvana and Kurt, I really wish he was here with us today; that would be so cool. I always wonder what he'd be doing today.

"I'm a drummer at heart, and my goal in life was to be a work-for-hire drummer. I even got endorsements over the years with major brand drum companies like Tama drums, Vic Firth sticks, Meinl cymbals, Evans drum heads, and Trick Drum pedals, and I traveled the world with famous and not-so-famous artists. I even played on cruise ships for a brief stint just to pay the bills as a drummer."

Paul laughs, and I can hear what he's really getting at. He'd built a legitimate career, checked all the boxes, played with big names, traveled the world—yet none of it compared to the pull he felt toward Nirvana. For him, getting onstage with this tribute band wasn't about imitation. It was about staying connected to the thing that made him want to become a musician—to the person who inspired him.

"There was always this part of me that could never let go of that high I'd get from listening and jamming to Nirvana. I always secretly wished I could be a grunge frontman in the vein of Kurt, but still original to carry on his legacy. I remember vividly sitting in my 1984 Volkswagen station wagon on the way to high school and hearing 'You Know You're Right.' I got so sad and angry. I could hear the music was spliced together, yet it was so beautiful and magical. I thought to myself, 'Man, someone has to carry on his work and help heal all of us fans.' I always wanted to do something heartfelt, honest, and pure.

"So I went ahead and started Tribute back in 2014 after I did my last touring version of the Broadway musical *Rock of Ages*. I was so scared and nervous when we started. I had to drink a whole bottle of red wine to get through my first show, and that show was at the legendary Cubby Bear in Chicago, Illinois, which is where Dave Grohl went to one of his first shows as a fan of music. About five hundred people showed up [when we played], and it was just a really good show. Ever since then—ten years ago—we've been doing it, on and off. After the lockdowns, we started playing a lot more and even started supporting the shows with a thirty-minute original set from an album I self-produced in 2021 titled *Bought and Sold* under the moniker 'Dead Original'—a name I came up with because people always said I looked like Kurt Cobain growing up." He laughs. "I use the name 'Dead Original' because I'll never be entirely original—maybe one day."

"That's awesome. You play all over the country, right?" I ask.

"Yup, pretty much. Since the lockdowns," Paul says. "We're even headed to Switzerland in March."

By this point, it was clear Paul wasn't just performing the songs—he was living inside the lore.

"I think he was ahead of his time," Paul says. "From what I've read online and read in books, he worked his ass off. He wanted to be in the spotlight for sure until the end. It was probably way too much success way too fast as they only have three albums."

"We know he had a lot that he struggled with, and you could tell that he was in a lot of pain, especially in the later shows," I say.

"I think he was pretty checked out towards the end," Paul says. "There are interviews of him saying how he wished he could have written music that was easier on him so he didn't lose his voice the next day . . . Kurt was a baritone in my humble opinion . . . I believe when you are a baritone who sings in tenor ranges, this can cause frustration because it's not as easy as it is for a tenor, so I believe that's why he was frustrated toward the end musically. Every night he was singing, he would pretty much sing until he blew his voice out."

Paul studied music theory at Berklee College of Music and Joliet Junior College, something he's proud of and quick to mention. (He laughs about the irony of it—a Berklee guy in a Nirvana tribute—and hopes Kurt would've gotten a kick out of it.) He reflects on the physical toll of Nirvana's live shows, especially Kurt pushing his voice to the brink. As a technical musician, it's easy for Paul to make sense of that strain in terms of range and technique—it's his way of processing how much Kurt gave of himself. The physical wear was real, but the exhaustion people saw toward the end went far beyond vocal cords. Chaos, pressure, scrutiny—those did the real damage. What Paul thinks matters most is the heart Kurt managed to still give through his music, and for someone who deeply appreciates Nirvana's message, that loss never fully goes away.

"As a fan of Nirvana, I'm hurt that he's not around. So, to me, doing the tribute shows is kind of like a healing process as a fan of Nirvana."

"To get out there and play is healing?" I ask.

"Yeah," says Paul. "To me, it's kind of cleansing, and it's been really cool to meet other fans of Nirvana. Our slogan with our tribute shows and opening the shows with originals is 'Make America Grunge Again,' and people are really, really digging it. They think it's cool and funny. Maybe there will be a grunge resurgence one day, who knows?"

The debate around tribute bands always straddles homage versus impersonation, sincerity versus spectacle. After talking with Paul, it's obvious he's not trying to *be* Kurt. He's processing loss—and he's doing it in a room full of people doing the same. Fans miss someone they never got to meet, and sharing a room with his music lets them feel that absence together. Say what you want about tribute culture, but the emotional reality underneath it is real.

Regardless, Paul understands the skepticism some people have toward tribute bands.

"I think Kurt would hate the idea of someone being in a tribute to him," Paul says. "Some people say it's creepy at times, and I agree with that. But for some reason, since I was a kid, something's told me, 'You have to do this, you have to do this right now.' And I think it's because of that—because people are hurt. They wish Kurt was around, as he was taken away too soon. They wish they could see him play. And that's kind of where we're at right now."

"You're preserving Kurt's memory," I say before mentioning that fans think he resembles Kurt. Whether it's the aesthetic or just people longing for someone who's gone, Paul hears it a lot.

"So we played a show in Tulalip Casino—it's near Seattle—and we went to the famous museum [MoPOP] and they let us in for free because they asked us if we were with Nirvana," Paul says, laughing. "The employees were all spooked out, too. I'm not making this up. They looked at me and thought I was related to Kurt Cobain. So they let us in for free."

As much fun as Paul has on the road with Smells Like Nirvana Tribute, playing shows and getting into museums for free, the decision to continue the band came from a much harder choice about another musical opportunity he ultimately had to give up.

At one point in his career, Paul was announced as the new drummer for Trivium, a high-profile metal band with a demanding touring schedule. They wanted him in Florida full-time, fully committed, but he felt himself pulled to continue Smells Like Nirvana Tribute.

"Any professional drummer would've held on and tried to stay with a band like Trivium because they are badass and travel the world," he admits. "But at the end of the day the inner child in me was like, 'No, I need to do this right now. Long live Kurt.'"

Do some people consider tribute bands sacrilegious? Sure. But entertainment requires a certain apathy toward critics; fans will always decide for themselves what feels authentic. And that's something I think Kurt would have respected. With Nirvana seemingly more popular than ever—especially among younger generations—legions of new fans never had the chance to see them in concert. Smells Like Nirvana Tribute offers those fans a place to come together and relive the energy of one of the greatest bands ever.

Chapter 26

"YOU KNOW YOU'RE RIGHT"

Brad Thomas

Jason Everman's early role in Nirvana initially pulled me toward Silence & Light, but once I learned the modern hard rock band was made up of other military Veterans, the importance of speaking with them became obvious to me. At first, I was simply following Jason's Nirvana connection, but learning that the band donates a portion of their profits to charity struck a deeper chord. Their mission reminded me of Walter, especially how they work to raise awareness for mental health struggles. Jason was interested in participating, but he was off the grid on a volunteer commitment and unreachable at the time. That's what led me to lead guitarist Brad Thomas, and to conversations about the music industry, mental health, and the cost of sensationalism.

Brad and I connected quickly, and it wasn't just because of the Nirvana thread—his volunteer work and unwavering stance on mental health drew me in immediately. A former Delta Force operator, Brad doesn't just spend his free time volunteering—he uses his music to highlight the importance of mental health alongside his bandmates. He was interested in this project from the outset, especially after learning about Walter. For that reason alone, his participation meant something deeper.

Our conversation naturally drifted toward the overlap between Kurt's impact, mental health awareness, and the kind of service Silence & Light dedicates itself to.[113]

★★★

"Persevere in the music industry . . . and maybe in the arts . . . I didn't understand this until I became a part of it, and still I'm such a fringe player in the music industry," Brad begins. "I mean, we're totally independent of everything. No help from anyone because we're an indie band. I feel like, rather than Kurt persevering, he was monetized and he was basically turned into a product. . . . I would think that part of his dissatisfaction with being so huge is that he realized that he'd become the commercial thing that he was seeking to rebel against."

"I agree," I say. "Kurt became a brand. He was no longer Kurt Cobain, the person, but Kurt Cobain, the product."

"Yeah," says Brad. "And I think that added to his depression and everything. I just think it was too much for him."

What Brad describes tracks with something I'd heard on repeat: Kurt's success was cyclical. He created out of necessity—mentally and emotionally—but the thing he loved eventually became a tug-of-war between creation and commodification.

"It's almost like, 'Well, I'm just going to quit my business where I've got fifty people employed and they're going to lose their jobs,'" Brad says. "You know, there's a lot of pressure in that regard. If you fold and walk away, there's that artist piece, which is that you're never really satisfied with the 'thing.' So there's a constant attempt to fix that thing to make it more like the way you envisioned it being. It's interesting to me, going from *Nevermind* and being as polished and literally perfect as it could possibly be to *In Utero*. It was not taking a step backward, but it was like, 'We're stepping back to *Bleach*.' Look at the Foo Fighters. They dropped their first record in '95, and everything has gotten better. Everything has gotten bigger, maybe not hits, but it just sounds more polished. Every album is better than the last. And that's his [Dave Grohl] attempt to fix all the things that he didn't like on the one before."

Brad instinctively called out the need to scratch an artistic itch—not just for self-preservation, but for growth. And the way he described stripping things back to their beginnings before pushing forward again . . . that's not just a musician's impulse. Veterans understand the cycle intimately: rebuild, recalibrate, move. Brad saw that same rhythm in Kurt—how he kept pushing himself forward even when he circled back to old ground, reexamining it with new eyes and reshaping it into something sharper.

As Brad and I continue to talk, I ask how Silence & Light came together.

"The impetus for the whole thing was when I retired from the military in 2010," he tells me. "I wanted to do something. I wanted to give back to the community . . . It was 2017, and I was driving into Manhattan to meet Jason [Everman], and a lightbulb went off and I was like, 'I'm gonna put together a band . . . I don't know what this is gonna be, but the idea is we'll release music and we'll take the proceeds from that and we'll contribute those to charitable organizations that we believe in.' So I'm excited now . . . and Jason's like, 'Hell yeah, I'm down.'"

Silence & Light came together out of necessity, much like Nirvana. Both were born from the need to create—to turn pain into art. And both understood the same core truth: fighting private battles while working to lift someone else up.

"I've had people contact me through social media," Brad says. "And they're like, 'Man, I heard you on this podcast, I checked out your music and this song brought me to tears because I was a police officer and I got injured in the line of duty and I really resonated with what you guys are doing.' I'm trying to be an example because there are all these Veterans—you know this all too well—there are people that are struggling, there are people that are killing themselves. What I'm trying to say is that I've lived all the dark stuff; I've gone through historic battles, been a part of incredible things, and lived all the same stuff that anybody that's out there struggling has lived through. I've done it. I've been there. I know the feeling. And if I can find a way to do something that's healthy, positive, and creative—and give back to the community—if I can do it, then anybody can do it. And I can promise you that if you give back to the community, you know you're going to feel an incredible sense of purpose from that. That's the thing that gets people across when they're contemplating doing something drastic—they have a sense of purpose. Like, 'I gotta take the dog to get washed because if I don't do this, then who's going to?' That's the thing that gets them across the line, so that's why I'm doing what I'm doing. It's not to be on the cover of *Rolling Stone* magazine to be like, 'My music is the best and look at me, I'm a rock star and used to be in the military.' I could give a fuck whether *Rolling Stone* picks up an article or anything else. I'm connecting with people. People are responding to me about what the music means to them or what my story means to them or what I'm doing. And that's all I care about."

As Brad talked about purpose and survival, I couldn't help but think of Walter. How could I not? Like Brad, Walter lived the kind of darkness most people only read about. But Brad found a way through—a way to turn that darkness into something that lifts others up, raises awareness, and channels support where it's needed most. And in their own way, Silence & Light honors not just people like Walter, but people like Kurt, too.

Our conversation turns toward the way people often overlook suffering until it's too late.

"I think that's the same thing that plagues the military—suicide," Brad says. "It's the same thing that plagues musicians and artists—suicide. It's one of those things where I think people view musicians as they're partying, they're doing this because it's the rock-and-roll lifestyle, assuming Kurt's using heroin because he's partying. But he was not that. He was a drug addict, yes, and he needed help—he needed somebody to get him help. And they didn't care about that. They cared about the product and everything else. If he had gotten help . . ." He pauses. "I've been involved in a lot of suicide stuff with military guys. There are multiple types of suicides. There's 'I want to end my life and I'm going to take my own life,' and there is also a version that I've seen that I don't think people talk about, and it's high-risk behavior. Kind of like living life on the edge: 'I'm going to do crazy stuff because I'm either chasing that same adrenaline rush that I got in a gunfight' or 'I'm going to do something that makes me feel so good that I crave just feeling good from that.' It might be heroin for a drug addict; it might be adrenaline for a non-drug addict. I have a friend that BASE-jumped to death. I'm not suggesting that he committed suicide. I'm suggesting that his behavior was so high risk that there was no need for that."

Brad's point was blunt, for good reason: people don't all break the same way, but they often break for the same reasons—trauma, the absence of anyone willing to intervene, or pressure they carry alone. Kurt felt it. Walter felt it. Countless service members feel it every single day.

For Kurt, that pressure was forward-facing, weighing on him both internally and publicly. In a lot of ways, Kurt represented the end of the polished musician in the mainstream.

"Heavy metal became more popular in the eighties, and even that got turned into a very corporate thing," Brad says. "MTV became a thing, so now we're putting artists in a music video and they've got to look good . . . So that got shoved down our throats to the point where it was like an imitation of an imitation of an imitation of an imitation. You're totally deluded. . . . There was this whole group of rebellious kids who were seeing very corporate hair metal all over MTV. I remember none of the angsty teenagers were being serviced. And then, all of a sudden, here's this guy [Kurt]. He's regular. He's plain. He's not wearing corporate uniform musician apparel, and it's raw, and you know it's just relatable, and he's writing things that you know an entire generation—multiple generations—could relate to.

And it was just perfect in my mind. It was a perfect storm. It was what the world needed right then . . . There was more to the guy than the negative, and maybe people can start to see that and be like, 'Okay, he really struggled, but we don't have to write people off as destined to join the "27 Club."' There were things that could have been done that weren't done. I think of those die-hard fans that kind of hold onto him like 'Man, that was just destined to happen to Kurt,' and that's not true. People didn't really try too hard to help him, because he was profitable."

"Nobody is beyond repair," I say.

That's the commonality—not destiny, not inevitability, not some "27 Club" myth, but a societal failure. Communities fail. Industries fail. And the ones who suffer most are the ones left carrying the weight alone. Artists, soldiers, everyday people, friends, family—all of them underscore why mental health advocacy matters.

Our discussion turns to gear, but not in a way that hinges on precision or recreating just a sound—it's about connection, about honoring the people who came before us. Brad isn't chasing accuracy so much as he's chasing a feeling, because that's what Kurt still does to musicians, even decades later: he pushes people to go after an emotion, not a carbon copy.

"I went out specifically and got some vintage guitar pedals that were the kind that Kurt used," Brad tells me. "The EHX and the Boss . . . there is a difference—there's a complete difference in tone between the vintage stuff and the new stuff . . . I used the Electro-Harmonix Small Clone Chorus pedal, and I didn't use it to copy the song, I used it to copy the kind of vibe and the tone. And that was something that twenty-nine years after Kurt's death is still inspiring me. It's one of my favorite tunes by them, 'Come as You Are.' . . . I feel like it's a perfect song because it has every element that just makes a song great, and when it ramps up and hits the heavy parts, it's just so good. It's a really kind of angsty, melodic solo, and that's the kind of tone that I was trying to emulate."

After Brad and I spoke, I took a moment to reflect on how many people Kurt impacted. Whether it's musicians purchasing vintage equipment to emulate a specific Nirvana vibe or people feeling at ease in their own skin because of Kurt's unapologetic attitude, his influence grows exponentially.

Kurt wasn't destined to die by his own hand. No one is. Help is available. On behalf of Walter and active-duty or Veteran service members, it's important to acknowledge mental health in the military by shining a light on suicide rates. And in honor of Walter, and every service member who never got to come home whole—or come home at all—it's more important than ever to keep talking about this, sharing it, and writing about it.

As reported by *PBS NewsHour*, "Since 9/11, more than 30,000 active-duty service members or Veterans of the post-9/11 wars have died by suicide. That is more than four times the number of those who have died in combat."[114]

You can visit veteranscrisisline.net if you know a Veteran in need.

Chapter 27

"BREED"

Jade Perry

WHILE I'D ASKED ALMOST EVERYONE I'VE INTERVIEWED ABOUT SENSAtionalism in the media, I hadn't actually asked a PR expert. So I reached out to Jade Perry, founder and director of Memphia Music Management in Bristol, England. She handles amazing bands from across the UK and has a fierce dedication to the music industry. I was also curious to hear the perspective of someone who understands the pressures artists face daily. And with so much public fascination surrounding Kurt, I knew a PR perspective could help contextualize the often-misunderstood connection between fame and perception. Working primarily with independent artists gives Jade a perspective on the music industry that feels far removed from its more corporate side.

Before I asked Jade to help me untangle the sensationalism that went into creating Kurt Cobain, I asked how she got into music.[115]

★★★

"How I got into music is a bit of a weird one," Jade says. "Quite in fitting with the themes of this book, my journey started because of grief. To deal with a grandparent's death, I listened to a lot of Johnny Cash, and within a year I was interviewing his daughter for a blog I had at the time. From there, I did PR for her book about her father. I got it onto the Rock & Roll Hall of Fame's blog. About a year after that, I found out she was book signing at a Johnny Cash Music Master's weekend alongside talks from his drummer, photographers, management, and so forth. So I scraped the money together and jumped on a flight. I met Johnny Cash's manager and found it really inspiring, but it never crossed my mind that I could manage or promote musicians. A music magazine found me on social media from my updates of the trip, and before long I was writing for them and meeting musicians, and the PR and management side of things organically grew from there."

I asked her about the pressures musicians face in the spotlight—how fame compounds vulnerability, and what that kind of exposure can do to someone like Kurt.

"This is a really hard one to answer as someone who doesn't have to personally deal with this feeling or experience, but I can't begin to imagine the pressure that musicians must feel, from their own expectations of themselves as well as the expectations of everyone around them and of their *perceived* expectations of their fans," Jade explains. "My work is currently centered around emerging artists and not global stars, so my experience of the 'spotlight,' so to speak, is on a very small scale. However, I've seen how hard musicians at this level have to work to get every opportunity they achieve, on top of having to have full-time jobs—it's crippling. I can't imagine at the start of Kurt's musical career that he could have ever dreamed Nirvana would have reached the heights that they did. Within three years, they went from playing gigs of thirty to forty people to playing 65,000-capacity venues; that's a very short period of time to get used to that level of fame, success, and adoration. Suddenly, a lot of people rely on you, you have a team of people pushing your music, and it soon goes from being your personal artistry to a commodity that's paying other people's bills. You go from writing music when the inspiration hits to constantly having the pressure to write to stay relevant and to keep to your end of a record deal. With social media placing importance on protecting our mental health now more than ever, I've seen countless statuses of late where musicians are claiming to be taking short hiatuses and time out for their well-being. That wasn't the case back then."

As Jade spoke, I kept thinking about how the pressures she described are amplified for the whole world to see when you achieve a certain level of fame. Social media only magnifies that, and I've often wondered how Kurt would have handled it. Would he have even bothered? The media's relentless accusations about his personal life already affected him in print; online scrutiny would have been even harsher, more invasive, and more incessant.

"We know the media plays a huge role in the entertainment industry," I say. "Nirvana was before the internet was big, but the media still did its damnedest to expose Kurt's personal life, even though he was outwardly irritated about the media's potshots and relentless assumptions about his marriage and substance abuse. Do you find that the media has a direct effect on a musician's mental health, in a sense? What could sensitive artists like Kurt have done to protect themselves from the media, if anything?"

"Music might be the only industry—at least that I've witnessed—where the media champions you when you're a small, hardworking, hungry artist, and the minute you reach any real height you are suddenly and completely open to ridicule," says Jade, candid in her response. "I'm not sure how anyone can really protect themselves from that. They say that to be in music you need a really thick skin, but the irony is many musicians are often fragile, emotional people. Music gets us through so many shit situations, breakups, grief—why is that? The people creating it are capable of invoking such deep feelings in us because they've felt them on an equally deep level. I don't think the change needs to come from the musicians; the media needs to take a really hard look at itself before putting people down and taking cheap shots at artists. We're all flawed; highlighting other people's flaws to the world is tactless."

The media's shift from celebration to ridicule is a tale as old as time, with artists across decades speaking out about critics eviscerating them in a never-ending cycle. Burnout rarely comes from one source alone. Endless touring, public scrutiny, parasocial culture, and media sensationalism all contribute to the pressure artists carry once fame enters the equation. And it doesn't stop with the media. Once you're in the public eye, a parasocial relationship forms—strangers start to believe they know you, and they feel entitled to weigh in on your every move. Kurt wasn't alone; he was part of a long pattern of sensationalism eclipsing humanity.

This makes me think of Kurt's interview with Kevin Allman in *The Advocate*. When Kurt was asked who he trusted now, his response was clipped and concise:

> "Uh—no one? *[laughs]* I've always kind of kept myself purposely naïve and optimistic, and now I've been forced to be really paranoid. Judgmental. Really defensive all the time. It's been hard for me to change my attitude."[116]

That was the cost of being seen by everyone and trusting of no one.

"What about losing creativity when trying to produce music that appeals to a wide range of listeners?" I ask Jade, curious about the pressure to write.

"Not quite relating to Kurt's era, but artists are required to wear more and more hats currently, especially when they don't have a team behind them," Jade says. "Not only are they musicians, which in itself is no small feat, they're also having to create a steady stream of content, being their own content manager, social media manager, merch designer, videographer, booking agent, PR agent—and for the very savvy—being their own producer. It's never been easy to make money from music unless you were a large act, though now it's harder than ever. Most musicians don't make enough from their music itself to make a steady living, therefore there's more of a demand to be on the road for longer as live fees and merchandise revenue is the main source of income, placing a lot of stress and demands on the artists with risk of fatigue, burnout, and the strain this can put on their personal and/or family lives. The pressures are endless; I couldn't have more respect for the people who choose to dedicate their lives to their creative endeavors. It's bloody brutal."

As I listen, I realize just how much the music industry demands from its artists, especially now that streaming has limited record sales. Now artists rely even more heavily on touring for income, pouring literal blood, sweat, and tears into life on the road while continuing to share their music with the world.

"Do you think Nirvana was able to straddle the lines between maintaining creativity and catering to a wide range of listeners?" I ask, curious about the pressure to create as their audience rapidly expanded.

"I think their long-standing, multi-generational legacy speaks for itself in that they absolutely did," Jade says. "What made them so popular to their audience at that time is that they were completely unlike any other band in the spotlight. Fans liked their individuality, that they were different. They were relatable en masse, and they did that by being completely and unapologetically themselves. If they were then to deliberately cater to an even wider audience, in search of fame that Cobain so frequently rejected, it really would have been counterintuitive, I feel."

Regardless of how Kurt felt about fame, it became a part of him. And no matter how deeply it bore into him, he refused to play by the rules—something that only added to his appeal.

"Kurt Cobain was a PR dream and a PR nightmare of equal proportion; it really was a toss of the coin," Jade says. "His empathy and general contempt for discrimination of any kind was a really great draw and won him a huge and dedicated fan base. He really advocated for women's rights and safety, went against gender norms, and he spoke out for marginalized, underrepresented groups. He had a way of making his audience feel seen, understood, spoken for, and safe."

Jade's absolutely right. Kurt's actions weren't performative—they were rare even then and still feel rare now, despite more artists speaking up. In an industry that has historically catered to self-preservation and detachment, his compassion wasn't just radical—it was an inspiration.

"There were some creative choices that would have made for PR nightmares, though, in the very same breath," Jade adds. "No matter how well-intentioned, I'm not sure a track entitled 'Rape Me' would go down too great in 2024, considering the size and age range of his audience and how readily available that track would be to stream to young children online now. The subject matter couldn't have been more in support of victims, granted, but I think that would be a PR disaster in this day and age."

"Do you have any other thoughts on what fame does to musicians?" I ask.

"Honestly, from watching what it's done to people in recent years, I wouldn't wish it on my worst enemy," Jade answers. "Let's be clear, there are very obvious perks: money, adoration, opportunities you'd never have otherwise . . . But the persistent beatdowns from the press, constantly having people comment on your personality, your looks, your behavior, feeling like people are constantly watching your every move, waiting for and relishing any downfalls and the opportunity to completely pick you apart must put you in the gutter. Not only that, but the continuous pressure to stay relevant and at the top of your game must be all-consuming once you have that taste of fame and respect for your art. I admire anyone that handles it with the poise and grace that Kurt Cobain managed to until he couldn't anymore."

Kurt was easygoing and kind in interviews, even when tired and met with repetitive questions. But he seemed to be one of the rare few who never let fame go to his head, which is ironic, seeing as he achieved more fame than most can even fathom. And fame—especially combined with life on the road—can be soul-crushing when mental health falls by the wayside.

In a study completed by the *Journal of Psychiatric Research* as part of the Tour Health Research Initiative's Touring Health and Wellness

Survey (2020), data showed that touring professionals had elevated levels of suicidality. They were also at risk for clinical depression, along with stress, anxiety, and burnout.[117]

Jade didn't know Kurt, but she sees artists struggle as they navigate this challenging industry. She helped me understand what artists go through and what role the media plays in deciding what parts of a person's life get the most attention. Apathy can keep the media from burrowing under your skin, but the paradox is that many artists—like Kurt—are too sensitive to wield it.

I was also reminded how Nirvana—and Kurt in particular—offered a lifeline to people who felt isolated and excluded, making them feel heard, appreciated, and accepted, even as he himself may have felt alienated by his newfound social status.

When framed alongside the pressures Jade described, his insistence on using his platform to defend and uplift others becomes even more remarkable. That's Kurt's lasting impact. And that's how he should be remembered.

Chapter 28

"BEEN A SON"

Antonino Tati and Juno Rylee Schultz

"Yes, Kurt Cobain was a grunge icon. He was also a gay rights hero." The title left little room for ambiguity.

The subtitle read: "I was a closeted Midwesterner in the '90s. Listening to Nirvana changed my life."[118]

The writer, Aaron Hamburger, author of *Nirvana Is Here*, and whose article permeated the mainstream above all the noise and click-bait, reflects on something besides Kurt's depression. Specifically, how Kurt positively affected him. And it was refreshing as hell to read.

Once you know what to look for, it's not hard to find articles that praise Kurt for standing publicly with communities that were often silenced. You just need to sift past the rumor machine and the clickbait.

I reached out to Antonino Tati, editor of *Cream Magazine Australia*, indie radio presenter, pop cultural commentator, and author of music interview anthology *There's Your Quote, Mate*. Antonino is insightful and perceptive. After years spent interviewing artists across genres while focusing on music, identity, and culture, I knew he'd help me better understand the societal underpinnings embodied by Kurt Cobain, particularly how his public values resonated within LGBTQIA+ culture.[119]

★★★

"I never really thought of Kurt Cobain or Nirvana as being champions for queer culture until I came across a copy of *The Face* magazine [UK] in 1993 on a newsstand that featured Kurt on the cover wearing a floral dress," Antonino recalls. "The caption read, 'In the court of king Kurt,' and here was this huge rock icon—probably the biggest in the grit-laden grunge scene—unshaven, hair tousled, wearing a pretty little dress, and branded a king. I loved the queer mess of it all, and whenever I'd publish a feature on queer style, I made sure to reference Kurt."

Antonino continues, "There were other times where Kurt insisted on wearing traditional women's clothing, either for the fun of it or to make a gender-deconstructing statement—but never to *make* fun of traditional femininity, like, say, a traditional drag queen might. Decades before Harry Styles was flouncing on stage in skirts and blouses, Kurt was brave enough to go full lingerie. While performing 'Dive' live in Rio in 1993, he wore a lace slip and tiara, taking the queen/king thing to the next level. If you're lucky, you might still find a clip of it on YouTube.

"Kurt's flirting with gender messing went way beyond the aesthetic. Many of his lyrics reveal a man who was either content to blur the lines of expected gender behavior or someone traumatized to a degree by a proverbial desire to crawl back into the womb. He certainly held high regard—if not a certain awe—for that place we were all born from. In 'Heart-Shaped Box,' he refers to this part of the female anatomy as something sacrosanct, a place where man is born from and forever aims to get back into. The lyric that speaks about Kurt climbing up an umbilical noose pretty much sums this notion up. The hint is also there in the title of one of Nirvana's most famous albums, *In Utero*."

But Kurt wasn't subtle about his views—especially when it came to calling out the people he never wanted in his audience.

In an interview with Jonathan Poneman for *Spin* magazine, Kurt said, "I don't necessarily want to go back and play clubs, but I would like to get rid of the homophobes, sexists, and racists in our audience. I know they're out there and it really bothers me."[120]

"Sometimes, he even took the blatant route in his lyricism about a certain sexuality, such as in 'All Apologies' with the lyric: 'What else should I be? All apologies; What else could I say? Everyone is gay,'" Antonino muses.

"Kurt was very much about the duplicity of things; in 'Heart-Shaped Box,' forlorn lyrics creep into a love song; the cheesiness of his Buddy Holly drag in the clip for 'In Bloom' while behind the scenes are crazy crossdressing and ambiguous cosplay. It's like he was trying to say, 'Man, if the one percent weren't so hung up about doing all this shit behind closed doors, we'd all just accept the freakshow and get on with trying to fix this world.' Kurt was in the music industry in the early 1990s—a time when diversity and tolerance of varied sexuality weren't celebrated socially. So, the pop stars of the day—Kurt, Shirley Manson, the Chili Peppers, PJ Harvey, even Courtney Love—they'd all be doing their darnedest to raise the velvet curtain on the kinky, sometimes corrupt goings-on of industry at large.

"While the spirit of Lennon remains inside the costume of the Walrus, Kurt's wardrobe was more of the Chameleon." There's that word again—*chameleon*. "Rock deity or damsel in this dress? Clean-cut pop pinup or drug-addled speaker in tongues? Devil with secrets of his own or angel and messenger of truth? You never really knew with Kurt, and he'd loved that you never knew. After all, killing off pigeonholing and pissing off the commandeers of industry seemed to play a part in his calling."

Antonino taps into an unfettered truth: Kurt was blunt yet baffling, and it made him timeless. He was also a seismic shift during a countercultural revolution, when the world needed more than a shake—it needed to be flung off its antiquated axis. Once people understood that someone had their back, it became safer to step forward loudly, clearly, and unapologetically. This is the true mark of a person worth celebrating.

And writers like Antonino remember him for exactly that essence—the unfiltered, honest persona and style that mattered far more than the tragedy that later consumed the headlines.

Antonino isn't the only person who remembers Kurt for his role as an LGBTQIA+ advocate. Many indie writers who were often underrepresented in the larger narrative around Kurt penned articles about music, identity, and counterculture. This led me to Juno Rylee Schultz, a writer featured in publications such as *Paste*, *Polygon*, and *Unwinnable*. Her article, "Don't Hurt Girls When You Dance (Or Any Other Time)," originally published under the name Juno Stump, reflects on Nirvana's *MTV Unplugged in New York* and includes a candid, powerful story from her own life—one that reminded me why we can't gloss over the lives Kurt positively affected. Juno's unfiltered account captures exactly what Kurt stood for, speaking to his permanence and undiluted inner beauty. She kindly let me reprint an excerpt here.

★★★

"Don't Hurt Girls When You Dance (Or Any Other Time)"
Juno Stump
April 5, 2024
Unwinnable Monthly #164's Cover Story

I don't know if Kurt Cobain would still be here today if he had the ability to inject estrogen instead of heroin, but I know his journal pages carry the same pain as me—and so many other women like me.

I grew up in a small world, just like Kurt Cobain but decades later, surrounded by the same kinds of family and people, and with the same kind of sorrows and wishes for myself and the world around me. Nothing felt right to me and everything felt wrong, around me and within me.

Growing up trans, queer, and closeted is hard for anyone, but it's even harder when you already know your parents don't love or accept you. This was the case for me. I tried to come out to my parents several times, as early as age four. My mom wouldn't listen. My dad called me a "faggot."

I already felt like I was on an alien planet, condemned to some strange, discarded flesh vessel, with just enough room for me in the corner, to waste away and think of another day, all while having the responsibility of inventing a stranger to keep me out of danger. All I could really do was not die while trying to hold on, with the hope that I would one day feel alive.

I didn't have any men in my life that felt right or worthy as guardians or role models when I was growing up. My feelings then, at ages four through nine, were that all men felt like a hostile force on a planet that everyone but them was trapped on. But that changed one day when I first heard Nirvana's songs and Kurt Cobain's words—and saw pictures of him and his swirling blue eyes that seemed to be home to familiar pain. I couldn't explain it entirely at first. I just knew right away that this man was different. My asshole dad seemed to be the norm, but Kurt Cobain was nothing like him.

I listened to all of Nirvana's albums on repeat while reading about Kurt Cobain online, on every credible website I could find. It was sometime in 2002, I was twelve years old and I had found my first hyper-fixation, a man who was not only cool but cared about marginalized people and complained about the same things that bothered me. I clung to every word I found in interviews, with the lyrics of songs hitting my brain like pure rain, washing everything artificially manufactured away. I didn't know how, but he was the first person that felt familiar. The first person that seemed to have the same pain. I'd never met a woman or man like me until I grew to learn about Kurt Cobain.

I disagreed with everyone who said Kurt's lyrics were just random words, including him, who, in an interview suggested fans stop asking him for meaning, instead imploring fans to just listen to the band's music and find their own meaning. I found that meaning, but I think it also might have been his.

I spent so many nights crying because I felt empty, isolated, alone—like I wasn't even alive.

I'd tried to forget I was trans and closeted, years after my parents had swiped away my fears and pain. It was impossible to forget but I tried nonetheless—like you would if you heard a major plot twist revealed in the theater bathroom, right before the movie you're about to see, trying to ignore that overheard detail, that character's death, that crucial part that affects everything—but it was stuck—stuck—stuck—stuck—stuck, just like a popcorn kernel behind your back-most tooth.

I wasn't allowed to remove the popcorn kernel, so I just tried not to think about it. I knew I was a girl. I knew I was trapped. My parents, God (???) and everyone I thought who would help me instead insisted everything was fine. I just needed to go to school, follow the rules, read my Bible, listen to God, and only play video games and music at a certain volume. Then, they assured me, everything would be okay. I would feel fine. I would feel great.

Nothing ever felt right and everything always felt wrong, but everyone said that was just me and not real. I just needed to stop acting weird. And then I would feel fine. Life kept moving, almost without me. I just wanted to feel okay. I just wanted to feel normal. I just wanted to feel right.

And many, many times I thought, if I could just make some changes to my body, then *maybe* I would feel okay. And if I wasn't successful, and started to need the help of a doctor, my parents would have to take me in, and maybe then, a doctor would hear me and help me.

This cycle continued. Everything was mostly about survival, saying the right things to fit in for safety, while I dealt with my predicament. I didn't know what else to do, outside of dying and trying again, which was something that always felt kind of, sort of on the table. I worried about God, mostly, but hoped He would understand. But I kept going, with the hope that I would eventually feel better, or at least a little okay.

Nothing really helped and nothing felt real until that first day I heard Nirvana. . . . All of a sudden, I felt a *little* grounded, a little present. I wasn't quite disassociating as much as I normally did. Not only did something finally feel real but it also felt familiar.

I immediately felt connected to nearly all of his songs and their lyrics, but especially tracks like "Dumb," "Something in the Way," "Sappy," "Even in His Youth," "Been a Son," and "You Know You're Right."

I didn't have all of the words to explain my predicament, yet. I tried to tell my parents with everything I had, from "God might be punishing me" to "My bones are wrong and are hurting me, inside and outside." That only got me slurs and abuse. I didn't have anything else, including anything resembling comfort or anything that encapsulated the pain I felt, until I heard the following words from "You Know You're Right," in the second verse of the last song Kurt ever recorded in a studio. In that verse, Kurt Cobain sang about the desire to sing about someone else. He then playfully referred to hot soup melting and male and female pronouns within the same breath. It felt so intentional.

Hearing those words against my heart, I knew that nothing was actually wrong with me—and that I just wanted to love and be myself. I held onto that as tightly as I could. The idea that I wasn't broken was enough to know I wasn't alone. And that was enough for now.

As the years passed, I dealt with my suffering by trying to numb everything with drugs and alcohol, much like Kurt Cobain did across much of his life. He had his music and tried not to feel. I had video games and did the same with my feelings. My popcorn kernel.

Kurt Cobain's *Journals*, released a few months after the release of "You Know You're Right" in 2002, containing chronologically organized pages from the musician's personal writings and notes. No single book could hold all of his jottings; he was always writing and filled up hundreds of notebooks in his life. *Journals* collected notes from the Nirvana years, giving fans a glimpse into Kurt Cobain's mind during his time in the spotlight.

Inside the book are nearly 300 pages of doodles, scribbles, rough drafts of letters to friends, important phone numbers, answers to hypothetical interviews, comic strips, song lyric drafts, and concept art for album covers, but also personal details about how he felt in his body, growing up and as an adult and how even with the fame, success, money and everything else, he still didn't feel right.

And that . . . helped me, alongside his music, as I went through the wrong puberty. As my bones grew, they hurt really bad, too, just like Kurt, and even though he wasn't here, knowing at least one other person had known what I felt like, tormented and suffering inside the walls of a stranger's fleshy prison, helped me a lot.

I didn't have all the language at this age. It was 2003, 2004, and 2005, in my small, Michigan farm town, and words like "trans" and "gender non-conforming" were just . . . not around me. I had Bible verses and whatever my public school taught me.

But I always had my suffering. I just didn't know how else to articulate it at this point. My parents already made me feel unsafe, traumatizing me for years, so telling anyone else was beyond me at that point.

I never did let go of that popcorn kernel that was stuck in my teeth. I just tried not to pick at it.

And I think that's what Kurt did too.

There's only so much you can do when you never feel right or like yourself. All you can ever feel is isolated. We may never know for sure, but I think there's a reason that so many trans women have been able to identify with Kurt Cobain's joy, pain, and suffering, so strongly.

Kurt Cobain suffered from a stomach problem his entire life, to the point that it agonized him almost daily. Despite attempts to get diagnosed by several doctors throughout his life, especially in his later years, he was never able to cure whatever ailed him. He tried changing his diet. He tried everything doctors suggested, but it never went away, only fading occasionally, during intermittent instances in his life. A few women in Kurt's family, including his mother, were briefly affected by debilitating stomach issues, but it always eventually subsided and calmed.

Kurt's stomach pain was the subject of many pages in his notebooks and came up in plenty of interviews. It's possible that this pain came from how Kurt felt about himself. Many trans people experience an assortment of issues and symptoms from dysphoria, including physical pain, especially while still closeted.

Kurt also hated his body, which affected the way he dressed in nearly every situation. This included rarely wearing shorts, hating how his knees and legs looked, unless the temperature was particularly high. He even wore long johns under jeans to the beach on more than one occasion. He complained about his body often, in his journals and to those around him.

Seeing another human being grappling with what might have been body dysphoria wasn't something I had ever experienced before. I didn't even know there was a word for dysphoria when I was a teenager. But here was someone else who was also upset about their body. Someone else that felt trapped. That thread of questioning and torment helped me know that I wasn't alone.

It wasn't in the songs, but seeing this in his journals, in his thoughts, and with penmanship that looked pained and frustrated . . . it couldn't be nothing.

Kurt Cobain would also often dress in drag, which included dresses and other female-coded clothing and makeup on many occasions, including for photo shoots and concerts. There were other rock stars, even Dave Grohl, Krist Novoselic, and Pat Smear in the band, who had worn or would wear eyeliner and lipstick, but Kurt just always looked much more comfortable, happy even, when dressing in drag and/or wearing makeup. It was even commented on by those who interviewed him and captured him on film, though I don't think they saw it in the same way as me.

Kurt consistently spoke highly of female artists, such as The Breeders, Shonen Knife, and Bikini Kill, throughout his life. Nirvana would tour with many of these bands.

Kurt always showed up for women, including in his political beliefs, even playing charity and benefit concerts that helped rape victims and empowered women. He was also outspoken, especially for his time, for how much women were oppressed by society. This extended to queer rights, which Cobain openly supported, even going as far as saying he wished he was gay "just to piss off the homophobes."

Kurt provided just one interview for Nirvana's 1992 release, *Incesticide*, a compilation album of outtakes and B-sides, and it was to *The Advocate*, a gay and lesbian publication. Kurt's support for queer rights and the band's opposition to racists and homophobes is something that's made clear in the piece.

Kurt loved performing music despite all the suffering he endured. He would often find joy and confidence from women around him, choosing to surround himself with feminist music and ideals. These punk rock ideals and Kurt's proximity of closeness and respect for Riot Grrrl bands, such as Bikini Kill, only served to amplify Kurt's contempt for macho men and male-dominated culture, which could be heard in interviews, read in album liner notes, and even during many of his songs, including "Very Ape," "Mr. Moustache," and "Territorial Pissings." He was gender non-conforming and constantly lifted women up, despite dealing with the clear-as-day body dysphoria, which is visible in nearly every photograph of Kurt Cobain.

There's just so much evidence to suggest that Kurt Cobain was a closeted trans woman who did the best they could, with the circumstances and trauma they had, while jamming through their hyper-fixation and trying to make the world a better place for other marginalized people, right up until the very end.

The LGBTQIA+ community and its allies typically try to avoid diagnosing people, especially if they're not here to speak up for themselves. It's part of listening to people when they introduce themselves and tell you who they are. But Kurt Cobain also has a page in his journals that reads, "Don't read my diary when I'm gone. OK, I'm going to work now. When you wake up this morning, please read my diary. Look through my things, and figure me out."

I think he would be okay with a girl like me finding catharsis in his pain, seeing his struggles, and taking something good from it. I think it would make him proud that a dyke like me was able to hit ages sixteen, twenty, and thirty with his help. And while he may be the only one that truly knows if he was a closeted trans girl, I know if he was here, he would be happy to learn that an untold number of trans women, cis women, non-binary people, queer people, and gender non-conforming people have found their days easier because of things he wrote, sang and said.

Kurt Cobain should have had the chance to grow some breasts. I'd rather have that than "All Apologies."

A world with trans rights would make less pain for people like Kurt Cobain, who was at the very least gender non-conforming, regardless of how you want to see him.

We should all be supporting laws and building communities that support people from all gender identities and sexual orientations. The anti-trans and queerphobic legislation sweeping across the nation can only lead to more people feeling isolated and alienated like Kurt Cobain. And if he was here today, he'd say something cool, like "God is gay" or "May women rule the world," but he'd also most certainly say "trans rights."[121]

★★★

Juno was incredibly brave in allowing me to reprint her words. Through her unflinching honesty, she shared how profoundly Kurt's message shaped her life. In turn, her words get to affect someone else—Kurt's message of inclusion coming full circle once again. He offered comfort at a time when she needed unconditional love and permission to exist as herself. I also saw the comparison: two people who persevered when the odds were stacked against them. Yes, Juno's words were gutting—but they were also a testament to resilience, and to what can happen when someone refuses to accept the cruelty of the world as inevitable.

Through her lived experience, my understanding of Kurt's legacy sharpened and deepened. His impact was never abstract to me, but after speaking with Juno and Antonino, I had tangible reinforcement of the reach and consequence of his convictions—particularly within the LGBTQIA+ community—and of the power in hearing, perhaps for the first time, that it's okay to be who you are. Kurt understood the weight of that message. Backlash was the last thing he cared about at a time when the world needed his razor-sharp, zero-bullshit megaphone.

Chapter 29

"SAPPY"

Darren Paltrowitz

As I delved deeper into Kurt's life, I began to form my own conclusions about the consequences of fame. The spotlight didn't just illuminate Kurt; it burned. There isn't enough access to mental health care—not for Veterans, not for artists, and certainly not for those who slip through the cracks. Can this book bring Walter or Kurt back? No. But can it help someone, somehow? I hope so.

After speaking with industry professionals who pulled back the curtain on how punishing the entertainment world can be, I wanted to hear from more writers who had spent years contextualizing artists under that same pressure. This led me to Darren Paltrowitz, author of *DLR Book: How David Lee Roth Changed the World* and host of the established podcast and interview series *Paltrocast*. His work explores how artists are consumed, celebrated, and often misunderstood by the media. While literature on Kurt Cobain is plentiful, I knew Darren's perspective would help me better understand Kurt's universal appeal—why his life, not just his death, continues to matter.

So I gave Darren a call to talk about the grunge icon, and what made him resonate so deeply with so many.[122]

★★★

"I think that there hasn't been a lot written about Nirvana's influence over the last twenty years," Darren begins. "Everything is about the last tragic days, or maybe just '91 to '94 with Kurt Cobain, because they [Nirvana] only had about three years of hugeness. International hugeness. And just in those couple of years, you got two studio albums, *Unplugged*, the B-sides record, all sorts of cameos. It's amazing how huge they were in three years. The Doors, I think, was four to five years, but Nirvana's really a record for how much they did, yet very little is talked about for the last twenty-ish years. And the influence of Nirvana is infinite."

"Some of the other artists that I've interviewed might not be super well-known yet, but they're from all over the world, and they showcase and celebrate Nirvana and Kurt Cobain," I say. "The band influenced all these people to just keep going and to make music. I mean, Nirvana just appealed to everyone."

"That makes sense," Darren says. "I think that Nirvana, being a pre-internet band, is one of those entertainment staples that everyone likes whether they are independent or mainstream. You see young people these days walking around with Nirvana shirts on that could not have been born within ten years of Kurt's passing. So they're [Nirvana] a rare multi-generational band that basically everyone likes. It's not an uncool corporate thing to like Nirvana the way that it might be for, say, Mötley Crüe. It's this big divide where people don't like that, but people can like Nirvana and Mötley Crüe, or just Nirvana. It's just a line-in-the-sand kind of band along the lines of The Beatles, The Rolling Stones. Very few bands are on that Nirvana level."

That disconnect between the public image and the real person is something Darren finds especially important.

"I think that when you read interviews or hear interviews from people who knew Kurt, as opposed to just liking his music, you hear about the depressed guy that we kind of assume was a creation," Darren explains. "In other words, he had different characters going on. The Melvins guys—I can't remember whether it was Dale or Buzz—was talking about how all that was entirely a character. That he [Kurt] was this fun, funny guy who could turn it on and off. So we hear that kind of stuff, and I find that usually the darker the music, the more lax and fun the person is. You realize that on stage, it's a character—except Dave Mustaine from Megadeth. Everyone else is super lax in the metal and punk worlds, I find.

"So tying in your book with my book, there are a few different Van Halen–Nirvana crossovers. One I can tell you is five or six years ago, there's footage of David Lee Roth watching sumo wrestling in Japan for fun, and he's talking everyone's ear off. He says to somebody, 'Hey, you know Kurt Cobain killed my career.' I'm paraphrasing, but he blames Kurt for killing his career, which is totally nuts. What killed David Lee Roth's career was bad decisions—because he fired management, changed up his sound in bad ways, and basically became a caricature of himself . . . But then towards the end of Kurt's life, there was a Los Angeles show where Eddie Van Halen was hanging out. He may have had a couple of drinks in him and he wanted to come on stage with Nirvana, but Kurt said no. It was because Eddie said a racist-ish thing and Kurt just did not want any part of that. Kurt was a feminist before feminism was cool. He was an equal-opportunity person who hung out with everybody, it seemed. He was anti-racism. Everything that the woke generation is going for, Kurt was woke before it was called 'woke.'"

Kurt was intentional about the shows he played and the people he associated with, regardless of who was headlining.

Darren continues, "Most people don't realize that when an artist is playing a tribute concert, some of the time—not all of the time, but some of the time, and in Nirvana's case—they were losing money to do it. Not only were they not taking payment, but they were paying crew salaries and they were paying for a hotel and things like that. So the artist is operating at a loss while fundraising to do that. You do hear bad cases where the artist is getting paid to do benefits and therefore the charity concert was still a money-making venture where they only had to give five percent to appease nonprofit law, but that's not what Kurt was, and that's not what Kurt did.

"So look at those three-ish years when he was alive and prolific and producing the Melvins album. He made cameos on other things. The average artist maybe puts out one album every three years, and you look at how much output Kurt had, and that we were still getting unreleased materials a couple of years ago. He was still doing the tribute concerts and he was still touring around the world, still doing interviews, and he had a kid in that period of time."

"And he was young."

"Yeah," Darren says. "He only lived to be twenty-seven. I think it speaks volumes as to how much he got done in those three years."

"I agree," I say. "People ask why Kurt didn't just quit if he was so depressed over being famous."

Darren offers his input. "I'm sure the man felt a lot of pressure from a lot of angles because so many people were feeding themselves off his creative output, and that's got to be a depressing thought . . . And when you become an industry-oriented band like that where there are . . . tens of millions of dollars coming in every year—you have that pressure while you have to write hit songs, while you have to be nice to everyone, and you can't be your old anonymous self, while you're a husband and a father. So I can't imagine how much pressure that guy faced."

What Darren described wasn't just fame—it was obligation.

"I think it's amazing and speaks to Kurt's determination, being unhoused and persevering to achieve that type of success," I say.

"Totally agree," Darren says. "Now, there are rumors that Kurt wanted to break up Nirvana and to fire Dave Grohl. That's been addressed to different levels of accuracy. I have no idea about any of that because, depending on the conversation, he loved Dave Grohl, he didn't love Dave Grohl. You also don't know if he was feuding with Billy Corgan, because they both dated Courtney Love, and they were both trying to be the voice of a generation—or not. There are so many things that we don't know because you have a bunch of egomaniacs telling their side of the story. I think that what we do know is Kurt was an original human being who wasn't following anybody else. He's very prolific. He fought for the things that he cared about, and a lot of critics have it wrong, but they want to tell a certain kind of sensationalized story."

What's often remembered is Kurt's pain. What surfaced again and again in these conversations, though, was something else entirely—a man who loved animals, hated assholes, and showed up for people who needed him. I even came across an article that commented on Kurt's "overlooked social activism," and that made me smile.[123] The world hadn't forgotten all the good he did.

That led me to the hardest question of all: whether anything could have been done to prevent Kurt's death.

Darren pauses for a moment to consider this.

"The tough part of that answer is I don't know what's true and what's not true, because Duff McKagan from Guns N' Roses was a Seattle guy; even though Guns N' Roses is thought of as this LA band, he's totally a Seattle guy," he explains. "And he claims that he had just seen Kurt at the airport that weekend and he was going to meet up with him. Michael Stipe was saying how he and Kurt were going to have this side project, and that was going to happen. And then Sammy Hagar from Van Halen, who has told a lot of tall tales, was talking about how he's singing about Kurt Cobain in a song, and I don't think Kurt liked anything that Sammy Hagar did. I think Kurt Cobain and Sammy Hagar couldn't be more diametrically opposed when it comes to artists. So I think he had a lot of fair-weather friends, but I do think that he had a lot of people who wanted to help."

As others have pointed out in previous interviews, withdrawal-related depression may have played a major role. Fame also complicated Kurt's relationship with the music scene he helped shape. Questions about authenticity, commercial success, and "selling out" followed Nirvana constantly, adding another layer of pressure during an already difficult period.

"'Selling out' is such a convoluted term," Darren says. "It means eighty different things to eighty different people. So just taking a record deal is not selling out, because getting a record deal is not the end of the rainbow; it's the beginning of the rainbow. That's when you actually have to start doing all the work. Most people think that because you're getting an advance, your life changes in this great way. The reality is that that advance is usually before the album budget, commissions, and taxes. You're splitting it three to eight ways with other members and whatnot, your equipment that you have to buy, you're probably buying your van.

"So a lot of artists think, *Oh, $700,000 advance* (which, by the way, happens no longer). And you think, *Wow, my life is over in a good way.* The reality is no, you're probably walking away with about six grand. It's something stupid like that. Nirvana did not have a huge record deal, so if anybody made out like bandits, it was Sub Pop Records who got the royalties. I think they call it an override, where Geffen took over the deal from Sub Pop, and Sub Pop was getting royalties on Geffen Records. I don't know how many titles, if it was all of them, or if it was just *Nevermind*, but Sub Pop probably made as much money as Krist Novoselic did."

Darren's comments about royalties and record deals mirror many of the frustrations penned in a *Baffler* article by Steve Albini in December 1993, aptly titled "The Problem with Music."[124] Steve's subtitle called it like he saw it: "Imagine a trench filled with decaying shit." Steve proceeded to describe the truth about what musicians encounter in the recording industry. I highly recommend reading this expertly written—and eye-opening—article.

"Nirvana was probably the biggest by far," Darren says. "And we got that *Bleach* thirtieth anniversary reissue. Supposedly, that's Dr. Dre's favorite rock album of all time—he works out to *Bleach*."

Darren's point underscores just how broad Kurt's appeal was. His music didn't belong to one scene, one genre, or one type of listener. It reached people across worlds—including artists operating at the highest levels of fame.

When I asked him what accounted for Kurt's unusually broad appeal, Darren framed it as a convergence of factors.

"A few things," he offers. "One, he was totally different from what was happening in the mainstream. Two, right time, right place when it comes to marketing for MTV and the other gatekeepers and tastemakers of the time to go, 'Hmm, I don't know if we want that second Trixter album.' People say that grunge killed heavy metal. I don't think that's fully true. I think that you just look at where things are, and nothing lasts more than five years. I can't think of one trend that really lasts a long time.

"So they were looking for something new, and the 'Smells Like Teen Spirit' video looked different from everything at the time. Everything was just totally different, so Nirvana was at the right place at the right time. And who were the people behind it? Danny Goldberg was one of the greatest minds in the history of the music business. He worked for Zeppelin when he was super young in the seventies, and then he was president of record companies ultimately. And I think Gary Gersh had signed Sonic Youth before them. So it was just really smart people behind Nirvana, on top of the music being that great."

When he mentions how great the music is, I think of the performance that left an enormous mark on music history.

"What about the *Unplugged* show? That's my favorite show," I say. "I think it was amazing that Kurt wanted to do all these covers from bands he loved and even brought the Meat Puppets with him on stage."

"I used to work for a management company that handled the Meat Puppets," Darren says. "Long story short, it was Kurt covering their stuff on *MTV Unplugged* that not only got them [the Meat Puppets] out of debt but got them a lot of money, got the record company to care, and got them a big new record deal. It all happened from *Unplugged*. And look at Pat Smear joining. When Kurt took on Pat Smear, he was the guy from The Germs, and that was ten years before that. So he [Kurt] wanted to take him on. Kurt helped elevate the Melvins by producing their album at a time where, yeah, the Melvins were doing okay, but he wanted to elevate them, too. And then you look at the bands he took on tour, like Shonen Knife from Japan. I think that Nirvana was their first big North American tour . . . He wanted to reunite the Wipers to take them on tour . . . So he loved these bands, and he wanted to make them money by covering them, or bringing them on tour, and elevating his scene, and going, 'These people love my stuff, maybe they'll love it, too.' How many artists in that position do that?"

Everything Darren said reinforced a truth I figured out while navigating this emotional walkabout to understand who Kurt really was. It also reinforced why his death still pulls so much focus, and what we can do to push back against the narratives that keep flattening a complex human life, shrinking him down to one reductive storyline.

Chapter 30

"ENDLESS, NAMELESS"

Gillian Gaar

Gillian Gaar conducted some of the most thorough research on Nirvana to date and is the author of definitive works like *Entertain Us: The Rise of Nirvana, Nirvana's* In Utero, and *Nirvana: The Biggest Rock Band of the '90s*, plus much more. We spoke candidly about Kurt's performance at *MTV Unplugged in New York* and what made the inscrutable punk rocker a worldwide sensation. Gillian also shared with me insight into Kurt's resolute nature, explaining how he wasn't someone who could be easily manipulated.[125]

★★★

"I had a friend who knew Lori Goldston [Nirvana's cellist in 1993]. That was how I was able to see *Unplugged*. She got me in to see one of their [Nirvana] regular shows a couple days beforehand. I remember we were given backstage passes, but they wouldn't allow us in right away. We had to wait for other people to finish before we could go in. Lori was leaving, so I said, 'Well, can we go out and have a drink?' She said, 'Yeah.' So she carried her cello back to the hotel, and then the friend I was with—and Lori—we just went to the bar at the hotel or something; we're sitting there at the counter having our drinks. At one point I said, 'I bet the band wishes they could be here instead of backstage having to do all the schmoozing.' And she said, 'You know, they probably do.' Her experience traveling with them really showed that side to her, how she had this freedom to go out and about and do stuff that they couldn't have."

Gillian then remembers the energy surrounding *Unplugged*, wondering if she'd even get in.

"I remember getting to the place and there was this long line, and you think, *Oh, will I get in?*" she explains. "But I got in, and it seemed like all the seats were taken . . . Then I heard someone say, 'There's a media section over here.' . . . It was these risers at the back, and I thought, *Oh good, you're overseeing everyone.* And even there they didn't have enough seats . . . I remember beforehand how some people just thought, *Oh, it's ridiculous. How could they possibly do an Unplugged because they're this noisy rock band?* I knew it was gonna work because they're good songs, so you'd just be hearing them without amplification . . . I think this was another deliberate thing; he [Kurt] wasn't gonna play his biggest hits, like 'Teen Spirit.' But they could have done a really interesting acoustic version [laughs], when you think of it."

She recalls how casual everything felt, with Dave Grohl wandering around with a Heineken in his hand. "Krist's wife I saw with Tinuviel, who cofounded the Kill Rock Stars record label, and they were looking for seats, and I thought, *Gosh, if they don't have seats reserved for them, no wonder the rest of us had a hard time.* I do remember my first impression on walking into that room was thinking it was like a funeral parlor. But not in any kind of morbid way. It just had this autumnal glow, and yeah, it did make me think of a funeral. Which we know now was Kurt's intention when talking to the set designer. He wanted all the stargazer lilies, and the designer goes, 'Like a funeral?' He said, 'Yeah, exactly.' He wanted that feel and whether that's foreshadowing or subconscious foreshadowing, who knows, but that was definitely in his head. Krist said this to me—he said this in other interviews, too—that Kurt's art was always twisted in some respect, whether that was songs or his sculptures or his illustrations. There was always something a bit twisted and dark about that. If you listen to the recording [of *MTV Unplugged in New York],* Kurt starts out . . . I remember kind of chuckling at this . . . he says, 'This song's off our first album. Most people don't own it' [laughs]. I thought, *Well, that's a little bit of snark dropped in there* [laughs]. By this time, you've sold millions of albums and yet you focus on the one that hasn't sold millions of albums."

I also took note of when Kurt made this comment, though I read it differently than Gillian. To me, it felt more like a humble remark from a man who didn't overestimate his fame—someone who understood that most fans simply focused on their mainstream success.

Her recollections of *Unplugged* also highlighted how unpredictable the setlist felt in the moment.

"I had no idea what they [Nirvana] were going to play. I certainly wasn't familiar with the Meat Puppets' songs . . . I mean, I know I read in someone else's description that there was kind of this tension in the air, but I didn't feel that myself. It was anticipation . . . And in between [songs], they're just kind of relaxed and chatting to each other and making jokes . . .

"I also wondered—and Lori told me she wondered this, too—that some of those *Unplugged* [shows], if they didn't get a song the way they wanted, MTV would make them perform it again. I think there was one—I forget which artist—but it went on for like three hours or something while they were taping all this. I remember thinking, *Well, do I want to stay here that long, even if this is Nirvana?* Lori told me later that she thought they [MTV] might make them do it again just because she knew they did that kind of thing, but obviously they didn't. They just went through it and that was that.

"They [the musicians] were probably more nervous than the audience was, frankly, because they never had a complete dress rehearsal. They'd rehearsed, but not just done the straight start-to-finish dress rehearsal. She said she really didn't like those cameras moving around because they're kind of constantly flying by you, which was sort of off-putting. She later said that because you're just so focused on playing and getting it right that she wasn't even sure how good her performance was—not until after it aired and people were saying, 'Oh, it was great.' The final song was 'Where Did You Sleep Last Night?' It was just really shattering. It still is."

"Did you ever meet him or talk to him [Kurt]?" I ask.

"I never did an interview with him, but I'll get back to that," Gillian says. "So I'm watching it [*Unplugged*] later and, of course, you see close-ups. (I was further back so I didn't have close-up shots of the band.) I remember looking at him [Kurt] and thinking, *Ah, there's something wrong.* I mean, at the time, I didn't know that he was pretty much a full-on heroin addict by then and that he needed drugs to get through that day. But there's kind of a deadness in the eye or that he's just not there. He's not fully present in the way that, say, you look at Krist's face—or any of the other band members' faces. In their eyes . . . you could see it in their eyes. And again, it wasn't like I had any . . . like I suddenly sensed, *Oh, no, this is gonna end in tragedy.* But those things, they left an impression.

"I remember that same fall, *Come as You Are* comes out—the book—and reading that and thinking to myself, *God, he [Kurt] talks about suicide a lot. . . .* Which didn't make me think, *Oh, that means he's gonna kill himself in a few months. . . .* but it stuck in my mind that's something he talked about a lot. Because you read that book, and it does come up regularly: 'I was so upset about such and such. I wanted to blow my head off or kill myself.' It's just a running theme throughout that book. And then coming into MTV [for *Unplugged*], it looks like a funeral, and you see his [Kurt's] eyes later and I think that was kind of in the back of my mind."

Gillian's memories recalled the often overlooked depths of despair; the gravity of hindsight, even when we're put in a position to live uncomfortably in the present. The emptiness in Kurt's eyes hits differently when you've pieced together his breaking points and his joys through the people who truly knew him, bridging the years and spanning a shared emptiness—loss and grief so profound.

Gillian circles back to whether she ever met Kurt.

"We [Kurt and I] actually didn't speak, but it's sort of a funny story. It was the weekend. I was going to some political march. I was going to play in the drum corps, so I had a snare drum with me. I went to this ATM machine. There's a guy there using it, and I'm waiting. This guy was kind of a scrawny guy, and he's in the most beat-up clothes you can imagine, and I thought it was some derelict, and I was thinking to myself, *Oh, that guy's getting out his last five bucks.* And he turned around and it was Kurt, and I did this huge double take, which he saw and which was embarrassing. I wanted to say, 'It's not just because you're Kurt, it's because I wrote you off as a bum' [laughs]. I didn't say anything; he was with some friends that came up and he kept looking at me and what caught his attention was the drum—he was looking at it. I almost went over to talk to him to say, 'Oh, yeah, I interviewed Courtney. It was a great interview, and I'm going to this march,' but by then, he had this reputation of not necessarily liking talking to the media and not really liking to be bothered. So I thought, *Oh, it's Saturday night. He's out with his friends, and I should just leave him alone.* So I did . . . Later, I realized that one of his heroin dealers lived about a block away from where we were, so maybe that's what he was getting the money for . . . or it was that area.

"The next time I saw him was backstage at the *Live and Loud* show because I was covering that. He was walking with Courtney, and he was completely out of it. I knew Courtney, so I talked to her, but he just couldn't even make a complete sentence, and I thought, *Oh, what's the show going to be like?* But that show was fine. It's a good, strong performance, and he did—all the band—they did interviews with MTV that day. They've used those clips again and again, and it's the day he's wearing the tinfoil leis and he seems perfectly fine there, too, in those interviews, maybe a bit tired. I just remember it was just such a difference from the guy backstage who couldn't even stand up or had a hard time standing up, Courtney supporting him, and then boom, he's out on stage and everything's fine.

"Alice Wheeler [photographer and close friend of Nirvana] had this story about that evening, too, because after the show she was hanging out by the stage. Kurt saw her and got her backstage with him because they knew each other from Olympia; she did the first photo session. So she went back to the hotel they were staying at—I think the Four Seasons—and Kurt's like, 'You know, get room service, get whatever you want. You know, it's all covered.' But she says that all the people around him were trying to get rid of her and make her leave, and he would say, 'No, no, I want her to stay here. You know, she's my friend.' But then he and Courtney, at one point, went into the bathroom for a really long time and that was when they managed to get her [Alice] out."

I always assumed fame meant relentless media scrutiny, but it also stripped Kurt of something more basic: friendship—real, familiar camaraderie at a time when he needed it most. The kind he needed most that night. And having that stripped away cut deeper than any headline ever could. Fame theoretically gave him the world—just not one he ever agreed to endure. And it was one more simple human necessity denied to him when the world around him felt dirty, diseased, and engineered to bleed him dry.

The more I learned, the clearer it became: Kurt was lonely in plain sight, in pain, and yet—despite all of it—utterly compelling.

"You see what Dave Grohl is like as a frontman, and then you see Kurt . . . You can really see the difference there," Gillian explains. "Kurt had, I guess—sounds kind of corny to say this, or trite—but just this sort of quiet intensity, you know, certainly in interviews. He's pretty much a laid-back guy and just very self-deprecating in the way he talks about himself and his work. But then you hear the songs and you hear something like 'Teen Spirit' and think of the ending—'a denial'—that's going on for however many times he says that and that tells you, yeah, he's not some soft-spoken little artist guy; there's more going on underneath the surface.

"I keep thinking of all the clichés, 'still waters run deep,' and that's really him, isn't it? When you think about it, especially if you just look at a picture of him—a picture pretty much from any time throughout his life—you know, he wasn't particularly tall and just dressing in these ordinary clothes and just seems like this very unprepossessing kind of guy. Yet he had this artistic drive in him that he had to get out whether it was just something more casual like putting the sculptures together or putting the videotape montages together or the cassette montages. Which is something I used to do . . . You do that when you don't have a full-time job and you're looking to occupy yourself. But you just see him focusing on that just kind of to the exclusion of everything else. I mean, he could have held down those jobs that he had—he did have day jobs. And he either got let go because he wasn't that good at them or he just didn't show up, but nothing . . . even being homeless didn't deter him from trying to create things.

"You think about when he moves in with Tracy later and she gets frustrated at one point that he won't help out around the house, and he offered to move out and live in his car, which was perhaps a bit of a bluff because he probably suspected she wouldn't let him do that. But had she said that was fine, I think he would have done that. I mean, he'd done that in Aberdeen, and Olympia would be kind of a similar type of town to be homeless in, not like New York City or Chicago or some scary urban environment.

"It's not really until the last year when I think heroin took over that you really see that [creative drive] stopping because you look at the *In Utero* album and about half those songs were written well before they recorded the album. Like 'Dumb'—that went back for years, and 'Pennyroyal Tea' as well. So he wasn't writing as much anymore. It was like that creative drive was getting burned out of him somehow. I think it's interesting that the real start of his heroin use coincides with the rise of Nirvana as a band. It's in that fall of '91 that he really starts becoming a regular heroin user, and it's interesting that this is happening at the time his band is progressively becoming the biggest band in the world. It's interesting [that it's] just at that time. I mean, it almost parallels it.

"I know Charley [Cross] talks about this somewhat in his book [*Heavier Than Heaven*], but you can really see it more in Everett's [True] book. He quotes Eric Erlandson talking about this, too. Kurt was seeing Mary Lou Lord for a bit, and then he was seeing Courtney, and Eric said something like, 'You know, you look at the choice and he went for perhaps the more exciting, dangerous choice. He chose the woman that wasn't going to mind that he did heroin.' No, she [Courtney Love] didn't start him on heroin. That's another thing that was kind of funny about how they got together; there are all these things about Courtney dominating him and manipulating him and all that, and certainly relationships have a dynamic that those outside it don't understand.

"But here's another thing about the quiet intensity. He could be a very determined and stubborn person. You couldn't tell him not to do something if he wanted to do it; if he wanted to do something, he was going to go ahead and be that way. He was not the person that could be totally manipulated like that. But then they said the same thing about Yoko and John Lennon. You know, he'd been with Mary Lou and asked her about heroin. She just said, 'I'm not at all interested in that.' And that wasn't going to dissuade him. It was like, 'Oh, okay. Well, I want to do it, so I'm going to.' And Courtney agreed to go along with that. In Charley's book, I think he quotes her as saying, 'I'll go back to this, I guess.'"

Speaking with Gillian reinforced what I'd learned throughout this process: Kurt was determined, almost to a fault. When he was standing in solidarity with the marginalized or making music, it helped him grow and create artistically. But when heroin entered the picture, that same resolution came at a price; one Kurt couldn't afford to pay. The problem was he wasn't someone who could easily be talked out of a decision once he had his mind set.

When Kurt channeled that determination into something positive, it came through loud and clear. Even as friends, family, and the media saw fame threaten to tear him apart, he still managed to play *MTV Unplugged in New York*. What he offered audiences was one of the most brilliant, if not harrowing, performances in music history.

Pain and art melded in a way that felt otherworldly, even as something unspoken lurked just beneath the surface. The room's ambiance, the look and feel of the stage, and even the songs Kurt selected—it all unfurled into an unbelievable performance. No, "Smells Like Teen Spirit" wasn't on the bill. Instead, Kurt leaned into a seamless blend of soulful covers and Nirvana originals, weaving in the old folk tunes he loved while somehow capturing the defiance of a misunderstood generation.

Concertgoers were privy to Kurt's innards through his overlooked confessional playlist—a carefully chosen setlist that reflected his influences and emotional landscape. His favorite songs were on display for all to appreciate, unaware that this would be one of the last times they'd watch a legend bare his heart and soul—or watch him at all.

Chapter 31

"ALL APOLOGIES"

MTV Unplugged in New York

It was November 18, 1993. Nirvana was about to perform their *MTV Unplugged in New York* special, one of the most intimate and celebrated concerts in music history. Almost a year later, on November 1, 1994, the live album would be released for public consumption—tragically, roughly seven months after Kurt Cobain died by suicide. But that evening carried more soul and grit than anyone could have expected.

Before the music could even command attention, Kurt's funeral-like décor transformed the concert into something strangely intimate. The walls were lined with rich textiles, the stage blanketed in black candles and stargazer lilies, setting the tone for the night's performance. *MTV Unplugged* was set to showcase a lighter side of Nirvana, if only in sound. What resulted was a far more intimate glimpse into Kurt Cobain himself. Even the setlist felt unexpected, his personal influences on full display.

A hushed audience absorbed their maudlin surroundings, bracing themselves for Nirvana. They congregated in the Church of Cobain, eager to revel in whatever he had in store. What ensued would become one of the most defining performances in music history.

★★★

Kurt addressed the audience, his voice breaking the anticipation that had been building in the room. His state of mind went largely unacknowledged—perhaps intentionally, perhaps not. In typical Kurt fashion, he wore a thoroughly loved cardigan and his Frightwig T-shirt. It reminded Nirvana fans that he was just a fan himself, someone who never failed to share the music that inspired him or the bands that affected him.

Kurt prepared for the show, "plectrum" escaping his lips as he organized the music on the stand—the notes for whatever song he held closest to his heart. Meanwhile, the gothic stage decorations were a stark contrast to his seat—a modest gray swivel chair was a reminder of his simplicity. He reached for his acoustic guitar—a 1959 Martin D-18E—the same guitar that would later become one of the most expensive guitars ever sold at auction.[126]

He looked around the stage and strummed absentmindedly, although nothing about Kurt was ever really unintentional. He addressed the audience, possibly feigning seriousness.

"Good evening." They greeted him in kind.

"This is off our first record," Kurt said. "Most people don't own it."

Watching Nirvana perform without a mosh pit directly beneath them was jarring.

"About a Girl" drenched the audience in sweet nostalgia, a reminder of how far Nirvana had traveled since the song's humble beginnings on *Bleach*, when they were still a scrappy underground band on Sub Pop.

Kurt picked up the loose pages at his feet and set them on his music stand before transitioning into "Come as You Are," the poignant chords matched only by his haunting vocals. Lyrics about not having a gun would take on new meaning later, but that night, they were simply part of the performance. The song concluded, and Kurt thanked the audience before making introductions.

"This is our friend, Lori Goldstein *[sic]*, on cello," Kurt explained. Dave added, "And this is our new guitar player, Pat."

"He's an—he's a certified honorary punk rocker . . . But he likes Queen better," said Kurt. The audience laughed, and he continued, preparing listeners for their next song.

"This was written by The Vaselines. Well, it's a, it's a rendition of an old, um, Christian song, I think. But we do it The Vaselines' way." A quick count-off and, without hesitation, the band performed "Jesus Doesn't Want Me for a Sunbeam."

Krist had traded his bass for an accordion, adding an old-world melancholy to the already emotive lyrics. Slowly and methodically, the band delivered a performance that would remind people just how much Kurt was capable of telling a story, even through someone else's song. He exuded power and permanence, and did so without ever leaving his chair. Even though the band was performing a cover, the words were more powerful than anyone understood at the moment. The lyrics alluded to a world that demanded all of Kurt—a man who was only twenty-six years old—a weight he carried quietly that night.

The song ended, and the band talked among themselves before Kurt tore into the opening of David Bowie's "The Man Who Sold the World." The delicate, poignant lyrics held special significance for Kurt who, at that moment, held the whole world in his hands. And in many ways, he sold the world on more than his music—he sold us all on a struggling kid from a small logging town who escaped with nothing more than his orange Dunlop Tortex picks and a desire to succeed on his own terms.

On stage, the rest of the band seemed more present in the performance, while Kurt appeared slightly detached and inward, frequently staring down at his lyrics as though absorbed in a world entirely his own. That mix of apathy and sadness became the unnamed band member, the dark shadow drifting across the stage. It threatened to drop him to his knees more than once, but he kept playing.

"Thanks. That was a David Bowie song," Kurt said, as the audience applauded.

"I didn't screw it up, did I?" he asked his bandmates. "Okay, but here's another one I could screw up. Am I gonna do this by myself?"

The band discussed their next song.

Kurt eventually saying, "Okay, well, I think I'll try it in a different key. I'll try it in the normal key. And if it—if it sounds bad, these people are just gonna have to wait. We'll do it over."

The audience laughed, and Kurt leaned into "Pennyroyal Tea," the lyrics that reminded us of his physical ailments, a concealed pain evident as he sang. The song also tackled the larger systemic issues Kurt was so vocal about, carrying multiple meanings, all depending on the listener. Yes, this was true of Kurt's lyrics in a general sense, but this performance held a deeper hurt. He seemed especially pained when singing about thievery, and it's hard not to shake the thought that he felt he'd sold out.

He finished the song, leaned on his guitar, and lit a cigarette.

"That sounded good," Dave said. Kurt absentmindedly pushed his hair behind his ears before firing back, "Shut up." The audience laughed again while the band members engaged in idle banter, discussing what to play next.

"Let's just play 'em back-to-back," Kurt said as they spoke among themselves. "Who cares? It'll be edited different. This is a television show."

He took a drag before putting his cigarette down.

"John," he said, "we're gonna do, um, 'Dumb' now, dummy." A moment later he began singing, his broken heart on display. Especially knowing Kurt's fate five months later, the words elicited a great deal of pain. But he claimed to be happy—the singular emotion we all hoped he truly was.

"I'm not like them / But I can pretend," Kurt sang.

The lyrics suggested he understood his own limitations but still needed someone to share his life with. Having the entire world at his disposal might have made it seem like he had more than enough people to confide in, but in reality, he may have had very few he trusted. The cello's somber quality made the song that much more poignant, each depressed note reverberating off his already melancholy lyrics.

> "Skin the sun, fall asleep / Wish away, the soul is cheap / Lesson learned, wish me luck / Soothe the burn, wake me up"

MTV Unplugged worked because Kurt resisted the temptation to turn the performance into a parade of Nirvana's biggest hits.

"Kurt stood for something," author Stephen Tow explained. "He represented the world of punk rock and underground music, then bubbling below the surface in a glossy MTV-dominated world. Even after Nirvana's enormous popularity, he continued to support the underground bands. A great example of that is the 1993 *MTV Unplugged* show where he didn't just play his 'greatest hits' but instead did covers of bands like The Vaselines and the Meat Puppets, even inviting members of the latter band on stage during the show to perform with Nirvana . . . I think that's so cool that bands like Nirvana supported artists from whence they came and got them some exposure."

"Dumb" ended, and the band readied themselves for the next number. "The reason we didn't want to play these two songs in a row—because they're exactly the same song," Kurt said. A muted chuckle ensued.

"Polly" echoed across the room, the intro familiar and evocative. Kurt never shied away from difficult subjects, and "Polly," a song about rape and torture, was no exception.

As with the misinterpretation of "Rape Me," Stephen Tow explained how "Polly" is often misunderstood.

"Kurt was deeply disturbed by that awful crime, so he wrote a song about it," Stephen said. "His genius was writing 'Polly' from the perspective of the attacker, which led some in the media to accuse him of being pro-rape when his band was the complete opposite, as you mentioned."[127]

As quickly as "Polly" began, it ended, making room for "On a Plain." Kurt's style was unassuming yet forceful; still, he often seemed unable to extend himself the self-love others felt for him.

"On a Plain" concluded, readying the audience for a song that needed no introduction: "Something in the Way." Kurt appeared subdued throughout the performance. In many ways, *MTV Unplugged* allowed Kurt to touch something elegiac and nostalgic. His face was stoic as he sang, a life of hardship reflected on his graceful features.

While the band took a short break and readied themselves for the next part of the show, someone in the audience yelled, "Hurry up!"

"Hurry up?" Kurt asked, looking into the audience. "Is that what you said?"

He took a sip of tea and smiled. The band continued to talk among themselves when, shortly thereafter, their musical guests joined them on stage to applause.

"These are the brothers Meat Puppets," Kurt said. "We're big fans of theirs." To his accompaniment, he said, "Strap on your *geetar.*"

He absentmindedly swiveled in his chair, thumbing through a *Lowest Common Denominator* "Special Edition! Winter 1993" program guide, the cover boldly claiming "WFMU's First Catalog of Curiosities!" Someone in the crowd screamed "Free Bird!"

Kurt looked up. "I've been waiting for that."

He focused on his program while the band and guests warmed up, eventually launching into "Sweet Home Alabama" and startling him. "Oh! What do we wanna do first?" he asked before slurring the lyrics to Lynyrd Skynyrd. The audience laughed and screamed as Kurt thumbed through his music sheets. "'K. Do you want to do 'Plateau' first?" he asked, nodding and dropping his program to the ground.

He turned in Krist's direction.

"What are they tuning, a harp?" he asked, taking a drag from his cigarette as the audience laughed again. "I thought we were a big, rich rock band," he continued. "We should have a whole bunch of extra guitars."

By this time, Kurt was sans guitar, ready to embrace "Plateau," holding up a lighter the way fans do—a pink Bic—his perpetual humor still infused with gravity. Certain notes sat just a little too deep for his voice, but that didn't stop him. He even took chances with a falsetto.

Eyes closed, he hummed into the microphone, his scratchy vocals the only reminder of his former self. *MTV Unplugged* let Kurt experience the music he loved with a childlike innocence.

The black candles continued to burn as he rocked back and forth in his chair, deep in thought, the instrumentals giving him a rare moment to simply reflect and be present. He tapped into a more introspective side of his creativity, embracing it. Meanwhile, the audience listened in silence before finally breaking into applause at the song's conclusion, Kurt joining in.

He took a drag on his cigarette, thumbing through his music as everyone joked on stage, introduced the next number, smiling.

"Cover your hair and your eyes then. 'K. This is called, 'Oh, Me,'" he said before singing without his guitar.

The lyrics in "Oh, Me" carry the quiet weight of something that may have been meant for his daughter, Frances Bean. Its words hint at one person's all-encompassing connection for another, suggesting that Kurt experienced an unconditional love that was born the day she was. The best part of Kurt was reserved for her and her alone, and this song felt like something he'd saved just for his child—unspoken but unmistakable. From that one song, I saw the happiness—the love—of a man who didn't just change the landscape of music, but for a coveted few, changed the trajectory of their lives—for good and forever.

Although he didn't write the lyrics, they seemed to carry the weight of his own ending.

But, in many ways, having a child made him eternal. The love Kurt had for his daughter became one of the few parts of him that could outlive tragedy.

In September 1992, Kurt spoke with Robert Hilburn.

> "I knew that when I had a child, I'd be overwhelmed and it's true," he said. "I can't tell you how much my attitude has changed since we've got Frances. Holding my baby is the best drug in the world."[128]

His comments about Frances Bean were among his most endearing qualities. I share a birthday with his daughter, and as a mother, I often think about what a turning point August 18, 1992, must have been for him.

"Oh, Me" ended, and the band prepared for their next song. Kurt cleared his throat.

"One more," he said. "This is called 'Lake of Fire.' All these songs are off their [Meat Puppets] second record," he added, careful to give proper credit. He appeared almost frail—knees together, fingers knotted—as he strained, but still hit every note. It was obvious how deeply he felt this song.

When the song ended, Kurt clapped and pointed as he spun around in his chair. How surreal it must have been for him, performing some of his favorite songs . . . *with* one of his favorite bands. This concert was his opportunity to play the songs that shaped him, giving him a platform to share those influences openly and intimately.

"That was the Meat Puppets," he said as they exited the stage.

"Any requests?" he asked. People screamed, "'Sliver'!" and Krist played the bassline.

"Lead Belly?" Kurt asked.

The audience continued to shout out requests, hell-bent on hearing more Nirvana.

"How are we supposed to play 'In Bloom' acoustically?" Kurt said, smirking. As Krist played the bassline, Kurt added, "I need a plectrum." A boyish grin spread across his face as he prepared for their next song.

They settled on "All Apologies."

> "What else should I be? / All apologies / What else should I say? / Everyone is gay / What else should I write? / I don't have the right / What else should I be? / All apologies."

His gaze trailed downward.

"I wish I was like you / Easily amused" carries a longing for simplicity and peace that's impossible to ignore. But beneath those lyrics is a glimpse of what Kurt wanted—a life where small things still felt meaningful, where curiosity survived, and where he could remain "forever in bloom" despite the weight surrounding him.

Fame led Kurt to resent an industry he once clamored to be a part of; it became an unavoidable byproduct of doing what he loved. There was no middle ground once Nirvana reached international stardom. Quitting wasn't an option anymore, forcing Kurt to press onward, not because he wanted to, but because he had to. As the evening wore on, so did the strain on Kurt. Witnesses watched the ups and downs of an entire life flash across the stage, reflected in shattered blue eyes. They saw something remarkable occur—a child once discarded by society reaching a fractured sort of self-actualization.

As he battled his celebrity status, he also battled becoming a brand, a commodity. "All in all is all we are," Kurt sang with closed eyes, Dave harmonizing beside him. He wasn't singing to the audience—not anymore. He was singing to himself, to the void, and to a future many feared he couldn't escape. Maybe, too, he was singing to his daughter.

The brilliance—and tragedy—of *MTV Unplugged* came at the price of a man slowly losing his soul before an intimate room of witnesses. When the song came to a close, the applause was uproarious, as if the crowd were trying to anchor him back to the world, holding him here a moment longer.

The band chatted idly, trying to decide on the show's final song as audience members screamed their requests. Kurt addressed the crowd.

"No, I'm sorry. This is—this is the last—this is the last song of the evening."

He laughed, smiling when Dave jokingly suggested they play "Jeremy." Kurt never hid his dislike for Pearl Jam as a band, despite liking Eddie Vedder as a person. He lit a cigarette as the band continued to mull over what to play. Someone yelled "Rape Me," and Kurt couldn't resist, tossing back, "I don't think MTV would let us play that," a nod to the network's past censorship. He followed it with a "Fuck you all. This is the last song of the evening."

"What is it?" Dave asked.

"This was written by—my favorite performer," Kurt said, turning to his bandmates as he continued. "Our favorite performer, isn't it? All of ours? You like him—the best?" Kurt nodded cheekily as the audience laughed. He was referring to Lead Belly.

Krist mentioned a donation basket going around because Kurt wanted to purchase Lead Belly's guitar—the same story Gary Lee told me during our conversation.

"Oh yeah," Kurt explained, laughing and grinning. "This guy representing the Lead Belly estate wants to sell me Lead Belly's guitar for 500,000 dollars." The audience laughed as Krist added more about the donation basket. Kurt went on, "Yeah. I even asked David Geffen personally if he'd buy it for me. He wouldn't do it." He smiled, shaking his head.

"Okay."

And then he played.

A quiet settled over Kurt as he disappeared into "Where Did You Sleep Last Night?" It was the kind of stillness that wasn't meant for a stage or a studio—it felt as if he was somewhere else entirely, following Lead Belly into a time and place that was completely his own. And in many ways, that space held the calm before the inevitable storm.

In the famous photo of Kurt holding up a Lead Belly T-shirt, the admiration is apparent—Kurt mirroring Lead Belly's same far-and-away look.

The song's instrumentals were easy to appreciate, but its lyrics were dark and twisted; it made sense that Kurt gravitated toward a piece with such complexities, so much weight. He sang with a distressed fragility—his face difficult to watch, yet impossible to look away from. Eyes closed, he channeled one of his favorite musicians, and it's wild to think how far he'd come from that simple moment posing with his Lead Belly T-shirt.

Kurt sang, screamed, and experienced music as if it were the first time he'd ever played it—fused to his guitar, the two inseparable. He was no longer on a stage in New York; he was "on a plain," one that no one else could touch. Eyes closed, he let out a primal scream that was as hair-raising as it was beautiful. He was in a trance, the audience waiting anxiously to see if he'd break or transcend. In a dreamlike state, he continued singing. Then he paused—remembering his whereabouts. His eyes sprang open, revealing another time and place, a place Kurt kept hidden for himself. He exhaled, closed his eyes again, and let the last note fall. The audience exhaled with him. He played with an awe-inspiring ferocity, channeling Lead Belly as he laid bare the full weight of his twenty-six years and poured it into the room.

And the audience bore witness.

"Thank you."

Kurt walked off stage last, cigarette in his mouth, signing autographs. The clapping faded into a quiet that was ceremonial, fragile. Everyone stayed seated; no one reached for the man whose music had affected them so deeply. Their shared silence said everything—they knew they witnessed something significant and singular. Devastatingly, it would be one of the last times anyone would ever see Kurt Cobain perform.[129]

That night, Kurt reminded the world that he wasn't just an artist; he was power and prose embodied, his talent—and his pain—emotionally exposed. Sadly, he offered the world only a glimpse of what he could do. Kurt had so much left in front of him, but we'll never know what he could have done with the life he deserved to keep living.

Kurt Cobain took his own life less than five months later, on April 5, 1994, alone in the greenhouse above his garage. He left behind a wife, daughter, and loved ones—more than he ever knew.[130]

★★★

"All Apologies"

"What else should I be?
All apologies
What else could I say?
Everyone is gay
What else could I write?

I don't have the right
What else should I be?
All apologies

In the sun
In the sun I feel as one
In the sun
In the sun
Married
Buried

I wish I was like you
Easily amused
Find my nest of salt
Everything is my fault
I'll take all the blame
Aqua seafoam shame
Sunburn with freezer burn
Choking on the ashes of her enemy

In the sun
In the sun I feel as one
In the sun
In the sun
Married
Buried
Married
Buried
Yeah, yeah, yeah

All in all is all we are."

—Kurt Cobain/Nirvana, produced by Steve Albini

Chapter 32

"OH, ME"

Epilogue

THIS PROJECT BEGAN AS A JOURNEY TO UNDERSTAND KURT COBAIN—not because I wanted to dissect his life, but because I hoped it might help me make sense of why Walter left us. I was never interested in unearthing hidden truths that Kurt would probably have preferred to stay buried. Instead, I wanted to know why society so often finds his death more interesting than the way he lived his life. I'm not naïve—I understand this happens when someone so prolific leaves not only tragically, but young. But it was always more than that. It was about what Kurt represented, and the people who are better because he existed. Kurt was never just "famous" in my world. He was my friends' friend, and someone I understood through the honesty of those who loved him. I remember Walter for his kindness and humor, and I wanted to offer that same sense of closure to those who still mourn Kurt.

At the time of writing this book, another round of Kurt's personal effects have gone to auction. Hopeful bidders emerge, desperate for a chance to be the proud new owner of an unopened pack of American

Spirit menthols or a stream of thoughts penned a little over a week before Kurt took his life. Owning one of his dingy old cardigans is one thing, but are the boundaries between remembrance and exploitation blurred or bluntly erased when a poignant page from his journals becomes fodder for the masses? One is seemingly innocuous; the other should give anyone with a conscience pause. You can sift through a virtual list of sold memorabilia, finding out just how much his personal thoughts were worth to those who demanded a piece of him.

A portion of the highest bidders claim to be fans; others call themselves collectors. Some simply have no comment. But the commonality is a morbid interest in owning a piece of Kurt's soul—the same soul the world felt they were owed some thirty-odd years ago even as he screamed at them to stay far away.

Writing this book wasn't just a project, it was life-altering and, in many ways, cathartic. I met some incredible people who taught me firsthand about Kurt Cobain, the man—not the monolith. Not the myth the world built around him, but about Kurt Cobain, the human being. He was still Nirvana's fantastical lead singer who changed the landscape of music as we know it, but he was also just Kurt—someone my friends once knew personally; someone they still mourn as if he left yesterday.

I learned about the man whose impact, even thirty years since his tragic suicide, continues to grow exponentially. I learned about the man whose unwavering spirit paved the way for countless individuals, shining a light on societal issues and letting the world know he understood what it felt like to be treated as stupid and contagious simply for being different. And I saw firsthand how impactful—how important—he truly was to so many people. No, I never had the chance to ask Kurt these questions myself, and that truth stung even more once my life naturally folded into the circles he once moved through. So, I learned about him the only way still possible: through the people who loved him and trusted me with their stories. Despite the obstacles I faced while writing this book, every moment has been worth it. I get to honor the ways Kurt inspired people to help others, even decades later, while refusing to let his suicide eclipse his life.

I often reflect on mental health awareness, how best to remove the stigma surrounding suicide, and how to have honest discussions about the subject. This book is intended to remind anyone experiencing a mental health crisis that they are not alone in how they feel, that help is there, and that people care. It's just a matter of reaching out and knowing they don't have to suffer in silence. Kurt Cobain experienced more in his short twenty-seven years than most people do in a lifetime, from a traumatic childhood and homeless nights to being a household name. And, as Danny Goldberg explained to me, depression and addiction were part of the pre-fame package. However, there is help, and having open and honest discussions about addiction and depression—no matter how difficult—might just save a life.

"I like that you're bringing awareness to suicide," musician and former Nirvana drummer Chad Channing once told me. "It's a serious problem in general and not just with musicians, as I know you are very aware of. It's tricky to try and figure out what triggers it for people. Peer pressures or the fear of failing. Homelessness, severe depression brought on by these thoughts as many other reasons I suspect. I know back in my touring days that being on the road was difficult for some and, of course, being easy to tap into drugs to help deal with the demands of the life."[131]

I think of the pressures Kurt faced and the obstacles the average person encounters every day. I heard heartfelt stories about how Kurt helped countless individuals overcome their personal trials and tribulations, even those who never met him. It was all part of his relatability.

"What was it about Kurt Cobain that stood out?" I'd ask, the answers amazing me time and again. Although I only set out to ask this question of others, I found myself answering it. What *was* it about him that stood out? To me, Kurt Cobain represented love and acceptance, regardless of race, gender, or sexual orientation. He was kind. He was wittily astute. He was massively talented. He was a genial human being.

And he didn't have to die, because suicide is preventable.

I've spoken to those who knew him best, and to those who often wonder if they knew him at all. Kurt Cobain is more than a man:

he's a movement, an inspiration, and a reminder that your roots—no matter how humble—and your struggles will not hold you back from changing the world.

Kurt offered us beauty and art, and because of that, we owe it to him to focus less on his depression and more on his lasting legacy. We can learn from his experiences to enact change, the same type of change he pushed for.

Kurt continues to live in today's generation of artists, his voice a whisper in every potent scream, an echo in every distorted power chord. In many ways, he's more popular than ever, museums displaying paraphernalia from his life with no way of knowing if he would have approved, scoffed, or simply had no opinion. Some people feel he's been monetized and reduced to a brand while others see exhibits as a way to feel connected to Kurt's enduring influence. Others simply want a connection to the man who made them feel heard. They understand that thirty years or thirty decades won't silence what he stood for. And that's something to celebrate.

★★★

Walter's often on my mind. Not a day goes by when I don't miss him and wish he had let us help him because I know we could have. Like Kurt, he struggled. Like Kurt, he was kind, compassionate, and a genuine human being. And, like Kurt, his suicide could have been prevented.

We need to speak openly and honestly about mental health. We need to remove the stigma surrounding suicide. And we need to know that we are not alone in how we feel and that there is always help and hope. There is always a way forward.

"I'm not like them / But I can pretend." Kurt's words.

Kurt was a son, husband, father, friend, and human being. And he was loved. His spirit is eternal, and his art is a reminder that there is no place for hatred in this world. He paved the way to "Come as You Are," and we must respect what he stood for: fairness and equality.

We can enact the same type of change he so desperately wanted. We must remember "Kurdt"—beyond just his end, in all his goodness—like I will remember Walter.

MENTAL HEALTH RESOURCES

According to the World Health Organization (WHO), "An estimated 3.8 percent of the population experience depression, including 5 percent of adults (4 percent among men and 6 percent among women), and 5.7 percent of adults older than 60 years. Approximately 280 million people in the world have depression. Depression is about 50 percent more common among women than among men. Worldwide, more than 10 percent of pregnant women and women who have just given birth experience depression. More than 700,000 people die due to suicide every year. Suicide is the fourth leading cause of death in 15–29-year-olds."[132]

According to Mental Health America (MHA), in 2023, "16.39 percent of youth (age 12–17) reported suffering from at least one major depressive episode (MDE) in the past year."[133]

MHA also explains that "[n]early half of Americans report often feeling alone (46 percent) or left out (47 percent). Children and teens are no exception. Over 2/3 of 11–17 year olds surveyed by MHA felt stressed out about loneliness."[134]

The harsh reality is that not everyone has access to appropriate medical care. For example, the majority of health plans offer an 80/20 split for covered costs. This means that patients unable to pay their 20 percent are often saddled with what can become insurmountable debt for themselves and their families. To further complicate matters, an estimated 14 million people in the US—about 6 percent of adults—owe more than $1,000 in medical debt, while three million (1 percent of adults) owe over $10,000.[135]

The 80/20 split is just one example of how cost affects access to care. Between deductibles, prescription pricing, and limited coverage for treatment—mental health included—many Americans face barriers long before they ever reach a doctor's office.

But what about those without *any* health coverage? As of 2024, 26.7 million Americans under the age of sixty-five lacked health coverage, with the uninsured rate for this group increasing to 9.8 percent.[99] Children are not exempt either—the uninsured rate for US children rose slightly to 5.3 percent in 2023. This increase reflected about 4 million children without insurance.[136]

We can learn from Kurt and Walter and remove the stigma surrounding mental health, depression, and suicide. Access to care remains a challenge for far too many people, but that doesn't mean people have to suffer in silence.

There are resources available. There are people who want to help. There is hope.

You are not alone.

★★★

If you or someone you know is experiencing a crisis or needs to talk, here are some available resources:

- **Help Center, Inc.**: 24-Hour Crisis and Suicide/Sexual Assault Confidential Line. Their website is **https://www.bozemanhelpcenter.org/** and their number is **406-586-3333.**
- **988 Suicide and Crisis Lifeline**: According to their website, "We can all help prevent suicide. The 988 Lifeline provides 24/7, free and confidential support for people in distress, prevention and crisis resources for you or your loved ones, and best practices for professionals in the United States." They have specific resources for the following: Individuals with Neurodivergence,

Black Mental Health, Maternal Mental Health, Youth, Disaster Survivors, Native American, Indian, Indigenous, and Alaska Natives, Veterans and Service Members, Loss Survivors, LGBTQI+, Attempt Survivor, Deaf, Hard of Hearing, Hearing Loss, and more. Connect via their website: **https://988lifeline.org/**.

- **Crisis Text Line**: Text **HOME to 741741** to connect with a volunteer crisis counselor. You can have free—confidential—support 24/7 by visiting **https://www.crisistextline.org/**. You can text, chat, or message on WhatsApp.
- **Maine Suicide Prevention Program (MSPP):** Maine Crisis Line: **1-888-568-1112 or 988.** According to their website, "Call, text, or chat. Free. Confidential. Available 24/7." Their website is **https://www.maine.gov/dhhs/mecdc/healthy-living/substance-use-and-behavioral-health/suicide-prevention.**
- **Veterans Crisis Line**: From their website, **"Dial 988 then press 1.** Free, 24/7, confidential support is a click away. The Veterans Crisis Line can help even if you're not enrolled in VA benefits or health care." Just visit **https://www.veteranscrisisline.net/get-help-now/chat/**.
- Teens can visit **Your Life Your Voice** at **https://www.yourlifeyourvoice.org/Pages/ways-to-get-help.aspx**. They can call **800-448-3000**. They can also text **VOICE to 20121**. According to their website, "Please know that this texting service is intended for pre-teens, teens, and young adults." There is also a mobile app (which is a mood journal) you can download called Your Life Your Voice, and you can also email them (but this can take 48 hours for a response).
- **The Trevor Project**: Their website is **https://www.thetrevorproject.org/**. They offer 24/7 support, 365 days a year, and you can call **1-866-488-7386 or text START to 678-678.** You can also chat with them from your computer. From their website: "Crisis counselors are trained to answer calls, chats, or texts from

LGBTQ+ young people who reach out on our free, confidential and secure 24/7 service when they are struggling with issues such as coming out, LGBTQ+ identity, depression, and suicide."

- **Society for the Prevention of Teen Suicide:** Their website is **https://sptsusa.org/**. According to their website, "If you or someone you know is in crisis, please call or text: **988**."
- Another excellent resource for teens is **Suicide Prevention Resource Center**, which you can visit at **http://www.sprc.org.** Their contact information: E-mail: **info@sprc.org.** Phone: **877-GET-SPRC (438–7772). NOTE (from their website): "SPRC is not a crisis center. If you're thinking about suicide, are worried about a friend or loved one, or would like emotional support, the 988 Suicide & Crisis Lifeline is available 24/7. You can call or text 988 or use their chat service."**
- **Mental Health America (MHA)**: From their website, "For people seeking help with mental health, crisis support, finding a warmline, navigating healthcare systems to work with providers, and finding support in your local community." "If you or someone you know is struggling or in crisis, help is available. **Call or text 988 or chat at 988lifeline.org.** You can also reach Crisis Text Line by texting **MHA to 741741**." Their website is **https://mhanational.org/get-help**.
- You can also visit **https://www.warmline.org/**. From their website, "Warmlines are the purest form of peer support. Warmlines (also known as peer support warmlines or peer-operated behavioral health warmlines) are phone, chat, or text lines that provide empathetic listening and peer support to individuals who may be experiencing distress or loneliness, or those seeking validation from a peer with lived experience who identifies with their concerns and can offer a confidential and non-judgmental space for connection and self-directed exploration of possible solutions and alternatives."

- For anyone in the UK or the Republic of Ireland, contact **Samaritans**: From their website: "We're the only organization collating suicide data for all UK nations and Ireland." "Whatever you're going through, a Samaritan will face it with you. We're here 24 hours a day, 365 days a year." Their website is **https://www.samaritans.org/** and you can contact them at: **116 123 for free**. You can also chat with them online, write them an email, or write them a letter.
- For a list of **International Suicide Hotlines**, visit **https://blog.opencounseling.com/suicide-hotlines/**.

Other Resources:

- **211**: From their website, "211 connects you to expert, caring help. Every call is completely confidential." Their website is **https://www.211.org/**.
- **Substance Abuse and Mental Health Services Administration (SAMHSA)**. Their website is **https://www.samhsa.gov/homelessness-programs-resources**. According to their website, "Homelessness Programs and Resources—The Substance Abuse and Mental Health Services Administration (SAMHSA) is one of the leading federal agencies addressing the issue of housing stability for individuals with serious mental illness, in addition to the U.S. Department of Housing and Urban Development (HUD) and the United States Interagency Council on Homelessness (USICH). On May 18, 2023, we joined other federal agencies as well as state and local leaders to launch ALL INside, a first-of-its kind initiative to address unsheltered homelessness across the country." You can visit **https://www.usich.gov/federal-strategic-plan/all-inside** to learn more.
- **ChildHelp (Prevention and Treatment of Child Abuse)**: Their website is **https://www.childhelphotline.org/**. You can call or text them at **800-422-4453**. You can also live chat

on their website or report child abuse. From **https://childcare.gov/consumer-education/child-protective-services**, "If you suspect that a child is being abused or neglected, or if you are a child who is being mistreated, call **800-422-4453** immediately. This ChildHelp National Child Abuse Hotline is available 24 hours a day, 7 days a week. The hotline can provide information on how to make a report."

ACKNOWLEDGMENTS

THERE ARE SO MANY PEOPLE I WANT TO THANK—THIS WAS DEFINITELY A group project in more ways than one. I'll try not to exclude anyone from being thanked, but if I do, please know I appreciate you, nonetheless.

First, my husband and son—I love you both more than anything. You've stood by me while I spent years writing this book and I couldn't have done it without you. You're my biggest supporters, my favorite humans, and you mean the world to me. I hope I make you as proud as you make me. Thank you for pushing me to be my best self and for inspiring me every single day.

Mom and Dad—I love you. Thank you for the help and support as I wrote this book. I'm grateful for everything.

Jack—thank you, I love you.

Lynn, Joe, Dee, Rachel, my grandparents, and my entire family—thank you. I love you.

To the extra special friends who helped make this book a reality: Thank you. This includes (but isn't limited to) Carlos "Cake" Nunez, Ryan Aigner, Mitch and Angie Holmquist, Misty Kuhl, and Amanda. Thank you from the bottom of my heart for all your help with this project.

Rodney Staton of LizardWorks Publishing, my book coach and friend—thank you for helping me when this project was just a concept, ensuring I put pen to paper daily.

Corevalay—thank you Phil Barbetta, Gerald Vitale, Chris Kozar, Richard Thomas, Brian Thomas, and Bryan Brenizer for being part of this, for your support, and for incredible music. You guys rock.

Jonny Keen and Jessica Noel Lee—thank you for your transcription services. I appreciate you.

To all the artists, musicians, authors, photographers, recording engineers, managers, executives, and everyone else featured in this book—thank you. You have been absolutely instrumental in creating a book that captures the best parts of Kurt. I could not have done this without you. You helped me honor Kurt and Walter.

Susan Collins—thank you. I am so grateful for all your help. You are truly wonderful.

Henry Diltz, Gilbert Blecken, and Daniel Bergeron—thank you for your kindness and support.

Tony Poukkula and family—thank you for being part of this. It's been a privilege working with you. You're all amazing.

Matthew Wells—thank you for preserving Kurt's memory in Aberdeen.

Tori and Marcia Kovach and Denny Jackson—thank you for creating a park in Kurt's honor.

Greg Hokanson, Aaron Burckhard, and Thurston Moore—thank you so much.

I'd also like to thank Zayac Media LLC, Colette Mancuso-Grisanzio of Forever Young Photography, Rob and Robin, my fellow Hothers, Al Kowalewski, Patrick DiPuccio, Phil Sutcliffe, Dennis Pelowski, Christina Ward, Ed, Ellen, Angela, Chrissy at Hal Leonard, and Steve Harris.

Stu Horvath—a huge thank you for all your help.

I'd like to add a special thank you to the legendary Steve Albini and his studio. Steve was one of a kind and is missed by all who knew him.

Thank you to Jesse McHugh, my senior editor at Skyhorse, for your unparalleled talent, and to the Skyhorse Publishing team for your insight, dedication, and unwavering support.

Thank you, Grandma and Grandpa. I miss you. I love you.

And thank you, Walter and Kurt. You inspired many, and you are both loved and missed.

BIBLIOGRAPHY

Aigner, Ryan. Personal interview.

Albini, Steve. Personal interview.

Albini, Steve. "The Problem with Music." The Baffler, December 1993. https://thebaffler.com/salvos/the-problem-with-music.

Alex, Michael. "MTV News." Video for MTV, October 18, 1993. MTV. https://www.livenirvana.com/interviews/9310unk/index.php.

Allman, Kevin. "The Dark Side of Kurt Cobain." *The Advocate*, February 9, 1993. https://www.livenirvana.com/interviews/9212ka/index.php.

August, John. "Healthcare Insights: How Medical Debt Is Crushing 100 Million Americans." ILR Scheinman Institute, Cornell University, October 21, 2024. https://www.ilr.cornell.edu/scheinman-institute/blog/john-august-healthcare/healthcare-insights-how-medical-debt-crushing-100-million-americans.

Azerrad, Michael. "Nirvana: Inside the Heart and Mind of Kurt Cobain." *Rolling Stone*, April 16, 1992. https://www.rollingstone.com/feature/nirvana-inside-the-heart-and-mind-of-kurt-cobain-103770/.

Barbetta, Phil. Personal interview.

Beato, Rick. "In the Room with Nirvana and Soundgarden: The Krist Novoselic, Kim Thayil and Jack Endino Interview." YouTube video, August 25, 2022. https://www.youtube.com/watch?v=tbrXN7x623U.

Beckner, Justin. "The Incredibly Disturbing Real-Life Story Behind Nirvana's 'Polly.'" *Ultimate Guitar*, July 2, 2022. https://www.ultimate

-guitar.com/articles/features/the_incredibly_disturbing_real-life _story_behind_nirvanas_polly-134482.

Blecken, Gilbert. "25 Years Later." *40 Minutes With Nirvana*, July 10, 2016. https://40minuteswithnirvana.wordpress.com/.

Blecken, Gilbert. "Live Nirvana Interview Archive." LiveNirvana.com, November 10, 1991. https://www.livenirvana.com/interviews/9111gb /index.php.

Caccamo, Mimmo. "London Calling." Radio Onde Furlane, October 27, 1989. https://www.livenirvana.com/interviews/8910mc/index .php.

Canning, Kirk. Personal interview.

CBC Radio Q. "Nirvana's MTV Unplugged at 25: Fascinating Facts About the Landmark Live Show." CBC Radio Q. https://www.cbc .ca/radio/q/blog/nirvana-s-mtv-unplugged-at-25-fascinating-facts -about-the-landmark-live-show-1.4908315.

CDC. "Notes From the Field: Firearm Suicide Rates, by Race and Ethnicity—United States, 2019–2022." Centers for Disease Control and Prevention, November 30, 2023. https://www.cdc.gov/mmwr /volumes/72/wr/mm7248a3.htm.

Channing, Chad. Personal interview.

Chiericozzi, Nick. Personal interview.

Cohen, Robin A., Diane M. Makuc, Amy B. Bernstein, Linda T. Bilheimer, and Eve Powell-Griner. "Health Insurance Coverage Trends, 1959–2007: Estimates from the National Health Interview Survey." Centers for Disease Control and Prevention, July 1, 2009. https://www.cdc.gov/nchs/data/nhsr/nhsr017.pdf.

Collins, Sara R., and Avni Gupta. "The State of Health Insurance Coverage in the U.S." *The Commonwealth Fund*, November 21, 2024. https://www.commonwealthfund.org/publications/surveys/2024 /nov/state-health-insurance-coverage-us-2024-biennial-survey.

Conner, Gary Lee. Personal interview.

Crisafulli, Chuck. "Kurt Cobain: Tribute to a Reluctant Guitar Hero." *Fender Frontline*, vol. 14, February 11, 1994. https://www.livenirvan a.com/interviews/9402cc/index.php.

Danielson, Kurt. Personal interview.

Danna, Jeff. Personal interview.

D'Onofrio, Brian, and Robert Emery. "Parental Divorce or Separation and Children's Mental Health." *World Psychiatry* 18, no. 1 (January 2, 2019): 100–101. https://www.ncbi.nlm.nih.gov/pmc/articles/PMC6313686/

Drescher, Jimmy. Personal interview.

Ehm, Erica. "Much: Our Last Time With Kurt Cobain (1993)." Video recorded at the Edgewater Hotel, Seattle, WA, August 13, 1993. MUCH Music. https://www.youtube.com/watch?v=PDgP4hN4OA4.

Emery, Matt. (1990, January 6). "Air Waves." KIRO 7. Retrieved from https://www.livenirvana.com/interviews/9001me/index.php on 6/23/2024.

Enriquez, Chris. Personal interview.

Euronews. "'A Broken Guitar of a Broken Musician': Nirvana Frontman Kurt Cobain's Fender Goes Up for Auction." *Euronews*, May 5, 2023. https://www.youtube.com/watch?v=7VKQ1cODSqg.

FAIR. "About/Mission Statement." Fairness & Accuracy in Reporting. Accessed June 22, 2024. https://fair.org/about-fair/.

Faulkner, Cathy. Personal interview.

Ferguson, Wm. "As They Were: Nirvana, Reading Festival, 1991." *The New York Times*, September 25, 2011. https://archive.nytimes.com/www.nytimes.com/interactive/2011/09/25/magazine/WTWT nirvana.html.

Gaar, Gillian. Personal interview.

Gale, Osty. "An Overview of the Victoria Clarke & Britt Collins Unofficial Biography Saga." LiveNirvana.com. Accessed June 22, 2024. https://www.livenirvana.com/documents/clarkeandcollins.html.

Garcia-Moran, Eva M. "Differential Fecundity and Child Custody." *Journal of Economic Dynamics and Control* 90 (May 2018): 156–170. https://www.sciencedirect.com/science/article/abs/pii/S0165188918300769.

Gardner, Josh. "The 15 Most Expensive Guitars Sold at Auction." Guitar.com, February 1, 2024. https://guitar.com/features/the-15-most-expensive-auction-guitars/.

Gehman, Pleasant. "Artist of the Year: Nirvana." *Spin*, October 3, 1992. https://www.livenirvana.com/interviews/9210pg/index.php.

Goldberg, Danny. Personal interview.

Government of Canada. "Opioid—and Stimulant-Related Harms in Canada." Canada.ca, March 27, 2024. https://health-infobase.canada.ca/substance-related-harms/opioids-stimulants/.

GroundGuitar. "Kurt Cobain's Fender Stratocaster (Sunburst, Reading Festival)." GroundGuitar. Accessed June 22, 2024. https://www.groundguitar.com/kurt-cobain-gear/kurt-cobains-fender-stratocaster-sunburst-reading-festival/.

Gunja, Munira Z., Evan D. Gumas, and Reginald D. Williams II. "U.S. Health Care from a Global Perspective, 2022: Accelerating Spending, Worsening Outcomes." *The Commonwealth Fund*, January 31, 2023. https://www.commonwealthfund.org/publications/issue-briefs/2023/jan/us-health-care-global-perspective-2022.

Hamburger, Aaron. "Yes, Kurt Cobain Was a Grunge Icon. He Was Also a Gay Rights Hero." *The Washington Post*, April 2, 2019. https://www.washingtonpost.com/outlook/yes-kurt-cobain-was-a-grunge-icon-he-was-also-a-gay-rights-hero/2019/04/01/00a62e24-50a3-11e9-8d28-f5149e5a2fda_story.html.

Hankey, Rick, and Jennifer Carr. "Kurt Cobain: These Kids Really Like Our Band." MTV.com, December 13, 1993. https://www.livenirvana.com/interviews/9312unk/index.php.

Hilburn, Robert. "Kurt Cobain (1992): Cobain to Fans: Just Say No." *Los Angeles Times*, September 11, 1992. https://www.latimes.com/entertainment/la-et-hilburn-cobain-1992-story.html.

Hilburn, Robert. "Storming Back From the Brink: The Pressures of Success Nearly Did in Kurt Cobain and Nirvana." *Los Angeles Times*, August 29, 1993. https://www.latimes.com/archives/la-xpm-1993-08-29-ca-29282-story.html.

Hirschberg, Lynn. "Strange Love: The Story of Kurt Cobain and Courtney Love." *Vanity Fair*, September 1992. https://archive.vanityfair.com/article/1992/9/strange-love.

HISTORY.com Editors. "Grunge Rock Icon Kurt Cobain Dies by Suicide." History.com, originally published November 13, 2009; updated May 27, 2025. https://www.history.com/this-day-in-history/april-5/kurt-cobain-commits-suicide.

Hodgkinson, Antony. Personal interview.

Holocaust Memorial Day Trust. "The Bosnian War." Holocaust Memorial Day Trust. Accessed June 22, 2024. https://www.hmd.org.uk/learn-about-the-holocaust-and-genocides/bosnia/the-bosnian-war/.

Home Alive. "Home." Home Alive. Accessed January 5, 2025. https://www.teachhomealive.org/.

Hubbard, Hanmi. "Nirvana . . . A Spiraling Vision." *Current*, April 22, 1989. https://www.livenirvana.com/interviews/8904hh/index.php#gsc.tab=0.

Hunter, Jane, and Trussell, Jessica. "Helping Preschoolers and Elementary-Age Children Adjust to Divorce." Extension: University of Missouri, April 2016. https://extension.missouri.edu/publications/gh6613.

Iansito, Michelangelo. Personal interview.

IMDb.com. *Kurt Cobain: Montage of Heck*. IMDb, 2015. https://www.imdb.com/title/tt4229236/.

IMDb.com. *Nirvana: Live at Reading (1992)*. 2009. IMDb. https://www.imdb.com/title/tt3189338/.

IMDb.com. *Nirvana: Unplugged in New York (1993)*. December 16, 1993. IMDb. https://www.imdb.com/title/tt0365559/.

Jones, Josh. "Read the Uncompromising Letter That Steve Albini (RIP) Wrote to Nirvana Before Producing *In Utero* (1993)." Open Culture, May 8, 2024. https://www.openculture.com/2024/05/read-the-uncompromising-letter-that-steve-albini-rip-wrote-to-nirvana-before-producing-in-utero-1993.html.

Julien's Auctions. "Kurt Cobain Handwritten Letter to David Geffen." Julien's Auctions. Accessed June 24, 2024. https://bid.juliensauctions.com/lot-details/index/catalog/177/lot/75727/KURT-COBAIN-HANDWRITTEN-LETTER-TO-DAVID-GEFFEN.

Julien's Auctions. "Nirvana: Kurt Cobain Smashed and Band-Signed Nevermind Era Fender Stratocaster Electric Guitar." Julien's Auctions. Accessed June 22, 2024. https://bid.juliensauctions.com/lot-details/index/catalog/454/lot/205635/x-kurt-cobain-smashed-and-rebuilt-guitar-signed-by-all-members.

Kuhl, Misty. Personal interview.

Kurt Cobain Equipment F.A.Q.The. "Guitars." *The Kurt Cobain Equipment F.A.Q.* Accessed June 23, 2024. http://www.kurtsequipment.com/.

Laudadio, Marisa. "Inside Story: Courtney Love and Daughter Frances Bean's Rocky Relationship." *People*, December 18, 2009. https://www.people.com/celebrity/inside-story-courtney-love-and-daughter-frances-beans-rocky-relationship/.

Leoncavallo, Ivano. "MTV News: The Week in Rock." Video for MTV, April 17, 1993. MTV. https://www.livenirvana.com/interviews/9304unk/index.php.

Lewman, Mark. "Nirvana Benefit Show." *Entertainment Weekly*, April 23, 1993. https://ew.com/article/1993/04/23/nirvana-benefit-show/.

Live Nirvana Concert Chronology. "Capitol Lake Park (Capitol Lake Jam), Olympia, WA, US." Live Nirvana Concert Chronology, August 20, 1988. https://www.livenirvana.com/concerts/88/88-08-20.php.

Live Nirvana Concert Chronology. "Cow Palace (Tresnjevka Women's Group Benefit), Daly City, CA, US." Live Nirvana Concert Chronology, April 9, 1993. https://www.livenirvana.com/concerts/93/93-04-09.php.

Live Nirvana Concert Chronology. "Dorm K208, The Evergreen State College, Olympia, WA, US." Live Nirvana Concert Chronology, October 30, 1988. https://www.livenirvana.com/concerts/88/88-10-30.php.

Live Nirvana Concert Chronology. "O.K. Hotel, Seattle, WA, US." Live Nirvana Concert Chronology, April 17, 1991. https://www.livenirvana.com/concerts/91/91-04-17.php.

Live Nirvana Concert Chronology. "Oakland-Alameda County Coliseum Arena, Oakland, CA, US." Live Nirvana Concert

Chronology, December 31, 1993. https://www.livenirvana.com/concerts/93/93-12-31.php.

LiveNirvana.com. "Tourette's." LiveNirvana.com. Accessed June 22, 2024. https://www.livenirvana.com/songguide/tourettes.html.

Long, Chris. "Nirvana." *Hollywood Rocks*, February 1991. https://www.livenirvana.com/interviews/9102cl/index.php.

Martin, Rachel, and Vince Pearson. "Reflecting on Kurt Cobain's 'Crystalline Understanding' 25 Years Later." NCPR, April 5, 2019. https://www.northcountrypublicradio.org/news/npr/709603031/reflecting-on-kurt-cobain-s-crystalline-understanding-25-years-later.

MHA. "Is Your Child Lonely? (For Parents)." Mental Health America. Accessed June 26, 2024. https://mhanational.org/your-child-lonely-parents.

Michaels, Sean. "Nirvana Singer's Hometown Says No to Kurt Cobain Bridge." *The Guardian*, July 29, 2011. https://www.theguardian.com/music/2011/jul/29/nirvana-singer-kurt-cobain-bridge.

Moore, Thurston. Personal interview.

Mouriquand, David. "Exploring Kurt Cobain's Overlooked Social Activism—30 Years Since His Death." *Euronews*, May 4, 2024. https://www.euronews.com/culture/2024/04/05/exploring-kurt-cobains-overlooked-social-activism-30-years-since-his-death.

National Conference of State Legislatures. "Youth Homelessness Overview." National Conference of State Legislatures, March 29, 2023. https://www.ncsl.org/human-services/youth-homelessness-overview.

Naureckas, Jim. "Kurt Cobain on FAIR: 'Tries to Expose the Truths.'" Fairness & Accuracy in Reporting, January 30, 2014. https://fair.org/media_criticism/kurt-cobain-on-fair-tries-to-expose-the-truths/.

Newman, Chayim, Ryan P. George, Tim Beitz, Zachary Bergson, and Vance Zemon. "Mental Health Issues Among International Touring Professionals in the Music Industry." *Journal of Psychiatric Research*, December 2021. https://www.researchgate.net/publication/357023032

_Mental_health_issues_among_international_touring_professionals_in_the_music_industry.

NIH. "Drug Overdose Death Rates." National Institute on Drug Abuse. Accessed June 24, 2024. https://nida.nih.gov/research-topics/trends-statistics/overdose-death-rates.

Nirvana—*In Utero* 30th Anniversary 8LP Super Deluxe. Nirvana Official Store. https://shop.nirvana.com/products/in-utero-30th-anniversary-8lp-super-deluxe?srsltid=AfmBOoqMqOOX1uj7H9kErg994Cr6NTCFs-VeHZl7LZpPQtAXJytt0hqj.

NPR. "Kurt Cobain's Broken Guitar Sells for Nearly $600,000." NPR, May 22, 2023. https://www.npr.org/2023/05/22/1177467481/kurt-cobain-nirvana-smashed-guitar.

Nunez, Carlos "Cake." Personal interview.

Nunez, Carlos "Cake," and Al Kowalewski. "An Interview With . . . Kurt Cobain." LiveNirvana.com, March 1992. https://www.livenirvana.com/interviews/9203akcn/.

Nunez, Carlos "Cake," and Al Kowalewski. "An Interview With . . . Kurt Cobain." *fLiPSiDE*, May 1992. https://www.livenirvana.com/interviews/9203akcn/#gsc.tab=0.

PACER.org. "Bullying Statistics: By the Numbers." PACER's National Bullying Prevention Center. Accessed June 23, 2024. https://www.pacer.org/bullying/info/stats.asp.

Paltrowitz, Darren. Personal interview.

Perry, Jade. Personal interview.

Peterson, Charles. Personal interview.

Phillips, Stephanie. Personal interview.

Poneman, Jonathan. "Family Values." *Spin*, December 1992. https://www.livenirvana.com/interviews/9210jp/index.php.

Poukkula, Tony. Personal interview.

Preston, Joe. "Matt Lukin's Legs and Snipehunt." 1989. https://www.livenirvana.com/interviews/89xxjp/index.php.

RIAA. "Gold & Platinum." Recording Industry Association of America. May 31, 2024. https://www.riaa.com/gold-platinum/?tab_active=default-award&se=Nirvana.

Robb, John. "On the Subs Bench: Nirvana." *Sounds*, April 22, 1989. https://www.livenirvana.com/interviews/89xxjr/index.php.

Romance, Laurence. "Fax'o." M6, August 10, 1993. https://www.livenirvana.com/interviews/9308lr/index.php.

Savage, Jon. "Sounds Dirty: The Truth About Nirvana." *The Observer*, July 22, 1993. https://www.livenirvana.com/interviews/9307js/index.php#Transcript1.

Scaramanga, Jenna. "The 15 Most Expensive Guitars of All Time." *Guitar World*, May 29, 2024. https://www.guitarworld.com/features/most-expensive-guitars-sold-at-auction.

Schewitz, B. "#173: Nirvana, In Utero (1993)." *Rolling Stone*, April 7, n.d.

Schifrin, Nick. "Study Finds Military Suicide Rates Highest Among Tank Brigades." PBS News, March 21, 2024. https://www.pbs.org/newshour/show/study-finds-military-suicide-rates-highest-among-tank-brigades.

Sevrin, Rebecca. Personal interview.

Share, Alex. Personal interview.

Soulsby, Nick. Personal interview.

St. Thomas, Kurt. "Nevermind: It's an Interview." DGC, January 10–11, 1992. https://www.livenirvana.com/interviews/9201kst/index.php.

Steve Albini. Wikipedia, last modified 2025. https://en.wikipedia.org/wiki/Steve_Albini.

Stump, Juno. "Don't Hurt Girls When You Dance (Or Any Other Time)." *Unwinnable*, April 2024. https://unwinnable.com/2024/04/05/dont-hurt-girls-when-you-dance-or-any-other-time-kurt-cobain-nirvana/.

Sutcliffe, Phil. "King of Pain." *Q*, no. 85 (October 1993). https://www.livenirvana.com/interviews/9307ps/index.php.

Tati, Antonino. Personal interview.

Thomas, Brad. Personal interview.

Thorfinson, Curtis Van Roland. Personal interview.

Tolbert, Jennifer, Sammy Cervantes, Clea Bell, and Anthony Damico. "Key Facts About the Uninsured Population." KFF, December 18,

2024. https://www.kff.org/uninsured/key-facts-about-the-uninsured-population/

Tow, Stephen. Personal interview.

Walker, Brett. Personal interview.

Walters, Darrin. Personal interview.

Wandtke, Paul. Personal interview.

Washington State Legislature. "RCW 26.20.030: Family Abandonment—Penalty—Exception." Washington State Legislature. Accessed January 5, 2025. https://apps.leg.wa.gov/rcw/default.aspx?cite=26.20.030.

Wells, Matthew N. "Kurt Cobain Book Author Wants to Save North Aberdeen Bridge." *The Daily World*, April 24, 2024. https://www.thedailyworld.com/news/kurt-cobain-book-author-wants-to-save-north-aberdeen-bridge/.

Wilkinson, Ryan, and Finkbeiner Law Firm. "Divorce Statistics: Over 115 Studies, Facts and Rates for 2024." Wilkinson & Finkbeiner, 2024. https://www.wf-lawyers.com/divorce-statistics-and-facts/.

World Health Organization. "Depressive Disorder (Depression)." World Health Organization. Accessed June 26, 2024. https://www.who.int/en/news-room/fact-sheets/detail/depression.

YaleNews. "Bullying-Suicide Link Explored in New Study by Researchers at Yale." YaleNews, July 16, 2008. https://news.yale.edu/2008/07/16/bullying-suicide-link-explored-new-study-researchers-yale.

Yarm, Mark. Personal interview.

ENDNOTES

Introduction

1 Gilbert Blecken, "Live Nirvana Interview Archive," *LiveNirvana.com*, November 10, 1991, https://www.livenirvana.com/interviews/9111gb/index.php.
2 Gilbert Blecken, personal interview.
3 Gilbert Blecken, "25 Years Later," *40 Minutes With Nirvana*, July 10, 2016, https://40minuteswithnirvana.wordpress.com/.

Chapter 1 – "Territorial Pissings"

4 Robert Hilburn, "Storming Back From the Brink: The Pressures of Success Nearly Did in Kurt Cobain and Nirvana," *Los Angeles Times*, August 29, 1993, https://www.latimes.com/archives/la-xpm-1993-08-29-ca-29282-story.html.
5 Mark Yarm, personal interview.
6 Jonathan Poneman, "Family Values," *Spin*, December 1992, https://www.livenirvana.com/interviews/9210jp/index.php.
7 Jane Hunter and Jessica Trussell, "Helping Preschoolers and Elementary-Age Children Adjust to Divorce," *Extension: University of Missouri*, April 2016, https://extension.missouri.edu/publications/gh6613.
8 Jon Savage, "Sounds Dirty: The Truth About Nirvana," The Observer, July 22, 1993, https://www.livenirvana.com/interviews/9307js/index.php#Transcript1.
9 Eva M. Garcia-Moran, "Differential Fecundity and Child Custody," *Journal of Economic Dynamics and Control* 90 (May 2018): 156–170, https://www.sciencedirect.com/science/article/abs/pii/S0165188918300769.

10 Brian D'Onofrio and Robert Emery, "Parental Divorce or Separation and Children's Mental Health," *World Psychiatry* 18, no. 1 (January 2, 2019): 100–101, https://www.ncbi.nlm.nih.gov/pmc/articles/PMC6313686/.

11 IMDb.com, *Kurt Cobain: Montage of Heck* (2015), https://www.imdb.com/title/tt4229236/.

12 Kevin Allman, "The Dark Side of Kurt Cobain," *The Advocate*, February 9, 1993, https://www.livenirvana.com/interviews/9212ka/index.php.

13 Jon Savage, "Sounds Dirty: The Truth About Nirvana," *The Observer*, July 22, 1993, https://www.livenirvana.com/interviews/9307js/index.php#Transcript1.

14 Jon Savage, "Sounds Dirty."

15 Joe Preston, "Matt Lukin's Legs and Snipehunt" (1989), https://www.livenirvana.com/interviews/89xxjp/index.php.

16 Kevin Allman, "The Dark Side of Kurt Cobain."

17 Sean Michaels, "Nirvana Singer's Hometown Says No to Kurt Cobain Bridge," *The Guardian*, July 29, 2011, https://www.theguardian.com/music/2011/jul/29/nirvana-singer-kurt-cobain-bridge.

18 Rick Beato, "In the Room with Nirvana and Soundgarden: The Krist Novoselic, Kim Thayil and Jack Endino Interview," YouTube video, August 25, 2022, https://www.youtube.com/watch?v=tbrXN7x623U.

19 John Robb, "On the Subs Bench: Nirvana," *Sounds*, April 22, 1989, https://www.livenirvana.com/interviews/89xxjr/index.php.

20 Chris Long, "Nirvana," *Hollywood Rocks*, February 1991, https://www.livenirvana.com/interviews/9102cl/index.php.

21 Thurston Moore, personal interview.

22 Euronews, "'A Broken Guitar of a Broken Musician': Nirvana Frontman Kurt Cobain's Fender Goes Up for Auction," May 5, 2023, https://www.youtube.com/watch?v=7VKQ1cODSqg.

23 Julien's Auctions, "Nirvana: Kurt Cobain Smashed and Band-Signed Nevermind Era Fender Stratocaster Electric Guitar," accessed June 22, 2024, https://bid.juliensauctions.com/lot-details/index/catalog/454/lot/205635/x-kurt-cobain-smashed-and-rebuilt-guitar-signed-by-all-members.

24 Jimmy Drescher, personal interview.

25 Rebecca Sevrin, personal interview.

26 Mark Yarm, personal interview.

Chapter 2 – "Negative Creep"

27 Nick Soulsby, personal interview.

Chapter 3 – "Stay Away"

28 Curtis Van Roland Thorfinson, personal interview.

29 Nirvana Official Store, "Nirvana—*In Utero* 30th Anniversary 8LP Super Deluxe," https://shop.nirvana.com/products/in-utero-30th-anniversary-8lp-super-deluxe?srsltid=AfmBOoqMqOOX1uj7H9kErg994Cr6NTCFs-VeHZl7LZpPQtAXJytt0hqj.

30 NPR, "Kurt Cobain's Broken Guitar Sells for Nearly $600,000," May 22, 2023, https://www.npr.org/2023/05/22/1177467481/kurt-cobain-nirvana-smashed-guitar.

31 Josh Gardner, "The 15 Most Expensive Guitars Sold at Auction," *Guitar.com*, February 1, 2024, https://guitar.com/features/the-15-most-expensive-auction-guitars/.

Chapter 4 – "School"

32 Tony Poukkula, personal interview.

33 Mimmo Caccamo, "London Calling," *Radio Onde Furlane*, October 27, 1989, https://www.livenirvana.com/interviews/8910mc/index.php.

Chapter 5 – "In Bloom"

34 Ryan Aigner, personal interview.

35 Rick Hankey and Jennifer Carr, "Kurt Cobain: These Kids Really Like Our Band," MTV.com, December 13, 1993, https://www.livenirvana.com/interviews/9312unk/index.php.

36 Brett Walker, personal interview.

Chapter 6 – "Where Did You Sleep Last Night?"

37 Misty Kuhl, personal interview.

38 Washington State Legislature, "RCW 26.20.030: Family Abandonment—Penalty—Exception," accessed January 5, 2025, https://apps.leg.wa.gov/rcw/default.aspx?cite=26.20.030.

39 Jonathan Poneman, "Family Values," *Spin*, December 1992, https://www.livenirvana.com/interviews/9210jp/index.php.

40 Matthew N. Wells, "Kurt Cobain Book Author Wants to Save North Aberdeen Bridge," *The Daily World*, April 24, 2024, https://www.thedailyworld.com/.news/kurt-cobain-book-author-wants-to-save-north-aberdeen-bridge/.

Chapter 7 – "Come as You Are"

41 Antony Hodgkinson, personal interview.

42 A mythical club of famous musicians—such as Jimi Hendrix, Janis Joplin, and Amy Winehouse—who all died at the age of twenty-seven.

Chapter 8 – "Frances Farmer Will Have Her Revenge on Seattle"

43 Charles Peterson, personal interview

44 Erinn Callahan, "On This Day in 1991, Nirvana Played 'Smells Like Teen Spirit' for the First Time Ever—and Grunge Music Was Never the Same," American Songwriter (April 23, 2025), https://americansongwriter.com/on-this-day-in-1991-nirvana-played-smells-like-teen-spirit-for-the-first-time-ever-and-grunge-music-was-never-the-same/.

Chapter 9 – "Scentless Apprentice"

45 Gary Lee Conner, personal interview.

46 Pleasant Gehman, "Artist of the Year: Nirvana," *Spin*, October 3, 1992, https://www.livenirvana.com/interviews/9210pg/index.php.

47 Michael Azerrad, "Nirvana: Inside the Heart and Mind of Kurt Cobain," *Rolling Stone*, April 16, 1992, https://www.rollingstone.com/feature/nirvana-inside-the-heart-and-mind-of-kurt-cobain-103770/.

48 Personal interview with Nick Chiericozzi of The Men.

49 Wm. Ferguson, "As They Were: Nirvana, Reading Festival, 1991," *The New York Times*, September 25, 2011, https://archive.nytimes.com/www.nytimes.com/interactive/2011/09/25/magazine/WTWTnirvana.html.

50 Rachel Martin and Vince Pearson, "Reflecting on Kurt Cobain's 'Crystalline Understanding' 25 Years Later," *NCPR*, April 5, 2019, https://www.northcountrypublicradio.org/news/npr/709603031/reflecting-on-kurt-cobain-s-crystalline-understanding-25-years-later.

51 Erica Ehm, "Egos & Icons: Nirvana," video for Much Music," LiveNirvana.com, August 13, 1993, https://www.livenirvana.com/interviews/9308ee/index.php.

52 Robert Hilburn, "Kurt Cobain (1992): Cobain to Fans: Just Say No," *Los Angeles Times*, September 11, 1992, https://www.latimes.com/entertainment/la-et-hilburn-cobain-1992-story.html.

53 GroundGuitar, "Kurt Cobain's Fender Stratocaster (Sunburst, Reading Festival)," accessed June 22, 2024, https://www.groundguitar.com/kurt-cobain-gear/kurt-cobains-fender-stratocaster-sunburst-reading-festival/.

54 LiveNirvana.com, "Tourette's," accessed June 22, 2024, https://www.livenirvana.com/songguide/tourettes.html.

55 Justin Beckner, "The Incredibly Disturbing Real-Life Story Behind Nirvana's 'Polly,'" *Ultimate Guitar*, July 2, 2022, https://www.ultimate

-guitar.com/articles/features/the_incredibly_disturbing_real-life_story_behind_nirvanas_polly-134482.

56 Nick Soulsby, personal interview.

57 Gary Lee Conner, personal interview.

58 Mark Yarm, personal interview.

59 Nick Soulsby, personal interview.

60 Chuck Crisafulli, "Kurt Cobain: Tribute to a Reluctant Guitar Hero," *Fender Frontline* 14 (February 11, 1994), https://www.livenirvana.com/interviews/9402cc/index.php.

61 The Kurt Cobain Equipment F.A.Q., "Guitars," accessed June 23, 2024, http://www.kurtsequipment.com/.

62 IMDb.com, *Nirvana: Live at Reading (1992)* (2009), https://www.imdb.com/title/tt3189338/.

Chapter 10 – "Sliver"

63 Carlos "Cake" Nunez, personal interview.

64 Carlos "Cake" Nunez and Al Kowalewski, "An Interview With . . . Kurt Cobain," *LiveNirvana.com*, March 1992, https://www.livenirvana.com/interviews/9203akcn/.

65 Recording Industry Association of America (RIAA), "Gold & Platinum," May 31, 2024, https://www.riaa.com/gold-platinum/?tab_active=default-award&se=Nirvana.

66 Michael Alex, "MTV News," video for MTV, October 18, 1993, *MTV*, https://www.livenirvana.com/interviews/9310unk/index.php.

Chapter 11 – "Rape Me"

67 Mark Lewman, "Nirvana Benefit Show," *Entertainment Weekly*, April 23, 1993, https://ew.com/article/1993/04/23/nirvana-benefit-show/.

68 Stephen Tow, personal interview.

69 Chuck Crisafulli, "Kurt Cobain: Tribute to a Reluctant Guitar Hero," *Fender Frontline* 14 (February 11, 1994),

70 Holocaust Memorial Day Trust, "The Bosnian War," accessed June 22, 2024, https://www.hmd.org.uk/learn-about-the-holocaust-and-genocides/bosnia/the-bosnian-war/.

71 Live Nirvana Concert Chronology, "Cow Palace (Tresnjevka Women's Group Benefit), Daly City, CA, US," April 9, 1993, https://www.livenirvana.com/concerts/93/93-04-09.php.

72 Mark Lewman, "Nirvana Benefit Show," *Entertainment Weekly*, April 23, 1993, https://ew.com/article/1993/04/23/nirvana-benefit-show/.

73 Ivano Leoncavallo, "MTV News: The Week in Rock," video for MTV, April 17, 1993, *MTV*, https://www.livenirvana.com/interviews/9304unk/index.php.

74 Erica Ehm, "Egos & Icons: Nirvana," video for Much Music, *Live Nirvana.com*, August 13, 1993, https://www.livenirvana.com/interviews/9308ee/index.php.

75 FAIR, "About/Mission Statement," accessed June 22, 2024, https://fair.org/about-fair/.

76 Jim Naureckas, "Kurt Cobain on FAIR: 'Tries to Expose the Truths,'" *Fairness & Accuracy in Reporting*, January 30, 2014, https://fair.org/media_criticism/kurt-cobain-on-fair-tries-to-expose-the-truths/.

77 Erica Ehm, "Egos & Icons: Nirvana," video for Much Music, *Live Nirvana.com*, August 13, 1993, https://www.livenirvana.com/interviews/9308ee/index.php.

78 Nick Soulsby, personal interview.

Chapter 12 – "Something in the Way"

79 Kurt St. Thomas, "Nevermind: It's an Interview," DGC, January 10–11, 1992, https://www.livenirvana.com/interviews/9201kst/index.php.

80 Jonathan Poneman, "Family Values," *Spin*, December 1992, https://www.livenirvana.com/interviews/9210jp/index.php.

Chapter 13 – "Serve the Servants"

81 Danny Goldberg, personal interview.

82 Munira Z. Gunja, Evan D. Gumas, and Reginald D. Williams II, "U.S. Health Care from a Global Perspective, 2022: Accelerating Spending, Worsening Outcomes," *The Commonwealth Fund*, January 31, 2023, https://www.commonwealthfund.org/publications/issue-briefs/2023/jan/us-health-care-global-perspective-2022.

83 Laurence Romance, "Fax'o," *M6*, August 10, 1993, https://www.livenirvana.com/interviews/9308lr/index.php.

Chapter 14 – "In Utero"

84 Steve Albini, personal interview.

85 Josh Jones, "Read the Uncompromising Letter That Steve Albini (RIP) Wrote to Nirvana Before Producing *In Utero* (1993)," *Open Culture*, May 8, 2024, https://www.openculture.com/2024/05/read-the-uncompromising-letter-that-steve-albini-rip-wrote-to-nirvana-before-producing-in-utero-1993.html.

86 "Steve Albini," *Wikipedia*, last modified 2025, https://en.wikipedia.org/wiki/Steve_Albini.

Chapter 15 – "Montage of Heck"

87 Jeff Danna, personal interview.

Chapter 16 – "Hairspray Queen"

88 Cathy Faulkner, personal interview.
89 Home Alive, "Home," accessed January 5, 2025, https://www.teachhomealive.org/.

Chapter 17 – "Lithium"

90 Gary Lee Conner, personal interview.
91 Scaramanga, Jenna. "The 15 Most Expensive Guitars of All Time." *Guitar World*, May 29, 2024. https://www.guitarworld.com/features/most-expensive-guitars-sold-at-auction.

Chapter 18 – "Paper Cuts"

92 Kurt Danielson, personal interview.

Chapter 19 – "Drain You"

93 Jimmy Drescher, personal interview.

Chapter 20 – "Polly"

94 Darrin Walters, personal interview.
95 Government of Canada, "Opioid—and Stimulant-Related Harms in Canada," *Canada.ca*, March 27, 2024, https://health-infobase.canada.ca/substance-related-harms/opioids-stimulants/.
96 National Institute on Drug Abuse (NIH), "Drug Overdose Death Rates," accessed June 24, 2024, https://nida.nih.gov/research-topics/trends-statistics/overdose-death-rates.
97 Michelangelo Iansito, personal interview.

Chapter 21 – "About a Girl"

98 Stephanie Phillips, personal interview.
99 Recording Industry Association of America (RIAA), "Gold & Platinum," May 31, 2024, https://www.riaa.com/gold-platinum/?tab_active=default-award&se=Nirvana.

Chapter 22 – "Smells Like Teen Spirit"

100 Chris Enriquez, personal interview.

101 Erica Ehm, "Egos & Icons: Nirvana," video for Much Music, *LiveNirvana.com*, August 13, 1993, https://www.livenirvana.com/interviews/9308ee/index.php.

102 LiveNirvana.com. "*Incesticide* Note." Accessed July 6, 2026. https://www.livenirvana.com/digitalnirvana/discography/nirvana/incesticide_note.html.

103 PACER.org, "Bullying Statistics: By the Numbers," accessed June 23, 2024, https://www.pacer.org/bullying/info/stats.asp.

104 YaleNews, "Bullying-Suicide Link Explored in New Study by Researchers at Yale," July 16, 2008, https://news.yale.edu/2008/07/16/bullying-suicide-link-explored-new-study-researchers-yale.

Chapter 23 – "On a Plain"

105 Lynn Hirschberg, "Strange Love: The Story of Kurt Cobain and Courtney Love," *Vanity Fair*, September 1992, https://archive.vanityfair.com/article/1992/9/strange-love.

106 Marisa Laudadio, "Inside Story: Courtney Love and Daughter Frances Bean's Rocky Relationship," *People*, December 18, 2009, https://www.people.com/celebrity/inside-story-courtney-love-and-daughter-frances-beans-rocky-relationship/.

107 Julien's Auctions, "Kurt Cobain Handwritten Letter to David Geffen," accessed June 24, 2024, https://bid.juliensauctions.com/lot-details/index/catalog/177/lot/75727/KURT-COBAIN-HANDWRITTEN-LETTER-TO-DAVID-GEFFEN.

108 Alex Share, personal interview.

109 Centers for Disease Control and Prevention, "Notes From the Field: Firearm Suicide Rates, by Race and Ethnicity—United States, 2019–2022," November 30, 2023, https://www.cdc.gov/mmwr/volumes/72/wr/mm7248a3.htm.

Chapter 24 – "Pennyroyal Tea"

110 Nick Chiericozzi, personal interview.

111 Robin A. Cohen, Diane M. Makuc, Amy B. Bernstein, Linda T. Bilheimer, and Eve Powell-Griner, "Health Insurance Coverage Trends, 1959–2007: Estimates from the National Health Interview Survey," *Centers for Disease Control and Prevention*, July 1, 2009, https://www.cdc.gov/nchs/data/nhsr/nhsr017.pdf.

Chapter 25 – "Lounge Act"

112 Paul Wandtke, personal interview.

Chapter 26 – "You Know You're Right"

113 Brad Thomas, personal interview.
114 Nick Schifrin, "Study Finds Military Suicide Rates Highest Among Tank Brigades," *PBS News*, March 21, 2024, https://www.pbs.org/newshour/show/study-finds-military-suicide-rates-highest-among-tank-brigades.

Chapter 27 – "Breed"

115 Jade Perry, personal interview.
116 Kevin Allman, "The Dark Side of Kurt Cobain," *The Advocate*, February 9, 1993, https://www.livenirvana.com/interviews/9212ka/index.php.
117 Chayim Newman, Ryan P. George, Tim Beitz, Zachary Bergson, and Vance Zemon, "Mental Health Issues Among International Touring Professionals in the Music Industry," *Journal of Psychiatric Research* (December 2021), https://www.researchgate.net/publication/357023032_Mental_health_issues_among_international_touring_professionals_in_the_music_industry.

Chapter 28 – "Been a Son"

118 Aaron Hamburger, "Yes, Kurt Cobain Was a Grunge Icon. He Was Also a Gay Rights Hero," *The Washington Post*, April 2, 2019, https://www.washingtonpost.com/outlook/yes-kurt-cobain-was-a-grunge-icon-he-was-also-a-gay-rights-hero/2019/04/01/00a62e24-50a3-11e9-8d28-f5149e5a2fda_story.html.
119 Antonino Tati, personal interview.
120 Jonathan Poneman, "Family Values," *Spin*, December 1992, https://www.livenirvana.com/interviews/9210jp/index.php.
121 Juno Rylee Schultz, "Don't Hurt Girls When You Dance (Or Any Other Time)," *Unwinnable*, April 2024, https://unwinnable.com/2024/04/05/dont-hurt-girls-when-you-dance-or-any-other-time-kurt-cobain-nirvana/.

Chapter 29 – "Sappy"

122 Darren Paltrowitz, personal interview.
123 David Mouriquand, "Exploring Kurt Cobain's Overlooked Social Activism—30 Years Since His Death," Euronews, May 4, 2024, https://www.euronews.com/culture/2024/04/05/exploring-kurt-cobains-overlooked-social-activism-30-years-since-his-death.

124 Steve Albini, "The Problem with Music," The Baffler, December 1993, https://thebaffler.com/salvos/the-problem-with-music.

Chapter 30 – "Endless, Nameless"

125 Gillian Gaar, personal interview.

Chapter 31 – "All Apologies"

126 Josh Gardner, "The 15 Most Expensive Guitars Sold at Auction," *Guitar.com*, February 1, 2024, https://guitar.com/features/the-15-most-expensive-auction-guitars/

127 Stephen Tow, personal interview.

128 Robert Hilburn, "Kurt Cobain (1992): Cobain to Fans: Just Say No," *Los Angeles Times*, September 11, 1992, https://www.latimes.com/entertainment/la-et-hilburn-cobain-1992-story.html.

129 IMDb.com, *Nirvana: Unplugged in New York (1993)* (December 16, 1993), https://www.imdb.com/title/tt0365559/.

130 HISTORY.com Editors, "Grunge Rock Icon Kurt Cobain Dies by Suicide," *History.com*, originally published November 13, 2009; updated May 27, 2025, https://www.history.com/this-day-in-history/april-5/kurt-cobain-commits-suicide.

Chapter 32 – "Oh, Me"

131 Chad Channing, personal interview.

Mental Health Resources

132 World Health Organization, "Depressive Disorder (Depression)," accessed June 26, 2024, https://www.who.int/en/news-room/fact-sheets/detail/depression.

133 Mental Health America, "Is Your Child Lonely? (For Parents)," accessed June 26, 2024, https://mhanational.org/your-child-lonely-parents.

134 Mental Health America, "Is Your Child Lonely? (For Parents)."

135 John August, "Healthcare Insights: How Medical Debt Is Crushing 100 Million Americans," ILR Scheinman Institute, Cornell University, October 21, 2024, https://www.ilr.cornell.edu/scheinman-institute/blog/john-august-healthcare/healthcare-insights-how-medical-debt-crushing-100-million-americans.

136 Jennifer Tolbert, Sammy Cervantes, Clea Bell, and Anthony Damico, "Key Facts About the Uninsured Population," KFF, December 18, 2024, https://www.kff.org/uninsured/key-facts-about-the-uninsured-population/.

INDEX

P

Q

R

X

Y

Z